in and around
St. Louis

in and around

St. Louis

ROBERT RUBRIGHT

Backcountry Publications
Woodstock · Vermont

An invitation to the reader

If you find that conditions have changed along these walks, please let the author and publisher know so that corrections may be made in future printings. Address all correspondence to:

Editor, Walks and Rambles Series
Backcountry Publications
PO Box 175
Woodstock, Vermont 05091-0175

Library of Congress Cataloging-in-Publication Data

Rubright, Robert.
   Walks and rambles in and around St. Louis / Robert Rubright.
      p.   cm.
   ISBN 0-88150-344-4
   1. Saint Louis (Mo.)—Guidebooks. 2. Saint Louis Region (Mo.)—
Guidebooks. 3. Walking—Missouri—Saint Louis—Guidebooks.
4. Walking—Missouri—Saint Louis Region—Guidebooks.
5. Illinois—Guidebooks. 6. Walking—Illinois—Guidebooks.
I. Title.
F474.S23R83   1995
917.78'660443—dc20   95–16437
                                               CIP

Published by Backcountry Publications
A division of The Countryman Press, Inc.
PO Box 175
Woodstock, VT 05091-0175

Printed in Canada

Book design by Sally Sherman
Maps by Alex Wallach, © 1995 The Countryman Press
Cover photo of *The Way,* by Alexander Liberman, courtesy of Laumeier
  Sculpture Park, St. Louis, MO
All interior photographs by Robert Rubright, unless otherwise credited

To my wife, Lynn, who helped in a million ways.
To my sons Dan and Ted, and to Gina.
To Ed and Martha Laue, incredible in-laws.

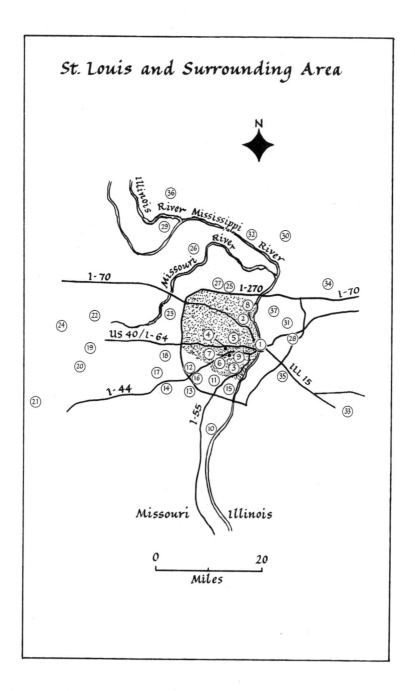

St. Louis and Surrounding Area

N

Illinois River

Mississippi River

Missouri River

I-70

I-270

I-70

US 40/I-64

I-44

I-55

ILL 15

Missouri   Illinois

0   20
Miles

Contents

NORTH ST. LOUIS AND ST. CHARLES COUNTY

ACROSS THE RIVER IN ILLINOIS

Acknowledgments

Dozens of people helped produce this trail guide, many walking the trails with me and pointing out historical landmarks, trees, wildflowers, and divergent paths; or passing along stories, anecdotes, and folklore. In particular, I acknowledge the help of Ramon Gass, whose curiosity about nature's wonders fills each walk to brimming, and of Howard "Dick" Miller, whose passion for regional history is nothing short of inspirational.

Others sharing their knowledge and enthusiasm along the trails include George Arnold, Bob Blain, David Bradford, Jack Buese, Anabeth Calkins, Ted Curtis, Cathy deJong, Edgar Denison, David Eschmann, Gloria Gambero, Manuel Garcia, Mark Hall, Mark Hodges, Dennis Hogan, Scott Isringhausen, Ken Kamper, Richard Keating, Bill Kloppe, Vernon LeClaire, Carl Lossau, Richard Love, John Madson, Bill Mockler, Jim Pona, Bruce Quackenbush, Frank "Chick" Severino, Sandra Shelley, Jim Struif, Daniel Skillman, Vince Stuart, Steve Tiemann, Terry Whaley, and Helen Wuestenfeld.

At the St. Louis Mercantile Library, Mark Cedek, Charles Brown, John N. Hoover, Dr. Jeffrey Smith, and Mary Ellen Davis were extremely encouraging and resourceful, as were Noel C. Holobeck and Anne Watts at the main St. Louis public library and Mary Seematter at the Missouri Historical Society. Francis "Bud" Barnes and Marshall Hier, fellow board members of the St. Louis Mercantile Library, offered useful insights. Historian and preservationist Esley Hamilton of the St. Louis County Department of Parks and Recreation was a key guide.

I'm grateful to the continuing generosity and support of professional staffers from the Illinois and Missouri Departments of Conservation; the Missouri Department of Natural Resources; the Illinois Nature Preserve System; National Park Service; and the US Army Corps of Engineers. Also, I am indebted to members of the St. Louis Audubon Society, the Webster Groves Nature Study Society, the

Nature Institute in Alton, and Gateway Trailnet, Inc. for ideas and historical perspective.

Thanks again to my son Ted for easing the computer technology that shores this book, and to my wife Lynn for trailsharing, initial editing, and incisive commentary.

Introduction

This is a book of urban walks. And suburban walks, and exurban walks. Even the fringe countryside is represented in a hike up a hill in Pere Marquette Park, 45 miles north of St. Louis, as well as a long stroll through the magnificent Shaw Arboretum, 37 miles due west of St. Louis in Gray Summit, Missouri. But essentially, this is a collection of urban walks that resonate with local and regional history; walks to make you proud to be living in Greater St. Louis, and to help you recall and reflect on our area's captivating past.

In this collection are 37 walks totaling nearly 119 miles, averaging 3¼ miles per walk. Ten are in Illinois; the remainder are in St. Louis, St. Charles, and Franklin Counties. Seven city parks are represented, as are five state parks; four St. Louis County parks; a national park; two Illinois nature preserves; one sculpture park; a re-created pioneer prairie; two islands—one in the Missouri River, the other an oxbow of the Mississippi; a school district's 98-acre outdoor classroom/urban forest—which may be the largest of its kind in America; and at least four distinct city neighborhoods: the Hill, Dogtown, parts of St. Louis Hills in south St. Louis, and the vintage utopian worker's village of Leclaire in Edwardsville, Illinois.

Assembling this trail guide, it amazed me to discover the many sights and surprises that can befall the curious walker. For example, on the St. Louis walks alone you'll stroll pink sidewalks, blacktops, back alleys, roads made for horse-drawn carriages, levees, grassy park knolls, river overlooks, and busy downtown streets. You'll walk beside floodwalls, tall buildings, national monuments, cemetery obelisks and mausoleums, 100-year-old trees, lily ponds, a Chinese gazebo, forts and parade fields, boathouses and fishing docks, vast sinkholes, exotic shrubs, old railway bridges, footbridges, the country's largest service station sign, towering bronze park statues, art deco–style homes and apartments, Madonna shrines, concrete Sicilian donkeys and carts, and a blacksmith shop.

You'll walk in places that once might have required a special invitation. These include the Olin Nature Preserve in Godfrey, Illinois, the one-time backyard of weapons and ammunition magnate John M. Olin, who invited friends and associates to shoot skeet on a sculpted limestone terrace overlooking the Mississippi River; the former home and grounds of Edgar M. Queeny, son of the founder of Monsanto Company, whose rolling estate is now one of St. Louis County's busiest parks; and the former summer retreat and working farm of Eugene D. Nims, once president of Southwestern Bell Telephone Company, at a place now known as Bee Tree County Park. It, too, commands a regal perch on the Mississippi River.

This book contains the first walk to the confluence of the Illinois and Mississippi Rivers at Calhoun Point across from Grafton, Illinois, the town that was arguably at the epicenter of national news coverage during the mammoth floods of 1993. It contains, as well, a 4½-mile stretch of the new Missouri linear park, the Katy Trail State Park. We hike a section rich in Daniel Boone history and lore; we end the walk on a piece of land that scholars believe is the only property Boone ever owned.

No doubt about it, this book is history-filled. Its details, facts, and anecdotes have been mined from oral histories (nearly 200 people were interviewed); the imposing regional collections of the St. Louis Mercantile Library, the Missouri Historical Society, and the main St. Louis public library; as well as corporate and private archives and personal scrapbooks. From readings of stimulating books on local history or nature, such as *Forest Park* by Caroline Loughlin and Catherine Anderson, *Up on the Mississippi* by the gifted John Madson, *Missouri Hiking Trails* by my good friend Ramon Gass, and dozens of other books and articles, I gathered a deeper appreciation of local and regional history and how it might interplay with my assembly of walks, hikes, and strolls.

You may have many reasons for wanting to leave your home to take a walk. My own reasons are: to solve a problem; to temporarily shirk household work; to daydream, especially about a lottery win; to get an early morning jolt, or, at night, to prepare myself for a more restful sleep; to pretend to shed weight; to socialize; to explore. As I grow older and perhaps wiser, it's the exploring that is more and more alluring. This is because all serious walkers, in my view, should be innately curious about their neighborhoods, their cities, their rivers, lakes, streams, and the surrounding countryside.

Several years ago, I asked my graduate students at Washington University in St. Louis to look out the classroom window and name the trees and flowers they saw. No one could identify a single species of flora! I repeated the exercise semester after semester with the same results: Bright, cheerful, and otherwise curious students simply could not put labels on common trees, shrubs, or wildflowers—or, by extension, most of the common backyard birds and butterflies. That revelation gave impetus to this book. I began to seek out my own panel of specialists to walk with me and describe what they saw. I walked with naturalists, wildlife biologists, forest entomologists, botanists, park rangers and superintendents, head groundskeepers, geologists, and nature writers. I joined both the Audubon Society and the Webster Groves Nature Study Society (as you should too) to learn about birding and botanizing and the great Mississippi River flyway. I discovered that just about every one of my 37 walks has its own historian, official or unofficial.

Every business, every institution is said to have a historian, or an archivist, or someone who can readily tell the story of the place, whether fact or folklore. The same is true for our hiking trails. As an example, I relied heavily on the late Alton lawyer Bruce Quackenbush, along with his friend Jack Buese, to tell me about Pere Marquette State Park near Grafton, Illinois. The pair hiked the park every Saturday morning for years; their knowledge of its hollows, over-looks, trail network, boulders, trees, and shortcuts was invaluable to park officials, and to me. Manuel Garcia is Bellefontaine Cemetery's unofficial historian; the cemetery staff relies on him to provide histori-cal data on permanent guests. I walked the cemetery with Manuel many times, and I've often seen him deep in research at the Missouri Historical Society. Ross Wagner, a former St. Louis University history professor, knows south St. Louis County like a charm. He's the expert whom the National Park Service calls on for information and opin-ions about Ulysses S. Grant's White Haven, or Grant's Farm across the street. I called on Ross, too, for his knowledge of Gravois Creek and the new Carondelet Greenway walking trail. And I spent many hours poring over Daniel Boone history with Ken Kamper, historian of the Daniel Boone and Frontier Families Research Association. As my main Katy Trail expert, his knowledge of Boone's ramblings and adventures on the Missouri River along the present trail is nothing short of amazing. This list of often unheralded experts and historians goes on and on.

The St. Louis area is filled with places to explore or become reacquainted with. I can't think of a better way to get to know the area than by hiking it. Walking is perhaps the simplest form of exercise and one of the most widely practiced. Even so, I have a few guidelines that you may wish to follow:

1 · Take along the proper guidebooks for birds, wildflowers, trees, or butterflies. Buy manuals with color photos, if possible. Bird binoculars, especially during spring and fall migrations, are helpful.

2 · Make sure that you will be safe on your walk. A sensible rule is to walk with another person or a group. On certain trails in this guide—Bellefontaine Cemetery, Forest Park (northeast end), and Riverfront Trail—you should not walk alone at all.

3 · Wear leg coverings in the summer since poison ivy and other poisonous plants abound on park and forest trails. Obtain a wallet card that identifies ticks, especially those that that may carry Lyme disease. And be sure your insect repellent is fresh, not last year's.

4 · In summer months, be wary about walking in high grass, which is often prime chigger habitat.

5 · If a trail brochure is available at the trailhead or visitors center, always take it. This book only supplements official trail guides.

Best wishes for 37 wonderful walks.

Resources

Arch (Jefferson National
  Expansion Memorial)
11 N. Fourth St.
St. Louis, MO 63102
(314) 982-1410

Babler State Park
800 Guy Park Dr.
Chesterfield, MO 63005
(314) 458-3813

Bee Tree County Park
St. Louis County Parks and
  Recreation Dept.
41 S. Central Ave.
Clayton, MO 63105
(314) 889-2863

Bellefontaine Cemetery
4947 W. Florissant Ave.
St. Louis, MO 63115
(314) 381-0750

Busch Conservation Area
2360 Highway D
St. Charles, MO 63304
(314) 441-4554

Cahokia Mounds Historic Site
Box 681
Collinsville, IL 62234
(618) 346-5160

Calhoun Point
Illinois Dept. of Conservation
RR 1, Box 182
Grafton, IL 62037
(618) 376-3303

Carondelet Greenway
Gateway Trailnet, Inc.
7185 Manchester
St. Louis, MO 63143
(314) 644-0315

Carondelet and St. Marcus
  Parks
St. Louis Parks, Recreation and
  Forestry Dept.
5600 Clayton Rd.
St. Louis, MO 63110
(314) 535-0100

Castlewood State Park
1401 Kiefer Creek Rd.
Ballwin, MO 63021
(314) 527-6481

Dogtown (no resource
  organization)

Emmenegger Nature Park
Powder Valley Conservation
  Nature Center
11715 Cragwold Rd.
Kirkwood, MO 63122-7015
(314) 821-8427

Fenton Parks and Recreation
Dept.
645 New Smizer Mill Rd.
Fenton, MO 63026
(314) 343-0067

City of Florissant
955 Rue St. Francois
Florissant, MO 63031
(314) 921-5700

Forest 44
Missouri Dept. of Conservation
2751 Glencoe Rd.
Glencoe, MO 63038
(314) 458-2236

Forest Park
Manager's Office
5600 Clayton Rd.
St. Louis, MO 63110
(314) 535-0100

Francis Park
(See Carondelet and St. Marcus
  Parks)

Golden Eagle River Museum
(314) 846-9073

Hill Neighborhood (no resource
  organization)

Horseshoe Lake State Park
3321 Highway 111
Granite City, IL 62040
(618) 931-0270

Howell Island
2360 Highway D
St. Charles, MO 63304
(314) 441-4554

Jefferson Barracks Park
(See Bee Tree Park)

Katy Trail State Park
Missouri Dept. of Natural
  Resources
PO Box 176
Jefferson City, MO 65102
1-800-334-6946

Knobeloch Woods Nature
  Preserve
Illinois Dept. of Conservation
Region IV Office
4521 Alton Commerce Pkwy.
Alton, IL 62002
(618) 462-1181

Laumeier Park
12580 Rott Rd.
St. Louis, MO 63127
(314) 821-1209

Leclaire Village (no resource
  organization)

Little Creek Nature Area
2295 Dunn Rd.
Florissant, MO 63033
(314) 831-7386

Marais Temps Clair Wildlife
  Area
Missouri Dept. of Conservation
PO Box 157
Warrenton, MO 63383
(314) 456-3368

Nature Institute Heartland
  Prairie
2888 Beltline Pkwy.
Alton, IL 62202
(618) 463-0766

North Riverfront Trail
(See Carondelet Greenway)

Olin Nature Preserve
(See Knobeloch Woods)

Our Lady of the Snows
9500 W. State Rt. 15
Belleville, IL 62223-1094
(618) 397-6700 or
  (314) 241-3400

Pere Marquette State Park
Box 158
Grafton, IL 62037
(618) 786-2204

Queeny County Park
(See Bee Tree Park)

Rockwoods Reservation
2751 Glencoe Rd.
Glencoe, MO 63038
(314) 458-2236

Shaw Arboretum
PO Box 38
Gray Summit, MO 63039
(314) 742-3512

Tower Grove Park
4255 Arsenal St.
St. Louis, MO 63116
(314) 771-2679

Wilson Park
2900 Benton
Granite City, IL 62040
(618) 877-3059

Two Feet
in St. Louis

*Joggers approach the north leg of the
Arch on a path bordered by ash trees.*

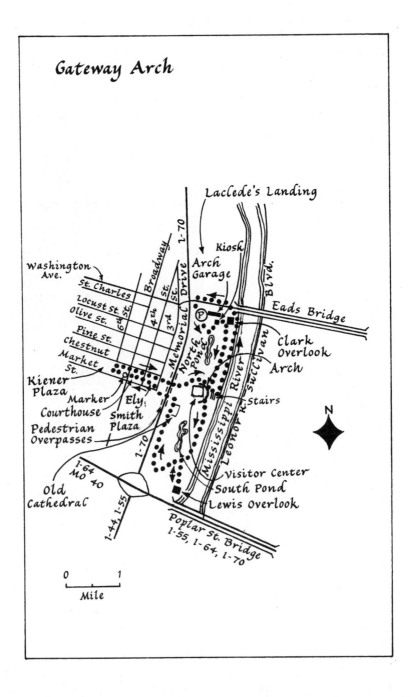

Gateway Arch

Gateway Arch

Location: St. Louis, Missouri
Hiking distance: 3 miles
Hiking time: 1½ hours
Bicycles: not permitted

Some visitors don't come to the 630-foot stainless steel Gateway Arch, America's tallest national monument, to ride to the top for the 25-mile view on a clear day. Instead, they come to walk or jog on the grounds of the Arch, formally known as Jefferson National Expansion Memorial and managed by the National Park Service. In this national park are 3 miles of curved, tree-lined walks (the curves match the curve of the Arch itself), 2670 trees, 7200 shrubs, and 700 square yards of flower beds.

To Jim Jacobs, gardener foreman, the Arch's 92 acres constitute an urban forest. "We're in an urban area; the whole park is built on fill; the trees and shrubs are selected and spaced according to a man-made plan," says Jacobs. Since the park is also considered a forest, it's not unusual that wild animals are sometimes seen here. "Once, we saw a deer jump off the top deck of the parking garage," says Jacobs. More recently, he says, he saw two baby foxes emerge from their hole by the south reflecting pond. Their fate is unknown.

"Hundreds of people come here daily to walk or run, especially during lunch hour," says Jacobs. "We saw Tommy Lasorda, manager of the Los Angeles Dodgers, running through here shirtless once. We have one regular during the summer who comes every noon, leaves his work clothes in a pile in an open field, and takes off. He waves to us sometimes."

Access

Take I-44, I-55, I-64, or I-70 into downtown St. Louis. Look for the Arch, then follow signs to the Arch parking garage, entered from Washington Avenue, just east of Memorial Drive. (There is a parking fee.) Park on the top level, where the walk begins.

Trail

From the bulletin board kiosk next to the garage, walk left to the William Clark overlook. From here, you can see Eads Bridge, which spans the Mississippi River, as well as Laclede's Landing to the north—the food and entertainment area that holds what's left of the old riverfront commercial district. Its street patterns date from the early 1800s. Permanently tethered to the riverbank is the SS *Admiral,* now a gambling casino. From 1940 to 1979, it was the largest river excursion boat in the country. It is built on the hull of a retired railroad ferry.

Eads, the world's first structural alloy steel bridge, was the first bridge in St. Louis to cross the Mississippi and the only bridge that James Buchanan Eads, a cousin of President James Buchanan, ever built. In May 1874, when it opened, 20,000 walkers paid 5 cents each to stroll its upper deck; the lower deck was for trains. (Currently, trains from MetroLink, the area's mass transit system, speed over the lower deck en route to East St. Louis.) To ease public doubts about its safety, bridge managers in mid-1874 sent 14 locomotives, each loaded with human passengers, across the span with no difficulty whatsoever.

Return to the kiosk, then walk south on the wide sidewalk in the direction of the Arch. Rosehill ash, the major tree species in the park, borders the sidewalks. Jacobs uses a computer to monitor tree strength, vigor, and vulnerability to insects. "We don't mass spray or mass prune," says Jacobs. "We treat each tree according to its needs." A well-known pioneer of ash borer (insect) control told Jacobs that the Arch urban forest has the best borer control program he has seen. Arch managers are very proud of that compliment.

The entire 40-acre original village of St. Louis, including its common fields, was located where the Arch is today. Memorable figures from history alighted from steamboats to walk up into the old village. Among them: Washington Irving; Alexander Hamilton; Daniel Webster, who was greeted by thousands in 1837 at the foot of Market Street; the Marquis de Lafayette; John James Audubon; and Senator Thomas Hart Benton of Missouri, who frequently took "the

*The Arch grounds include a pleasant tree-lined walkway
along the Mississippi River.*

river boat" from Washington, D.C., to St. Louis between sessions of
Congress.

Once you arrive at the Arch, walk up, pat its sides, and gaze
skyward. "The Arch moves when the clouds move and you feel, as
you look up, a touch of vertigo along with the awe," writes William
H. Gass, St. Louis essayist, novelist, and philosopher. Along hand-cut
Italian granite blocks, ramps descend to the door of the underground
visitors center, which contains America's largest national park museum, a thriving bookstore, and tram cars that carry passengers up to
the Arch observation tower. There are 1076 stairs to the top of the
Arch, but they're used only in emergencies.

From the Arch, walk south on the sidewalk that parallels the
river. Notice the vast greenspace west of the Arch; groundskeepers
call it "the land between the legs." It is seeded with "Arch ground
mix" (major ingredient, Arboretum bluegrass), sold at local nurseries
and seed stores.

Continue on the sidewalk to the Meriwether Lewis overlook in the park's extreme southeastern corner, a spot few tourists visit. On view from here are the Poplar Street Bridge (opened in 1967) and a warehouse district somewhat similar to the warehouse area razed to make room for the Arch. After viewing from the overlook, retrace your steps and take the sidewalk west toward Memorial Drive. Turn north onto the Memorial Drive sidewalk and walk to the Basilica of Saint Louis, the King—the oldest Catholic cathedral west of the Mississippi. It is the fourth Catholic church to be located on this site since 1770; some say this is the only piece of ground in St. Louis that has never been sold. The present building dates from 1830.

At Market Street, turn left to cross Memorial Drive. Stroll through Luther Ely Smith Plaza, a bright pocket park favored by office workers and tourists. "On a nice day," said one visitor, "office workers come here in shifts; you have to take a number and run for a bench." The park is named for the St. Louis visionary who in 1933 proposed a combined monument to Thomas Jefferson, the Louisiana Purchase, and the opening of the West beyond the Mississippi. In 1947, Smith organized a contest to select the architectural design that best depicted his concept. Of 172 entries, Eero Saarinen's was chosen. It wasn't until the summer of 1967 that the Saarinen Arch was completed and ready for visitors. Vice President Hubert H. Humphrey helped dedicate it in May 1968.

From the west side of the pocket park, walk west across Fourth Street and, if it's open, through the east door of the Old Courthouse, a major Greek Revival building that dates from 1826 and has looked the same since 1862. Some say its Italianate dome influenced the design of the national capitol dome in Washington, D.C. In the 19th century, the courthouse held slave auctions on its steps; two Dred Scott trials also took place there. Senator Thomas Hart Benton delivered his prophetic "Westward the Course of Empire" speech here, calling for a transcontinental railroad. In this building Henry Clay tried unsuccessfully to auction some land in 1846; Ulysses S. Grant set free one of his slaves in 1859; and President Grover Cleveland was given a reception in 1887. After walking through the courthouse, admiring its incomparable rotunda, and viewing any current exhibits, walk out the west door and west across Broadway to Kiener Plaza.

Facing Broadway in midblock is a red granite boulder marking the approximate start of America's first westward trail, Boone's Lick, or St. Charles Rock, Road. Following the War of 1812, the trail was used by settlers, largely from Kentucky and Virginia, as the only westward expansion route this side of the Mississippi. The 150-mile road to a salt mine owned by sons of Daniel Boone eventually became a link to the Santa Fe, Oregon, and California Trails. Walk through the plaza to the overlook near the 500-seat Morton D. May amphitheater and fountain cascade. Then retrace your steps through the plaza, passing the bronze statue of *The Runner*. Harry J. Kiener, who donated $200,000 for the fountain and statue, was an executive who had run the half-mile event in the 1904 St. Louis World's Fair.

Walk east on Chestnut Street toward the Arch, and recross Broadway with the Old Courthouse on your right. Continuing east, cross Fourth Street, then Memorial Drive. Back on the Arch grounds, take the wide walk that curves to your left past the Arch's underground shipping/receiving building. By the north leg of the Arch, walk down the 64 grand stairs—where each step "is a vista," said Saarinen—to Leonor K. Sullivan Boulevard, named for the congresswoman from St. Louis who helped secure federal funds and approvals for the Arch.

Walk to the reviewing stand on Leonor Sullivan Boulevard and scan the levee and granite paving blocks that compose it. The blocks were laid after 1877, replacing limestone pavers that had become worn and powdery after heavy traffic during the steamboat age.

Walk north on Leonor Sullivan Boulevard, past a row of bald cypress trees, to Washington Avenue. Turn left. Walk up the hill until, just before Memorial Drive, you reach the wide walk that bends back to the kiosk by the parking garage. En route, cut across the grass to the north reflecting pond.

For awhile, large goldfish swam in the pond, but they didn't take to it as well as do the frogs and ducks of today. A small Kentucky coffee tree on the east bank started as a sapling from a tree on the grounds of the historic George Rogers Clark home in Louisville, Kentucky. Clark's Revolutionary War victories at Kaskaskia, Cahokia, and Vincennes provided America's main claim to territory west of the Mississippi. "We think having the Clark tree here is appropriate," says Jacobs.

With some 2.5 million visitors a year, not including those who come for the July 4 Fair of St. Louis, the Arch turf can take a beating. "We find that the worst damage comes on weekends the Chicago Cubs play the St. Louis Cardinals in St. Louis," says Jacobs. The baseball stadium is about three blocks away; many of the fans park on the levee or adjacent lots and hike to it over the Arch property. "Those Chicago fans can be pretty spirited," says Jacobs, who takes it all in stride.

Bellefontaine Cemetery

Location: St. Louis, Missouri
Hiking distance: 1⅔ miles
Hiking time: 1½ hours
Bicycles: not permitted

Bellefontaine Cemetery, which opened in 1850 in what was then a rural area, owned the area's largest collection of trees. People called Bellefontaine a sacred place, a pensive silent forest. "If you fly over Bellefontaine today, it still looks like a forest," says Carol Resch, secretary in the cemetery office. The property's 305 acres contain at least 105 kinds of trees, pin oaks and tulip poplars the most abundant.

In the mid- to late 1800s, St. Louisans visited Bellefontaine to stroll its serpentine paths, marvel at its lush plantings, and read monuments for inspiration. Rural cemeteries were a phenomenon created to partially accommodate "a growing urban population in need of recreation," state Kenneth T. Jackson and Camilo Vergara in *Silent Cities.* Cemeteries as forests and sculpture gardens are said to have inspired the American park movement as well as the profession of landscape architecture.

Nearly 14 miles of curvy, landscaped roadways wind through Bellefontaine, which has more than 84,000 permanent guests and room for about 60,000 more. The cemetery's first superintendent, Almerin Hotchkiss—who was on the job for 46 years—devised the roadways, assigning them names with somber overtones such as Balm, Autumn, and Sunset. He called one section of fancy mausoleums Repose Hill.

Calvary Cemetery, at 477 acres, is Bellefontaine's immediate, and larger, neighbor to the west on West Florissant Avenue. Among its 315,000 interments are playwright Tennessee Williams, General

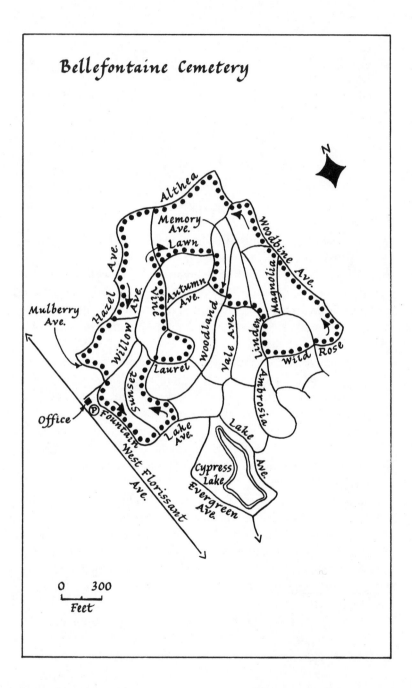

Bellefontaine Cemetery

William Tecumseh Sherman, and Dr. Tom Dooley. Since the cemeteries are contiguous, it is not unusual for funeral processions to turn into the wrong front gate!

Bellefontaine's most famous landmarks are probably the Louis Sullivan–designed Wainwright tomb; the monument to General William Clark who, with Meriwether Lewis, led the 1804–1806 expedition to the Pacific Northwest; and the pink Gothic mausoleum of Adolphus Busch, a founder of Anheuser-Busch, Inc. Our walk passes only the Busch tomb.

Access

From downtown St. Louis, take I-70 west to exit 245B, West Florissant Avenue. Upon exiting, merge to the right onto West Florissant for the 0.6-mile ride to the cemetery's Willow Gate entrance on your right. Park near the gatehouse, where you can obtain a free map that includes an optional 2½-hour driving tour of Bellefontaine. Booklets on Bellefontaine history and highlights are for sale.

Trail

Leaving the cemetery office, walk across Fountain Avenue. In the Walters lot near the corner of Fountain and Willow is the grave of **"Scrappy Bill" Joyce** (1867–1941). In August 1897, as the New York Giants player-manager, Joyce hit four triples in one baseball game, a record that still stands. "Bill was as fearless a base runner as Ty Cobb," one obituary said.

Walking east on Fountain, you'll soon find the **Norman J. Colman** lot on your left. Once a Missouri lieutenant governor, he was named by President Grover Cleveland the nation's first Secretary of Agriculture. When Fountain bends left, the **William Prufrock** grave appears. As a child, poet T.S. Eliot noticed the intriguing surname above the William Prufrock furniture store in St. Louis. Later he used it in his poem "The Love Song of J. Alfred Prufrock."

Cross Sunset Avenue. (Off to your right is Cypress Lake, one of Bellefontaine's two human-made lakes.) Bear left on Woodland; the Carpenter lot is on your right. On your left, under some tall trees in the Blair-Graham plot, is the grave (embellished by a Celtic cross) of

Major General Francis Preston Blair Jr. A pro-Lincoln Republican, Blair was ironically the Democratic vice-presidential candidate who ran against U.S. Grant during Grant's first presidential try. "He's one of my favorite politicians out here because he always said what he felt; he never weasled," says Manuel Garcia, a retired *St. Louis Post-Dispatch* proofreader whose hobby is the cemetery. Members of the Graham family, who rest nearby, left funds to establish Graham Chapel on Washington University's main campus.

Turn right onto Laurel, a curvy stretch. Off to your left is the tall red granite obelisk of **Senator Thomas Hart Benton,** who died in 1858. The state's first senator after Missouri joined the Union, his robust oratory and powerful voice for westward expansion placed him among Senate peers such as John C. Calhoun, Daniel Webster, and Henry Clay. Benton once wounded Andrew Jackson in a duel, but later became a staunch Jacksonian. Almost diagonally across Laurel, the **Frederick Dent** monument, resembling a neatly stacked stone pile, is about 30 steps in from the curb. Dent died in the White House in 1873 while visiting his daughter, Julia, wife of President Grant. The Grants accompanied the body to Bellefontaine for the burial. (Incidentally, the Grants purchased burial plots for themselves at Bellefontaine near the Dent family, "but probably gave the plots away to other family members," says Grant historian Kim Little.)

Turn right on Woodland, which soon becomes Vine. On your right is the red granite headstone of architect **George I. Barnett,** flanked by two worn marble tombstones. He designed the governor's mansion in Jefferson City and some original buildings at the Missouri Botanical Garden in St. Louis. Stay on Vine; pass Lawn. Down a few plots on your right is **Samuel Hawken**'s tombstone, a rifle etched into it. He perfected the design of, and manufactured, the .50-caliber rifles that bore his name, and that were used by Buffalo Bill and Kit Carson. Turn around. Walk back to Lawn on Vine, and turn left.

On your right on Lawn is the family plot of fur trader and western traveler **Robert Campbell.** His Rocky Mountain Fur Company competed with John Jacob Astor's American Fur Company in the early days of western trading. The Campbell home at 1508 Locust is a downtown St. Louis landmark. Next door, on your right, is the

Poet T.S. Eliot liked Bellefontaine resident William Prufrock's last name so much he invented "J. Alfred Prufrock," immortalizing that old St. Louis family.

family plot of **James Yeatman,** first president of Bellefontaine's board and a founder of both the St. Louis Symphony Orchestra and the St. Louis Mercantile Library. A Yeatman grandson's will provides for fresh flowers to be placed at the monument each Sunday between February and September. Other Bellefontaine lots have similar provisions. Across from the Campbells and Yeatmans are members of the **Taylor Blow** family. Blow was the last owner of slave Dred Scott before the court set Scott free. In the plot are the remains of Joseph C. Blow. Garcia, the historian, says he is unable to find details of the life of "Joe" Blow.

Turn right on Autumn Avenue, then left on Memory Avenue (no sign for Memory was visible when we walked) by the William Renshaw monument on your left. Upcoming on your left is the marble tombstone of **James B. Eads** (1820–1887), who built St. Louis's first bridge across the Mississippi; it was America's first structural steel bridge. He also built submarines to salvage wrecks from the river bottom, then developed ironclad, steam-driven gunboats to secure the western rivers for the Union in the Civil War.

Keep strolling straight ahead on Memory, crossing both Woodland and Vale Avenues. As you walk uphill, Memory Avenue magically changes its name to Memorial Avenue. Turn right on Linden. Off to your left, topped by the "Angel of Hope," is the tall monument to **Colonel John R. O'Fallon** and his family in Bellefontaine's largest family unit. Banker-philanthropist O'Fallon, first president of Missouri Pacific Railroad, donated land for St. Louis University and the original Washington University medical school. On the side of the O'Fallon plot facing Linden Avenue, under holly trees, lies **Luther Ely Smith** (1873–1951), a civic-minded lawyer who initially advocated the Jefferson National Expansion Memorial, better known as the Arch. At the intersection of Linden and Wild Rose, northwest corner, are the parents of the late St. Louis–born actor Vincent Price. Turn left on Wild Rose. **Trusten Polk**'s gravesite is on the right corner. A pre–Civil War Missouri governor, he was a US senator for 53 days before being expelled in 1862 for his pro-Southern sentiments. He then served the Confederate army as a colonel. Next to Polk is the **General Stephen W. Kearny** plot; 40 members of his family are there. In the 1840s Mexican War, he led American forces that conquered present-day California and New Mexico.

Continue on Wild Rose; cross Memorial. On your left, behind two rows of red granite markers in the Kretschmar family lot, is the grave of **Roswell Field,** a St. Louis attorney and father of the poet Eugene Field. Turn left onto Woodbine; you'll stay on it for a long stretch, crossing Tulip, then Magnolia. On your right just beyond the intersection with Balm is the mausoleum of tobacco magnate **John E. Liggett.** His partner in Liggett & Myers Tobacco Company, George Myers, is also buried in the cemetery. Behind Liggett is **Major General John Pope,** who lost a major Civil War battle at Bull Run. Nearby lies Pope's father, **Nathaniel,** an Illinois territorial congressman whom some consider the "father" of Chicago, since in 1818 he established the northern boundary of Illinois to include Chicago's present site. At left on Woodbine, just beyond Vale Avenue, is the $250,000 (in 1913 dollars) red granite Gothic mausoleum containing **Adolphus and Lilly Busch.** In a comparatively inconspicuous grave behind the mausoleum lies the founder of Anheuser-Busch, Adolphus's father-in-law, **Eberhard**

Anheuser. Next to the Busch tomb on Woodbine is the grave of **Susan Blow,** who in 1873 founded America's first kindergarten in a south St. Louis school.

Across Woodbine from Busch is **Captain Isaiah Sellers,** a famous Mississippi River steamboatman who allegedly knew by heart all 1200 miles of the river between St. Louis and New Orleans. He wrote the "River Notes" column for the *New Orleans Picayune* using the pseudonym "Mark Twain." After Samuel Clemens satirized the Sellers column, it was said that Sellers never wrote again. Clemens adopted the "Mark Twain" pseudonym himself in 1862, two years before Sellers died.

Walk left on Lawn, then right on Aspen, to Althea, turning left. Set back to your left on Althea is the grave of **Susan Magoffin,** the second woman to ride the Santa Fe Trail. "We always thought she was the first until the March 1991 *National Geographic* came out," says Garcia. "The town of Magoffinville, Texas, named for her brother-in-law, later changed its name to El Paso," he adds. Near the Elks Rest monument, a sizable tomb capped by an enormous full-antlered elk (this section contains remains of many area members of the Loyal Order of the Elks), is the unmarked grave of St. Louis Mayor Washington King, who ran the city for one year in the mid-1850s. His is one of some 20,000 unmarked graves at Bellefontaine.

Stay on Althea; pass Vine. Shortly after, on your right, is the tomb of **Richard King** (1860–1922), whose father founded the celebrated King Ranch in Texas. Pass Meadow, then bear left on Hazel, passing Poplar. Under a white granite obelisk on your left (look closely, there are many obelisks in this section) is **Thomas Jefferson Whitman** (1833–1898), brother of poet Walt Whitman. Directly across Hazel from Whitman, in behind the red granite–bordered Reber family plot, is the modest gravesite of **William Chauvenet,** second chancellor of Washington University and a co-founder in 1845 of the US Naval Academy, where he was a professor of math and navigation.

Finish the walk by taking a left on Mulberry and a right on Willow, again passing, on your left, the grave of "Scrappy Bill" Joyce, the long-forgotten baseball hero.

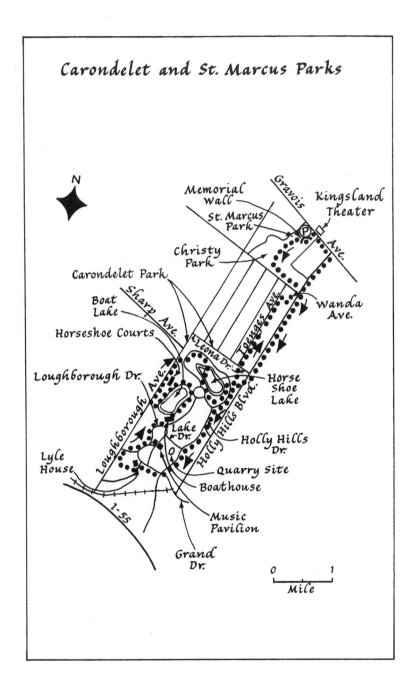

Carondelet and St. Marcus Parks

Carondelet and St. Marcus Parks

Location: St. Louis, Missouri
Hiking distance: 3 miles
Hiking time: 2 hours
Bicycles: permitted

Carondelet Park was nearly named Independence Park because it was dedicated on July 4, 1876, the 100th anniversary of US independence. It was designed with wide roadways, and wide terra-cotta gates on its four corners to accommodate horse-drawn carriages. In Carondelet's early days, there were two soccer fields, three baseball diamonds, a ¼-mile running track, a limestone quarry mined by St. Louis workhouse prisoners, an aquarium, a railroad station, an enormous concrete equestrian statue of explorer Hernando de Soto that had been displayed at the St. Louis World's Fair, and canoeable lakes. In 1923, the first bus service in the area began when the People's Motorbus Service offered double-decker rides from the park into downtown St. Louis. The park property had been part of a Spanish land grant to Amos Lyle, whose grandson inherited it and erected a home in 1842 on what was then called Lyle's Pasture.

St. Marcus Park was an active cemetery from 1856 to around 1961 when its sponsor, the St. Marcus German Evangelical Church, ceased to maintain it. Later, the church decided to abandon the property and transfer between 800 and 1000 perpetual care burials to the New St. Marcus Cemetery farther west on Gravois. Vandalism beset the deserted cemetery in the 1960s. As a result, most of the headstones were damaged and obelisks toppled. Army reserve units and other volunteers helped clean up the grounds. The land, which still contains nearly 15,000 burials, was almost sold to a shopping center developer until the neighborhood improvement association and local politicians successfully blocked the plans. Dedicated in 1972 as a passive park, there are no recreational facilities or picnic tables. Park department people once suggested that visitors might take "slow cadence walks through the grounds."

Access

From the intersection of Hampton Avenue and I-44, take Hampton Avenue south to Gravois—about 5 miles. Turn left on Gravois; drive to the 6600 block. Park in front of St. Marcus Park, across the street from Kingsland Theater.

Trail

Inside St. Marcus Park, examine the six low limestone walls that contain small headstones and fragments retrieved after the vandalism of the 1960s. Rod Tiemann, a neighborhood leader who fought the shopping center proposal, got the idea for the headstone arrangement, which he calls a "chronological wall," from a Pulaski, Tennessee, cemetery. He and his wife were among those who persuaded city officials to adopt the idea.

After strolling among the lonesome pines and yews and the damaged obelisks on the hard-edged turf, walk to the rear of the cemetery and down the hill to the green strip known as Christy Park, dedicated in 1910 "for boulevard purposes." Stretching linearly from Kingshighway on the west to Holly Hills Boulevard, it has been a city park, albeit a skinny one, since 1954. Turn left on the paved path. Once you arrive at Holly Hills Boulevard, turn right. Walk 4 long blocks to the northern edge of Carondelet Park in a neighborhood of 1920s and 1930s brick bungalows.

Inside the park, at Leona Street, whose curbs might hold the finest sycamore tree specimens in all St. Louis, jog to your right to access Holly Hills Drive, a no-sidewalk road that will convey you to Grand Drive, about 4 city blocks ahead. Horse Shoe Lake, on your right, is a sinkhole that was enlarged and filled in the 1890s to accommodate anglers and people who enjoy sitting on its banks to meditate in the shadows of the beautiful pines and spruces.

Most of the park's 19 sinkholes lie along Holly Hills Drive. In

A photo taken in the 1920s shows the now-razed St. Louis, Oak Hill, & Carondelet railway station near the present Holly Hills Drive bridge in Carondelet Park. (St. Louis Department of Parks, Recreation, and Forestry archives)

1907, the city park commissioner warned that "sinkholes are extremely dangerous and should be carefully guarded." Just before Grand Drive, on your right, is the old quarry, also known as the "bear pit" or "sauerkraut bowl." Quarry limestone helped pave some of the park's first roads. Depleted of stone, the quarry became a deer and animal paddock. Later, the city supply commissioner sold 19 deer and 4 elk from both Carondelet and Forest Parks to August A. Busch for his animal collection at Grant's Farm on Gravois Road. In the 1940s, recalled the late St. Louis botanist Art Christ, "We used to go to the old quarry for Halloween parties after walking in the park with the St. Louis Hiking Club."

Stay on Holly Hills Drive to Grand Drive. Walk west on Grand Drive, cross a busy street, and enter the grounds embracing Lyle House, the eight-room white frame residence built for Alexander Lyle, who was accused of being a Southern sympathizer during the Civil War. After those charges, "Lyle and his family (which included

14 children) are said to have made a hasty departure from the old homestead under the cover of darkness," a local newspaper reported. The Lyles never returned to the home, which eventually became the parkkeeper's residence and is now headquarters of the Carondelet Park Pinochle Players Club.

Pinochle is played at Lyle six days a week. The club's only living founder, Ray "Boom Boom" Blase, says that its most exciting, and saddest, moment was when original founder Martin Stefin died while holding "a trump 1500 in his hand. That's one of the best hands you can have." In its first year, 1959, the club had 150 members, but it's now down to around 50. It seeks recruits. "We'll even give free pinochle and gin lessons," Blase promises. "And, if you're 90 years old, you don't have to pay dues."

Follow Lyle House's front sidewalk; it curves west past the backyard through a stand of spruce and pine trees and ends at Loughborough Avenue. Turn right on Loughborough Avenue. At the paved bike path, walk right. Pass the park music pavilion, built in 1898. From there, follow Loughborough Drive (*not* Loughborough Avenue), which winds north inside the park toward the 1918 boathouse on Boat Lake. Two tunnel-shaped pergolas extend into the lake alongside a T-shaped casting dock. If fishers aren't on the dock or out on the pergolas, it's likely the park's ducks and geese are. A south St. Louis tradition is feeding the ducks. After looping the lake, turn right on the bike path that runs abreast of Loughborough Avenue. Walk north to Leona Drive.

A 12-court horseshoe area is a 50-year-old landmark along your way. Probably the largest such facility in the city, it is maintained by the 190-member Greater St. Louis Horseshoe Club, which sponsors league contests on summer Tuesday evenings. "We take care of the courts, the wooden backboards, fences, and pegs, and we mow the grass," says Ken Sykora, a club officer. "We always have to fight for more lighting."

Just beyond the horseshoe courts, a grove of Austrian pines "flat and thinning at the top and dying of old age," according to forest entomologist Ramon Gass, backdrops the nearby playground-restroom complex. Gass estimates that the pines were planted in the early

1940s. Near the intersection of Loughborough and Sharp Avenues are six ailanthus trees. "That's the tree that grows in Brooklyn, you know," explains Gass. "Its gray bark looks like that of a beech tree; we sometimes call the tree 'elephant leg.' " It has a third name, "tree of heaven," which refers to its speedy skyward growth, often up to 10 feet a year until it reaches about 60 feet.

Leave the bike path at Leona Drive; turn right and walk down the hill to the rim of Horse Shoe Lake. Walk to the east along the bank, then up and over the footbridge, then back down to the bank until you reach Holly Hills Drive, where you must turn left and begin the walk back to Gravois. For variety, you might follow Toenges Avenue north. Just past Parkwood Place, pleasant, shady Toenges dead-ends at an alley. Turn right into the alley, then follow it as it jogs left by some backyard beware-of-the-dog signs. Don't worry; the dogs are fenced in. At Wanda Avenue, turn right for the short hike to Holly Hills Boulevard. Turn left and walk to Gravois, where you must make another left to reach your car.

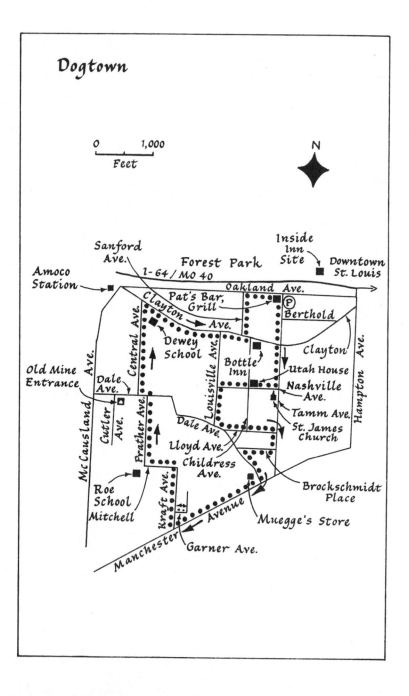

Dogtown

Dogtown

Location: St. Louis, Missouri
Hiking distance: 3⅔ miles
Hiking time: 1½ hours
Bicycles: permitted

Dogtown gained distinction in the wake of the 1904 St. Louis World's Fair, which was located just to the north in Forest Park. Besides the fair, nearby clay mines and factories and hefty influxes of Irish, German, and Italian immigrant workers shaped the neighborhood that exists today, which is roughly 50 percent Irish, with many Germans and Italians.

How did Dogtown get its name? Two theories prevail: (1) When Forest Park was about to open in 1876, Irish immigrant squatters and small-time coal miners who lived on park land were forced to move, so they drifted to the present Dogtown area, their pet and hunting dogs wagging behind them; and (2) The Igorot, a Philippine aboriginal tribe exhibiting at the fair, scavenged Dogtown's rolling hills for dog meat, a common food for them, when they couldn't obtain enough from fair managers. The first theory is most accepted; in fact, some stories suggest that Dogtown area property owners needed dogs to protect their possessions from marauding World's Fair-goers. "A lot of people move into the neighborhood today thinking you have to have a dog to live here," says Bob Pierce of the Clayton-Tamm Business and Merchant's Association.

Dogtown, roughly bounded by Hampton, Manchester, McCausland, and Oakland Avenues, was known as Cheltenham before 1900. In 1852, Cheltenham was the terminus of the first set of rail tracks west of the Mississippi River, and from 1853 to 1864 it was home to the alleged first socialist enclave in America, Etienne Cabet's Icarian community.

World's Fair memories linger near Oakland and Tamm. The Cheltenham entrance, 1 of 10 gates into the fairgrounds, was opposite Tamm. East of the entrance was the world's largest hotel (to that date), the $400,000, 2257-room Inside Inn, developed by E.M. Statler of the future Statler hotel chain. Rooms rented for $1.50 to $7.00 a day, with free fair admission. The place was billed as "the hotel in the wilderness" because of an adjacent virgin oak forest. Corridors in the yellow pine, burlap, and stucco building were half a mile long. Rooms had wooden semaphore arms to flag the bellboys stationed at each corridor intersection. Here, Statler developed the concept of a bath in every room. It was Statler who allegedly first said, "The customer is always right." After the fair, the inn was demolished.

Access

From downtown St. Louis, take MO 40/I-64 to Hampton Avenue South, exit 34C. Drive south on Hampton for one block. Turn right onto Clayton Avenue, then one block later jog right onto Berthold Avenue. Drive past the Deaconess Hospital complex to Tamm Avenue; turn right. Drive one block north to Oakland Avenue and park. The walk begins at Pat's Bar and Grill.

Trail

Walk south on Tamm to Clayton Avenue. From 1926 to 1932, Clayton Avenue was designated as US 50/66. Legendary Highway 66 crawled through Dogtown, made a left turn at McCausland, then pushed south toward Manchester, where it turned right, destined for the Great Southwest. Some older buildings around Clayton and Tamm are made from wood salvaged from World's Fair buildings, though new exteriors hide the original material. In the 1930s, Empire Field, a large baseball diamond, was located at the northwest corner of Clayton and Tamm, where Chuy Arzola's Tex-Mex restaurant is today.

At 1208 Tamm is Seamus McDaniel's bar and restaurant. For years, it had been O'Shea's Shamrock Bar. Jack O'Shea, a one-time Missouri legislator, was supposedly the first area bar owner to dispense corned beef and cabbage on St. Patrick's Day. A great sportsman, he once tried to promote boxing matches in the yard behind his bar. "Every bootlicker interested in local politics came around O'Shea's," recalls attorney William Quinn, a lifelong Dogtowner. Down the block, in front of 1218 Tamm, the pastor of St. James the Greater Catholic Church erected in the 1930s a small ring to coax local youngsters into tuning up for the annual Golden Gloves boxing competitions.

St. James the Greater Catholic Church, at Tamm and Nashville, has been the major Dogtown institution since 1861, though the present church building dates only to 1928. St. James was called the "World's Fair church." Its pastor offered Sunday mass to fair employees and baptized a baby, Louisiana O'Leary, born in a fair concession stand. "The World's Fair is being held in St. James the Greater parish," its members boasted. Nowadays, the church's membership is about one-third Irish.

Turn right onto Nashville. One block west on your right, at 6457 Childress, is the white frame Utah House that represented the state of Utah at the World's Fair. "When the fair was over, the house was cut in half, put on logs, and pulled by mules to the present site," says James Adler, who lives across the street. Continue west on Nashville, noting the three pristine-condition white frame shotgun houses at 4456, 4458, and 4489 Nashville. Continue down the hill to Louisville Avenue; turn left and walk south in former clay mine country to Dale Avenue. Turn left at Dale. Walk to an intersection, then take Lloyd Avenue uphill all the way back to Tamm.

After turning right on Tamm, walk a short block to Brock-schmidt Place. Turn right and walk past a row of late-19th-century, almost quaint brick homes (there is no sidewalk here) to Dale Avenue. Turn left on Dale and walk to Manchester Avenue.

Turn right onto Manchester Avenue. Here, around 100 years ago, were flourishing clayworking plants that produced fancy firebricks, decorative tile, and, at one time, more sewer pipe than any other plant in America. "About a third of Dogtown is built over old clay mines," estimates architect William Ziervogel, a Dogtown native. Throughout the area, mule-drawn carts pulled up heavy loads of rich Cheltenham clay from the deep mines, most of which had closed by 1930.

At Dale and Manchester, near the present Tech Electronics building, was Muegge's grocery store and federal post office. It is said that Ulysses S. Grant, then a farmer in southwest St. Louis County, would "wassail" at Muegge's in the 1850s—he'd stop by for a drink every now and then.

Across Manchester, site of the St. Louis Marketplace, is the former home of Scullin Steel Company, which occupied 12 city blocks and employed hundreds of locals from 1898 to the 1970s. After walking 3 blocks of irregular length on Manchester, turn right onto Kraft. Ramble up the sidewalk through a picture-book working-class neighborhood where chain-fenced front yards contain religious shrines, plaster donkeys, pink flamingos, and many live dogs. As you walk up Kraft, don't overlook the picturesque row of brick flats with varying porch designs on the north side of Garner Avenue. Seventy-five to 100 years ago, this area was considered part of the River des Peres valley and floodplain, although the river never flowed through what is now Dogtown. Above the floodplain is an area of glades, plateaus, and ridges. Locals called these "the bluffs." On these bluffs are streets named Glades and Plateau.

Turn left at Mitchell, then right on Prather. Behind the home on the southeast corner of Prather and Plateau is a single tree formed from a silver maple and a catalpa.

Walk downhill in former clay mine territory to Dale Avenue and turn left. Turn right off Dale onto Central Avenue. Walk—mostly uphill—6 blocks north to Clayton Avenue.

Just before turning right onto Clayton, look out to your left at the large Amoco sign over LeClaire Stevenson's service station on Skinker Boulevard. The 75-foot structure may be the tallest service station sign in America, says Stevenson. It costs Amoco about $1000 per month to illuminate the sign, a replacement for a same-sized Standard/Red Crown sign erected in 1928 to entice Highway 66 traffic. That older sign was so heavily illuminated by hundreds of large lights that it required its own electrical substation. "Visitors from all over America come to see our sign," says Stevenson.

Walk east on Clayton. One day in the fall of 1945, students at Dewey School rushed out the front door to wave as President Harry S Truman rode by in a political motorcade, recalls former pupil Vince Stuart. At Childress and Clayton, a pair of large, chocolate-brown bottles (they resemble milk bottles from the 1930s) rise from a modest one-story building. "That place used to be the Bottle Inn," recalls Dogtown musician Nick Mucci. In the 1930s and 1940s, the spot was popular as a restaurant, bar, dance hall, and beergarden. In another incarnation, in the early 1960s, the building housed "The Candles" restaurant. The Childress-Clayton corner was near the site of the last coal mine to operate in Dogtown. Backtrack one block west, then turn right on Sanford Avenue and walk along the sycamore-lined sidewalk to Oakland Avenue. Turn right onto Oakland.

In order to relieve traffic pressure on Oakland, a sunken artery known as the Oakland Express Highway opened in 1936. In the late 1930s, with traffic still comparatively light, the highway closed briefly each year for the Soapbox Derby, which attracted hundreds of self-propelled model cars created by St. Louis youngsters. "Drivers got annoyed when Highway 40 was shut down so that a 6-foot starter ramp, stretching across the highway, could be erected near Hampton," recalls Ziervogel, a soapboxer himself. From the ramp, the model cars coasted down the hill west to the finish line just beyond the Tamm Avenue overpass. "Kids came out of the woodwork to enter the derby," says Ziervogel.

Your walk ends back at Tamm near Pat's Bar and Grill, formerly McDermott's, and earlier, Pete's Place. "When I was a boy, you could walk north past Pete's Place, cross Oakland, walk on a rickety bridge over a creek, and you'd be in Forest Park," recalls Joseph McMahon, once a vice-president of the International Fire Fighters union. "Back in those days, Dogtown was looked on as being on the other side of the tracks. Today, it's in its ascendancy."

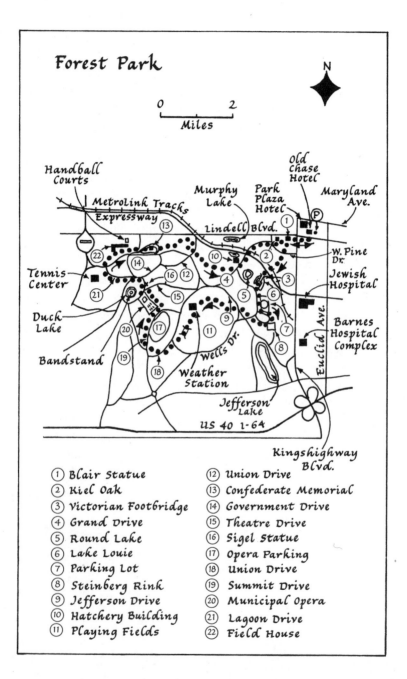

Forest Park

0   2
Miles

N

Handball Courts

MetroLink Tracks

Expressway

Murphy Lake

Park Plaza Hotel

Old Chase Hotel

Maryland Ave.

Lindell Blvd.

W. Pine Dr.

Jewish Hospital

Tennis Center

Duck Lake

Bandstand

Barnes Hospital Complex

Euclid Ave.

Wells Dr.

Weather Station

Jefferson Lake

US 40 I-64

Kingshighway Blvd.

① Blair Statue
② Kiel Oak
③ Victorian Footbridge
④ Grand Drive
⑤ Round Lake
⑥ Lake Louie
⑦ Parking Lot
⑧ Steinberg Rink
⑨ Jefferson Drive
⑩ Hatchery Building
⑪ Playing Fields
⑫ Union Drive
⑬ Confederate Memorial
⑭ Government Drive
⑮ Theatre Drive
⑯ Sigel Statue
⑰ Opera Parking
⑱ Union Drive
⑲ Summit Drive
⑳ Municipal Opera
㉑ Lagoon Drive
㉒ Field House

Forest Park

Location: St. Louis, Missouri
Hiking distance: 3 miles
Hiking time: 2 hours
Bicycles: permitted on paved paths, roads

As the Democratic National Convention met in downtown St. Louis on June 24, 1876, Forest Park officially opened. Many curious delegates took the 45-minute carriage ride to see what was and still is America's second largest city park, after Philadelphia's Fairmount Park.

Nearly half wilderness, the new property was designed as a driving park for carriages. By the late 1800s, the park was attracting bicyclists as well as walkers, who called bicycles "silent steeds" and "road hogs." Shortly, the first dedicated bike path opened. In 1911, the US national championship bike race was held in the park.

The St. Louis World's Fair, which drew 20 million visitors in a 7-month stand in 1904, was the park's great growth catalyst. For this mammoth event, fair officials planted 1,679,000 trees, shrubs, and vines (how many survive today, do you suppose?) and constructed 1576 buildings and other structures, mostly of ivory white plaster-of-paris material called "staff," on wooden frames. So rugged was the material, says Max Storm, founder of the 1904 World's Fair Society, that "it took only two full-time employees to maintain all the buildings during the course of the fair." Many existing park streets are World's Fair legacies, such as Government Drive, which ran near Government Hill, site of the Missouri and US government pavilions, and Wells Drive, named for Rolla Wells, mayor of St. Louis during the fair.

The first police cars in St. Louis were deployed in the park in 1902 to check reckless drivers. The police vehicles were called "skiddo cars." In 1909 aviator Glenn H. Curtis made what were perhaps the first airplane flights west of the Mississippi—seven short take-offs and landings on the cricket field near the present Jefferson Memorial building at Lindell and DeBaliviere.

In 1919, the St. Louis Municipal Opera debuted. Described as "a people's theater," it had the world's largest stage and the first stage amplification system. Popular entertainers, including W.C. Fields, Eddie Cantor, Cary Grant, Bob Hope, and Grace Kelly, all played "The Muny."

Access

From the intersection of US 40/I-64 and Kingshighway, drive north on Kingshighway to Lindell Boulevard. Park near the intersection. Walk to the Blair statue near the park's southwest corner, where the walk begins.

Trail

Begin the walk at the triangular island where Senator Francis Preston Blair Jr. (1821–1875) sits on his bronze horse. The one-time Missouri senator was a Civil War Union general, then an 1868 US vice-presidential candidate. In 1885, his friend General William Tecumseh Sherman was among the 15,000 guests at the statue unveiling. South of the statue are the Koplar Family Fountains, sharing space in the Lucy and Stanley Lopata Plaza, with a monument to the first Jewish settlement in America.

Walk directly south; cross West Pine Drive. Find the paved path that leads to a footbridge over the Wabash Railroad tracks, now used by MetroLink, the light rail transit system. Forty years ago, 18 daily Wabash passenger trains, including the "Blue Bird," the "Banner Blue," and the "Midnight Limited," chugged under the bridge en route to and from Chicago, Kansas City, Omaha, and Detroit. Walk over another footbridge spanning Forest Park Expressway, then over an 1885 black iron, wooden plank footbridge that bisects a small lagoon (known as "Lake Louie" in honor of former parks commissioner Louie Buckowitz). Walk left on the paved bike path to Steinberg Skating Rink.

A gift of nearly $750,000 from the Mark C. Steinberg Charitable Trust made possible the rink, which opened in 1957. "My

In 1920, a motorist prepares a campsite in Forest Park. (Forest Park archives)

grandmother [Mrs. Mark C. Steinberg] used to stay at the Hotel Pierre in New York, where she could look out her window at the skating rink in Central Park," says John D. Weil. "She never skated herself, but she wanted a rink like that for Forest Park." Near the rink is a 1927 bronze statue, *Joie de Vivre,* by renowned sculptor Jacques Lipchitz, a friend of the Steinbergs.

Return to the bike path. Walk left to Wells and Jefferson Drives. Walk west on Jefferson; a traffic island will be on your left. Turn left and walk straight up the grassy hill to the ball diamonds. Turn right; follow the edge of the diamonds west to a red granite marker, a remnant of the early 1900s St. Louis Meteorological Station on the site. Still on the lawn, walk left, then head down the hill and across a crumbling stone bridge. From the Union-Summit Drives intersection, hike up Summit to the rear of the St. Louis Municipal Opera. Gaze across 12,000 empty seats to the giant stage, half the length of a football field.

In 1923, President Warren G. Harding, in town for a Rotary convention, arrived at The Muny midway into a performance and was

A footbridge passes over the old Wabash Railroad (now MetroLink) tracks on the northeast edge of Forest Park.

immediately introduced on stage by St. Louis mayor Henry Kiel. Six weeks later, Kiel interrupted another Muny production to announce that Harding had died suddenly in San Francisco. The rest of the show was canceled; the audience left, stunned. In June 1927, Charles A. Lindbergh, just back from his solo flight across the Atlantic from New York to Paris, visited The Muny. He sat through part of *The Princess Pat,* a Victor Herbert operetta, when the pit orchestra launched abruptly into the French and American national anthems. Lindbergh was escorted to center stage. He bowed, said nothing, and returned to his seat.

Stroll down The Muny's east walkway, then its Hall of Fame, where plaques celebrate stars who have played the theater. Walk around the colonnade and ticket area. Observe the art deco box office design; the massive bronze chandelier; and the terrazzo floor, with 37 color shades and symbols representing Muny production themes.

Cross Theatre Drive to view the Nathan Frank bandstand on Pagoda Lake. Walk east to see the city's first equestrian statue, the

1906 bronze General Franz Sigel. A German native, Sigel became a schoolteacher in St. Louis. During the Civil War, he headed the all-German Third regiment of the US Volunteers, stationed at the US Arsenal in downtown St. Louis. He participated in the Camp Jackson Affair in St. Louis in 1861, then fared poorly later that year in the battle of Wilson's Creek in southwest Missouri. After losing a battle to a small Confederate force at New Market, Virginia, in 1864, he resigned his major general's commission. His statue in Forest Park, the first addition to the park in the wake of the 1904 World's Fair, was dedicated in 1906 as a "memorial to all German-Americans who fought for the Union" in the Civil War, writes William C. Winter in *The Civil War in St. Louis.*

Walk west along Government Drive, then bear to your right and join Lagoon Drive. Straight ahead are the Dwight Davis tennis courts. In their book, *Forest Park,* authors Caroline Loughlin and Catherine Anderson write that new gaslights around the courts in 1917 drew curious St. Louisans who sat in their automobiles and gawked. Police had to direct traffic. Turn right on the sidewalk that runs north to the Field House on Grand Drive.

Atop the Field House is the remaining lower segment of the clock tower (in place from 1892 to 1903) from the Lindell Railway Pavilion, once a major streetcar stop and the park's early north central entrance. Walk through the Field House, then turn around and exit through the front door, turning left to take the sidewalk past the handball courts.

Walk east to the traffic circle that contains the 1914 bronze Civil War Confederate Memorial. St. Louis aldermen declared at the time that no Confederate soldier or weapon could be depicted on the memorial since St. Louis had been a Union city. From the east end of the traffic island, cross Confederate Drive. Walk on the grass through a grove of white birch trees and past a closed stone restroom facility. Turn left; hike north to the paved bike path, then walk right on the path toward the 1876 Victorian residence of Joseph C. Cabanne, later the parkkeeper's home, and now the headquarters of the St. Louis Ambassadors, a civic booster group. Walk around the building, then continue east on the bike path, crossing Union Drive.

On your right, protected by black iron grating, stairs lead to the Metropolitan Sewer District entryway to the River des Peres watershed system. Two 29-foot pipes, 40 feet below ground, carry storm water under the park. On your left and right are lagoons or fish hatchery lakes, managed until 1947 by the US Bureau of Fisheries. The eleven 5-foot-deep lakes were created when the park opened in 1876. Note the pointed protuberances or "knees" near the base of some of the bald cypress trees along the lagoons. The "knees" take in air for the trees' water-lodged roots.

At Grand Drive, walk left. On your left, before the bridge, is the 1938 limestone fish hatchery building, topped by a fish-shaped weather vane. The building is now a maintenance office. Cross West Pine Drive and access the sidewalk to the Blair statue. On your left is a burr oak planted in memory of Henry Kiel, mayor of St. Louis from 1913 to 1925. While mayor, he headed the Municipal Opera Association, got to meet President Harding and Charles Lindbergh, and greatly advanced the cause of Forest Park.

Francis Park/ St. Louis Hills Art Deco Walk

Location: St. Louis, Missouri
Hiking distance: 2 miles
Hiking time: 1½ hours
Bicycles: permitted

Welcome to a neighborhood of pink sidewalks, art deco apartments and duplexes, and well-tended homes from the 1930s and 1940s. Francis Park is the centerpiece of the neighborhood. It lies in the heart of St. Louis Hills, a subdivision created by builder Cyrus Crane Willmore.

"If you bought a lot from Mr. Willmore, you got a bed of roses and a Japanese elm tree as extras," recalls Vincent Micotto, who subcontracted for Willmore. "Mr. Willmore specified slate or red tile roofs on his homes, but he didn't enforce that as much as he did the pink sidewalks. He thought pink meant affluent."

To James Shrewsbury, the St. Louis alderman who represents St. Louis Hills, pink sidewalks can be nightmarish. "I hadn't been in office very long before I got a call from a constituent who screamed that his neighbor was putting in a white sidewalk. He pointed out to me that our walks here are predominantly pink.

"Pink is expensive," continues Shrewsbury. "Whether you are doing one or two sidewalk squares or 900 square feet of sidewalk, you have to buy a whole truckload of pink cement. Since you can't use pink concrete anywhere else, any leftover concrete has to be dumped."

In 1887, Missouri governor David R. Francis bought 377 acres in the area. He called the property "fine truck gardening land." On his land was a tenant farmer, an old home, barns, outbuildings, and some

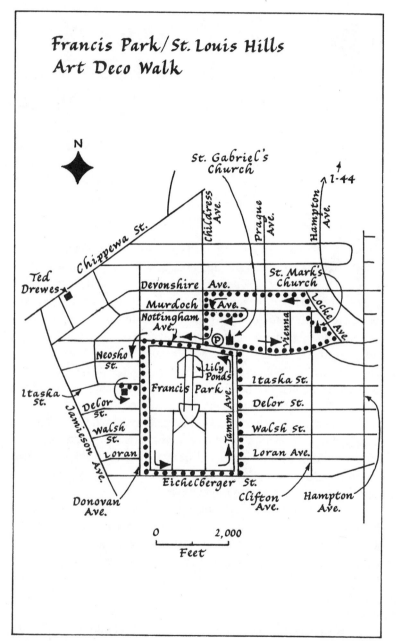

Francis Park/St. Louis Hills Art Deco Walk

chickens. In the early 1900s, he considered the farm for the site of the 1904 St. Louis World's Fair, which he headed, but nixed the idea because the place was so inaccessible.

In 1917, Francis gave 60 acres to the city to establish a park, but World War I intervened, delaying development. Eventually, in 1923, the park was dedicated and handed over to a supervised detachment of first offenders from the St. Louis City Workhouse so they could live there and "develop" the ground. In 1929, Willmore purchased much of the remaining Francis land for his subdivision.

Willmore was a superb promoter. Walter Tracy, in *St. Louis Leadership 1944,* says that Willmore probably acquired a promotional flair as a college undergraduate. "The first university homecoming in America was held at the University of Illinois when Willmore was student president of the University athletic association," Tracy notes.

In the summer of 1930, during the Great Depression and a miserable heat wave, Willmore took out a six-page advertising section in the *St. Louis Star-Times* to push the formal opening of a "master model home" in St. Louis Hills. Within 2 months, more than 100,000 people had filed through the home at 6226 Itaska.

For the subdivision opening, Willmore requested that "a movie man" be on hand to take "an extensive panorama of the crowds so that St. Louisans will have a chance to see themselves in the movies." Major movie houses showed the short film, now apparently lost, laments a St. Louis Hills historian, attorney Joseph Hanses. Later, the Home Owner's Institute of New York recognized Willmore and St. Louis Hills as "the national leader" in subdivision promotion. Today, some say, with tongue in cheek, people move to St. Louis Hills mostly for its proximity to the Ted Drewes frozen custard shop on Chippewa Street.

The annual 5K Run for the Hills and its companion Fun Walk (once around the park)—events that attract 600 ramblers, 75 percent of whom are thought to be year-round Francis Park hoofers—raise money for park improvements in a unique partnership with the city. So far, the sponsoring St. Louis Hills Home Owners Association, matched by alderman Shrewsbury's 2-for-1 contribution of city funds, has helped provide a new playground, dozens of new dogwood and other trees, and new trash receptacles.

Access

From US 40/I-64 in the central west end of St. Louis, get off at the Kingshighway South exit. Take Kingshighway South to Nottingham Avenue, about 3.2 miles. Turn right. Drive 6 blocks west to Tamm Avenue. Park in the middle of the St. Gabriel the Archangel Catholic Church block.

Trail

Start your walk in front of St. Gabriel's Church, its steeple resembling a 1930s Manhattan skyscraper. "I was with Archbishop John Glennon when he tried to talk Mr. Willmore into buying the whole block on Nottingham for St. Gabriel's," recalls Vincent Micotto, "but he only bought half the block."

Stroll east on Nottingham, which Willmore once described as "the prize apartment spot in St. Louis." Many of its apartment buildings retain strong art deco motifs and features. Popular from about 1925 to 1940, art deco architecture embraced such features as glass blocks, zigzag brick patterns, brick bands, curved corners, casement and circular windows, and concrete designs and flourishes near doors and windows.

The apartment at 6263 Nottingham (at Prague) typifies art deco: porthole window, curved glass blocks, brick bands on the face of the building. It's a favorite of the St. Louis Art Deco Society, which conducts walks in the area. At 5845 is the intriguing Vedder apartment building, constructed in 1938 for $20,000. All six units have penthouses. Old-style venetian blinds hang throughout the building.

At the Vedder, turn left onto Locke Avenue, then cut down the alley behind the apartment complex. Turn right at Clifton Avenue, where you'll immediately encounter the imposing St. Mark's Episcopal Church, one of "the very few examples in the world of Modernist design before World War II," reads *A Guide to Architecture in St. Louis* by George McCue and Frank Peters. The white-brick building, de-

Near Francis Park on Nottingham Avenue is the 1938 Vedder apartment building, rich in art deco architectural features, including penthouses.

signed by Nagel and Dunn, cost $75,000 to construct, including the land. Turn left from Clifton onto Devonshire.

At 6352 and 6358 Devonshire are, respectively, the August and September 1936 *McCall's* magazine national homes of the month, quite an honor for St. Louis and the aggressive Willmore Organization that built them. Note the art deco sailboat in a large circular window at 6360. This home was designed by Francis G. Avis, who blueprinted 400 other residences around St. Louis, including the Moorlands section of Richmond Heights, another art deco stronghold.

Turn left on Childress, then walk to Murdoch, turning left again. In 1936 *McCall's* magazine called the white-brick home at 6359 Murdoch "a gentleman's home . . . typical of Monterey houses of California." Backtrack to Childress; turn left, walk to Nottingham, then turn right.

Three buildings on this block showcase art deco motifs. At 6347 Nottingham is an over-the-door fluted concrete geometric pattern; at 6449, a Western theme in stained glass; and at 6475, corner wraparound windows and a curving glass-block wall.

Walk left on Donovan by Nottingham School, which isn't art deco but is impressive for its colorful front entrance mosaics. Turn right on Itaska to see the eight-sided home at 6520 with casement windows and ashlar concrete by the front door. "This may be the most unique home in St. Louis Hills," says David Eschmann, former Art Deco Society president, who points out that each side differs in length. Retrace your steps to cross Donovan and enter the park. Turn right onto the park sidewalk.

On uncharacteristically white sidewalks, hundreds hike the 1¼-mile circumference of the park daily, some several times in succession. Forester Ramon Gass, familiar with the grounds for 50 years, identifies the trees as he walks around the park. Across from 5221 Donovan is a grove of bright green white pines, mixed with Scotch pines with their orangish bark. Opposite Walsh Street, a grove of tall persimmons partially fills a yawning sinkhole.

Walk left on Eichelberger, then left again on Tamm Avenue. Park handball courts are off to your left; a European white birch stands near the sidewalk. A huge grove of Norway spruce trees is opposite Walsh Street. Across from 5220 Tamm is a lone Japanese pagoda tree; to its left, a Chinese chestnut. Opposite Delor are four mature arborvitae trees.

Turn left on Nottingham for the last half block of the walk. A colony of black locust trees is near the corner. At midblock, sidewalks lead to the lily ponds where just-married couples liked to have their pictures taken in the 1940s and 1950s. Bald cypress trees border the pond on both sides. From here you can either walk around the park again or return to your car and call it a day.

The Hill
Neighborhood

Location: St. Louis, Missouri
Hiking distance: 3½ miles
Hiking time: 2 hours
Bicycles: permitted

Nearly 95 percent of the Hill's 6500 residents are of Italian descent, mostly from Lombardy and Sicily. Most are Catholic, shown by statues of the Virgin Mary and of St. Francis in front yards and on porches, and by the strong central presence of St. Ambrose Catholic Church, the community religious and social center.

Many Hill homes are "shotguns": one room wide, one story high, tidy, frame or red brick. Some are set back to the alley. Some lots support two homes, one fore, one aft. Some yards yield spectacular gardens. Throughout the Hill, small businesses blend organically with neighbors on what appear to be purely residential blocks.

How did the Hill begin? In the 1830s, rich clay deposits were discovered beneath St. Louis's highest ground, which is in the Hill neighborhood. "Nowhere in the United States is the soil so perfect for fine clay and terra-cotta brick products," wrote a local geologist. In the 1880s, the clayworks and brick factories attracted European immigrants, mostly Italians and a few Germans. The largest terra-cotta, press brick, fire brick, and sewer pipe factories in the United States were all built on or near the Hill. The father of T.S. Eliot, whose *Old Possum's Book of Practical Cats* inspired the long-running musical *Cats,* was president of one company, Hydraulic Press Brick.

Access
At I-44 and South Kingshighway (exit 287), take Kingshighway south to Shaw Avenue. Turn right on Shaw; drive to Marconi. Take

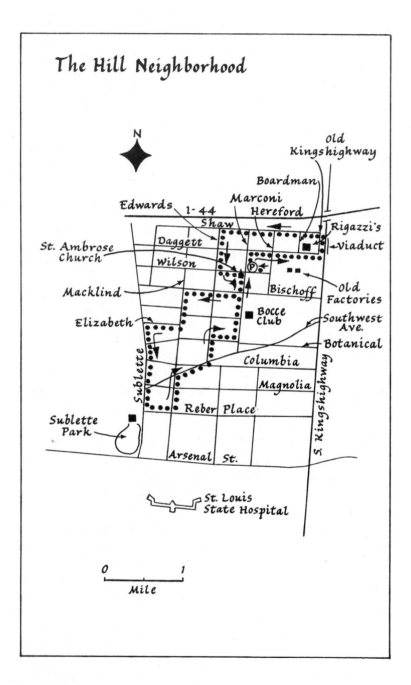

The Hill Neighborhood

a left at Marconi. Drive to Wilson Street and park near St. Ambrose Catholic Church. The walk begins at St. Ambrose Church School on Wilson.

Trail

In front of St. Ambrose School, look across Wilson to a row of mostly brick "shotgun" houses. "These are basically three-room homes where the front door is aligned with the kitchen door so you can literally fire a gun straight through the place," says Frank "Chick" Severino, local historian and tour guide. Many Hill homes are brick because 30 to 40 percent of the locals once worked for the brick factories. The brick home at 5117 Wilson kept goats in the postage stamp–sized yard until 1960, says Severino. Neighbors bought the goats' milk, which, due to the minuscule "pasture," must have been skim!

If you look to your right, toward the corner of Wilson and Hereford, you'll see Dominic's restaurant, originally the Achillies-Berra tavern, which catered to employees of the neighboring Magic Chef stove plant. Later, as Andreino's, the restaurant hosted visiting celebrities such as Sammy Davis Jr., Johnny Carson, Dean Martin, Frank Sinatra, and Jack Benny. Magic Chef was previously called American Stove. "So many Hill people worked there, it was nicknamed Italian Stove," says Severino. Magic Chef bragged that it was "the world's largest gas range manufacturer."

Walk west on Wilson; turn right at Marconi. At the corner is Amighetti's Bakery and Gelateria, a bakery since 1917, a restaurant since about 1975. Founded as a confectionery by Lombardian immigrants from Verona, Amighetti's has been on Wilson Street since 1921 and in its current building since 1929. One early visitor in the 1930s was Primo Carnera, Italy's "Ambling Alp," who was the world heavyweight boxing champ for about a year until Max Baer defeated him in 1934. "The priest across the street at St. Ambrose brought him over," recalls Lou Amighetti Jr., the founder's now-retired son, still excited as he describes the celebrated visitor.

Across Marconi, the two white frame homes have double basements, one atop the other, an arrangement that helped shield moonshining operations during Prohibition. "Many people bought homes, then jacked them up and put in a second basement," explains Severino. Walk one block north on Marconi to Daggett; turn right on Daggett.

At 5040 Daggett, look in on Imo's Pizza's meat and sausage processing plant and toppings center. At 4945 is Rigazzi's Restaurant, started in 1955 by John Riganti and Lou Aiazzi (hence the blended "Rigazzi's"). At 4941 is the art deco–inspired former research building of Magic Chef, whose low brick plants were across the street. Farther east on Daggett, a glass-enclosed shrine of the Virgin Mary sits in the rear of an abandoned parking lot next to Sala's restaurant, closed in 1976 after 65 years. Sala's sued the city in the 1930s when the Kingshighway viaduct opened nearby and allegedly hid the restaurant from passing motorists. Sala's told the court it lost 66,000 customers the year the viaduct opened. The city paid $41,000 in damages.

Turn left on old Kingshighway and walk north to Shaw, turning left. At Shaw and Boardman (southwest corner) is the Shaw playground site. "We called it the Sahara Desert because it had no trees and the park supervisor sat under a fly tent," says Severino. At 5041 Shaw is the former Spam's store, which sold lemon punch in the 1930s and 1940s. Up the street, in the next block, its name etched in concrete over the front entrance, is the one-time Family Theater. "They used to leave the side doors open in summer since there was no air-conditioning," recalls Severino. Across Shaw is J. Viviano and Sons Grocery Company, once Rau's clothing and shoe store. "At Rau's, you put what you purchased in a basket. The clerk wrote the bill, then sent the basket on a pulley up to the store balcony where they wrapped the merchandise and wrote the receipt. You could leave just as soon as they sent the basket back down," says Severino.

The former Big Club Hall is on the southwest corner of Shaw and Marconi. The building opened in 1897 as "North Italy America Club" (NIAC), the social center for immigrants from Lombardy. For many, it was the place to drink beer and find entertainment on Sunday after church. (The Sicilians' social center, now headquarters for The Pasta House Company, was at 1924 Marconi Avenue.) Toasted

Redbrick shotgun houses line Botanical Street in the Hill neighborhood.

ravioli, invented in St. Louis, was supposed to have debuted commercially in the 1940s at Angelo's on the Hill restaurant at 5226 Shaw, now Charley Gitto's on the Hill.

On the next corners are Fair Mercantile Furniture Company, in the same location since 1915 (but closed in 1995), and the 7 Steps Tavern, here since 1888. Open at 6 AM, 7 Steps has a potbellied stove and a walk-in icebox. For decades, local legend says, a 7 Steps employee who worked at nearby St. Louis State Hospital brought ice from the hospital each noon to pour over the saloon's beer supply.

Turn left onto Edwards. On the northwest corner of Edwards and Daggett stood the Rose's Garden saloon. Yogi Berra brought New York Yankee teammates for beer and bocce in the saloon's rear courts, which remain. John Volpi and Company, Inc., cattycorner to the Rose saloon since 1902, makes prosciutto ham (long a favorite of customers Zsa Zsa Gabor and Frank Sinatra) and salami and sells the meats along with cheeses and pastas. Cross Daggett; continue south on Edwards.

Near Wilson is Missouri Baking Company, opened in 1909. "It

was always called the Missouri Bakery because at that time it wasn't fashionable to be Italian," a second-generation co-owner of the place says. Today, says Jo Arpiani of the bakery, "we always put in our ads, 'Gambaro and Arpiani's Missouri Bakery.' "

Turn left onto Wilson. Zia's Restaurant was once Ribaudo's and, earlier, Consolino's grocery and dry goods store. "It has a double basement," notes Severino. Walk east on Wilson, a Hill showcase block with manicured lawns and homes. At 5225 is a cigar-chewing concrete wine maker. "I have one of these statues in my living room," Severino reveals.

Turn right on Marconi; walk to Bischoff and turn right. At 5225, at the rear, is Tony Ranciglio's potbellied stove–heated black-smith shop, in business without interruption since 1906. In its prime, it employed four smiths and four wagon-wheel makers. Now it produces ornamental fences and railings as well as special construc-tion tools.

Stay on Bischoff; walk to Macklind, then turn left. Walk to Elizabeth and turn right. Jack Buck, the St. Louis Cardinal baseball broadcaster, lived in an apartment at 5405 Elizabeth in the late 1950s. Yogi Berra lived at 5447 Elizabeth, says his friend Severino. "From a backyard shed, Yogi ran the Stags athletic club, a softball-soccer organization for kids about 13 and 14. Across Elizabeth, at 5446, was Joe Garagiola's boyhood home."

Turn left on Sublette. Fassi's Market and Bar on Sublette is where both Joe and Yogi fetched pails of beer for their fathers many evenings after work. Continue south 2 blocks to Magnolia. At Mag-nolia, look right toward the end of the block to St. Aloysius Catholic Church, spiritual home to German Catholic settlers in the area. At left is Cunetto's Restaurant. In the 1950s it was the Brass Key nightclub with an all-girl orchestra and terrazzo dance floor. Earlier, it was Rigoletto's nightclub, which packed the house with smashing stage shows on weekends. Continue south another block straight to Reber Place, the Hill's only boulevard.

Sublette Park, where Berra played American Legion baseball, is at the southwest corner of Reber and Sublette's intersection. The land immediately west of the tennis courts may be the highest point in St.

Louis, as Severino and others insist, and as engineers from the Metropolitan St. Louis Sewer District confirm. Walk east on Reber Place to Macklind. Turn left on Macklind and follow it to Southwest Avenue. Cross Southwest to Columbia Avenue; walk to Henry Shaw School. From the Shaw play yard, Berra allegedly hit fly balls that bounced off the roof of the Columbia Theater, now a private residence at Southwest and Edwards.

From the schoolyard, walk left on Edwards, then right on Botanical Street, with its rows of picturesque, redbrick shotgun homes. Turn left on Marconi. On the right is the former McQuay Norris plant, which made piston rings. In September 1945, the *St. Louis Post-Dispatch* reported that during World War II the company made a "secret weapon rated as second only to the atomic bomb." McQuay's radio proximity fuse was "credited with breaking up the German Belgian Bulge offensive and stopping the [German] buzz bomb attack," said the *Post-Dispatch*.

Nearby is the 450-member St. Louis Bocce Club, a refurbished McQuay Norris building. "Our three courts are used constantly by men and women, some of whom have taken over bocce," states Severino, club secretary. From the club, it's a short way to St. Ambrose Church and the end of your walk.

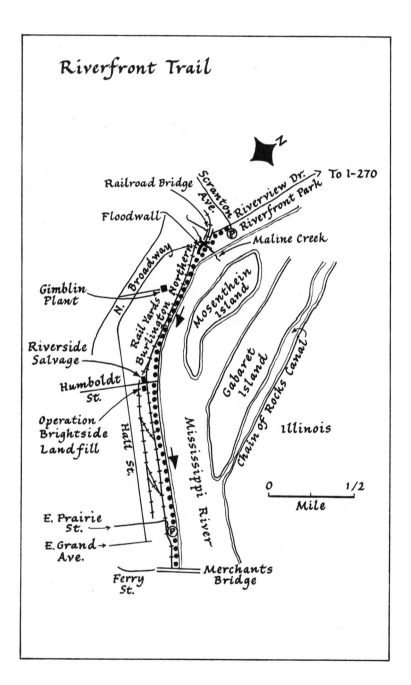

Riverfront Trail

Riverfront Trail

Location: St. Louis, Missouri
Hiking distance: 5 miles one way
Hiking time: 1½ hours
Bicycles: permitted

Most St. Louisans are familiar with the 1½-mile "central riverfront" near the Arch and Laclede's Landing, but are hazy about the remaining riverfront north and south of downtown. This right-bank, downriver walk introduces you to 5 miles of northside riverfront and its floodwalls and levees, part of the city's new Riverfront Trail, which someday will extend from North Riverfront Park down to Bellerive Park in south St. Louis, about 19½ miles.

In the past 60 years, lofty proposals for taming the north riverfront have been offered, and rejected: Put in an airport, develop another Coney Island (like the one in New York), build a scenic highway, reserve land for a World's Fair site. In 1966, however, the St. Louis city planning commission had a good idea—develop a riverfront bike- and walkway to make the riverside more inviting and accessible. Twenty years later, the city got serious, ordered a feasibility study, and committed some resources. It was former St. Louis mayor Vincent Schoemehl who pushed hard for trail development; it was Gateway Trailnet, Inc., and its planning director Jim Pona, who originally advocated the trail and helped obtain grants.

Historically, this stretch of the river was one of the most frequent sites of steamboat accidents because, at low stages, the rocks on the bottom stuck out like sawyers and cut away away the bottoms of boats, says Claude N. Strauser, chief of the potamology (science of rivers) section for the US Army Corps of Engineers, St. Louis district. The Chain of Rocks Canal, begun in 1946 and completed in 1953, was built to circumnavigate this harrowing stretch of the river near the Missouri shore.

Access

In north St. Louis County, take I-270 East to exit 34, Riverview Drive—the last exit in Missouri. Drive south on Riverview for about 3 miles. Just south of Scranton Avenue, turn left into the south parking lot of North Riverfront Park. If you don't want to walk 10 miles round-trip, two cars are required; leave a car at the south end of the trail, then drive back to the North Riverfront Park to begin your hike.

You can reach the second parking area by driving south on Riverview, turning left onto Hall Street, and driving south on Hall to East Prairie Street, just before Grand. At East Prairie, turn left; drive east, then south. Cross the railroad tracks. Make a right turn onto the levee road and park.

Trail

From North Riverfront Park, a linear recreation area that floods occasionally, walk south on the paved trail next to Riverview Drive. On the left is a city street department yard that stores surplus granite curbstones, some dating from the early 1800s. Today, this stored granite is used to patch existing curbstones, especially in downtown St. Louis and the near north side.

After crossing Maline Creek, the trail turns left at the concrete floodwall. In 1955, Maline Creek was called St. Louis County's worst public health hazard due to its open sewage and general stench. When the Metropolitan Sewer District formed, its first project was a trunk sewer on the 12-mile stream, whose mouth lies slightly to the east of the Maline bridge. Meanwhile, the $130 million floodwall project, which included levees, was completed in 1968. It's the "biggest of its kind ever authorized by Congress" and "the largest job ever undertaken by the City of St. Louis," local newspapers crowed. The project included 7 miles of floodwalls and 4 miles of levees and was meant to protect 3100 contiguous acres from floods.

Walking south atop the levee, you pass the Metropolitan Sewer District's storm-water pumping stations—Gimblin, at the 1¼-mile point on the trail, and Baden, at 2¼ miles. Both stations pump storm water into the Mississippi in underground pipes. The Baden plant, which can pump 2 million gallons a minute, is one of America's largest stations, says Jack Kearns, MSD pump station manager.

At the 2-mile point, abandoned railroad ties lie stacked off to the right near what once was the St. Louis terminal facility and general offices for the Missouri-Kansas-Texas (M-K-T or "Katy") Railroad. The spire on the right horizon marks Holy Cross Church in Baden; its height equals that of an 18-story building. Incoming pilots at Lambert St. Louis International Airport use the spire as a visual guidepost. In 1950, the entire Trapp family, immortalized in the musical *The Sound of Music,* gave a concert at the church and signed the guest register.

Along here, birdwatchers spot eagles and other uncommon species in midwinter. Railroad workers observe an occasional coyote or deer. The levee was once part of the river. To build it to its average height of 20 feet, workmen in the 1960s hydraulically pumped sand, clay, and rock chunks from the Mississippi to the levee site, their pumps often running 24 hours a day.

To the right of the trail, the parallel tracks constitute the Burlington Northern (BN) Railroad main line. In 1948, Harry Truman's campaign train passed through there, says Bill McLain, who began a long career with BN in 1947. "President Eisenhower came past here in 1954 heading into Union Station, and later on, so did President Lyndon Johnson."

Near the Humboldt Street crossing is Riverside Salvage, Inc., an auto junkyard with two Rottweiler guard dogs, Stan and Henry. About 1100 old cars rest in neat rows, most with their hoods up. Customers are plentiful, most searching for replacement carburetors. "People think that if anything is wrong with their car, it's the carburetor," says Dennis Sullivan, manager.

Bankside is Albericci Construction Company's river facility where four mitre gates, each weighing 140 tons, were constructed in work barges and floated to the new Alton Lock and Dam #26 farther upstream. The construction cranes on the shore weigh from 150 to 200 tons each.

At Humboldt is the city's Operation Brightside clean landfill, accepting only brick, concrete, and dirt, mostly from building contractors. "Our landfill generates revenue to help the city fund new beautification projects," says Mary Lou Green, executive director. "We hope to plant flowers up and down the trail in the future."

Mosenthein Island lies opposite Humboldt Street; here, in 1959, the US Secretary of the Army turned the first shovelful of dirt for the giant floodwall/levee project. Four miles long, about 1½ miles wide, the island is named for Mary Mosenthein, who lived there with her six children from 1883 to 1904. Since then, few humans have called Mosenthein home, though visitors have been plentiful. In the 1940s, sandy beaches on the Illinois side beckoned sun worshipers who ferried over from Humboldt Street every Sunday afternoon.

In 1936, Major Albert B. Lambert, taught to fly by Orville Wright and in whose memory Lambert Field was named, advocated a close-in airport. Reclaim Mosenthein Island by filling in the river and connecting it with the Missouri shore, he urged. That idea was a flopperoo, as was a 1966 city planning commission proposal that Mosenthein become a bistate park with a motel, golf course, and restaurants.

In 1947, two local developers sought support to create a second Coney Island and a possible future World's Fair site on Mosenthein. Their futile plan called for surplus government oil barges to be converted into replicas of Chinese junks and pirates' galleons, and anchored at the island as restaurants and dance floors.

At the 3⅓-mile point, the trail forks. You must now take the path to the river side of the floodwall. This last section of the trail takes you past floodplain trees such as cottonwoods and sycamores, and underbrush that nearly blocks the river view in summer.

As you walk, you pass under three conveyor systems that carry coal and grain to waiting barges for transshipment through the river network. After passing the ADM Growmark terminal grain elevator, the trail comes within a few feet of the river, the closest to the Mississippi that you'll be.

Around here, the Mississippi flows by at about 3 to 4 miles per hour, and two or three times that fast if the river is low; this, says Strauser of the Corps of Engineers, is because the lower stages have a steeper slope due to the rock bottom. If all the silt and mud that flow past this midbanks point over 24 hours were removed, the suspended material (sands, silts, and clay) could cover 1000 acres 6 inches deep. Following a flood, about 12 million tons of suspended material could be removed from the Mississippi in a single day, he says.

At Ferry Street, under the 1889 Merchants Bridge, the trail ends; you must turn around and return to North Riverfront Park unless you have a car waiting. (A 3-mile extension from this trail to the Arch is in the planning stage.) Merchants Bridge was built as an alternative to Eads Bridge, which also carried trains on its lower deck and then through a smoky, sooty tunnel into downtown St. Louis.

At Ferry Street, you can look out toward Gabaret Island, which lies south of Mosenthein Island. Gabaret's southern tip marks the entrance to the Chain of Rocks Canal, which allows river transportation to bypass the shallow, treacherous water near the Missouri side of the river. There have been plans galore to develop this island, too. A land trust controlled by the Granite City (Illinois) Trust and Savings Bank advertised the island for sale in the *Wall Street Journal* in 1977. The place could be turned into a gambling casino or an international trade exposition site, the ad said. "Research indicates this could be the largest single real estate development in the entire Midwest," it babbled. Nothing happened.

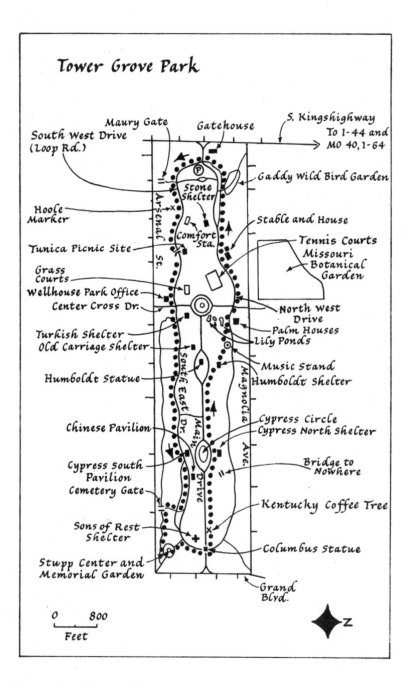

Tower Grove Park

Maury Gate

Gatehouse

S. Kingshighway
To 1-44 and
MO 40, 1-64

South West Drive
(Loop Rd.)

Gaddy Wild Bird Garden

Stone Shelter

Hoole Marker

Stable and House

Comfort Sta.

Tennis Courts
Missouri
Botanical
Garden

Tunica Picnic Site

Arsenal St.

Grass Courts

Wellhouse Park Office
Center Cross Dr.

North West Drive

Turkish Shelter
Old Carriage Shelter

Palm Houses
Lily Ponds

Humboldt Statue

South East Dr.

Music Stand
Humboldt Shelter

Chinese Pavilion

Main Drive

Magnolia Ave.

Cypress Circle
Cypress North Shelter

Cypress South Pavilion
Cemetery Gate

Bridge to Nowhere

Sons of Rest Shelter

Kentucky Coffee Tree

Stupp Center and
Memorial Garden

Columbus Statue

Grand Blvd.

0   800

Feet

Z

Tower Grove Park

Location: St. Louis, Missouri
Hiking distance: 3 miles
Hiking time: 1 hour
Bicycles: permitted

In 1868, hardware merchant–philanthropist Henry Shaw deeded the city 202 acres of oblong terrain on its western boundary for a magnificent park designed for carriages, buggies, horseback riders, and strollers. He named the park, now 289 acres, for his nearby country home, Tower Grove, then enclosed it with a wooden fence that stayed in place until 1920.

To catch the fancies of wide-eyed visitors, Shaw installed in the early years three monumental entrances for carriages and pedestrians; elaborate gatehouses; a colorful music stand; a stable; ornamental pavilions to comfort strollers and picnickers (some call the structures "gazebos"); 12 wellhouses with buckets for thirsty horses; ponds and greenhouses; major bronze statuary; and at least 10 bridges, made from stone, cedar, or cast iron. He planted 200 kinds of trees, including a grove for every species he hoped would thrive in St. Louis; in all, he planted nearly 20,000 trees and shrubs. In 1883, David MacAdam wrote that with every few steps, on a park walk, a different view, an ornamental structure, or a work of art would meet the eye.

English-born and widely traveled, Shaw took the gentle terrain and added the physical features that best suited its contours. This mixture was described as "gardenesque" or "cultivated"; it was of European influence, inherently Victorian. Nowadays, Tower Grove Park is considered America's best surviving gardenesque park. Along with Central Park in New York, Boston Common, and Boston Public Garden, it is a National Historic Landmark, designated by the US Department of the Interior.

"The road-base in the park is probably as fine as any in the world . . . costing at the rate of $60,000 per mile," wrote Camille N. Dry in 1875. The next year, *Saint Louis Illustrated* gushed about the park's busyness: "Upon the boulevard [probably Main Drive] . . . high-blooded horses may frequently be seen moving as if winged."

Shaw, the park's first superintendent, set many rules. One was: No funeral processions through the grounds. Ironically, the first to break the rule—in 1889—was Shaw himself. His 75-carriage funeral cortege slow-clopped through the park, then turned toward Missouri Botanical Garden, where he reposes to this day.

"No park in the Mississippi valley has the ensemble of features that Tower Grove has," says John A. Karel, director since 1987. "None has as much Victorian architecture. And our remarkable collection of trees (now 320 different varieties) makes us one of the most significant urban forests in the United States."

Access

You can reach the park by driving 1.7 miles south on South Kingshighway from US 40/I-64; or 0.8 mile on South Kingshighway from I-44. Turn left into the park. Drive through the 12-foot-wide west carriage entrance, flanked by 40-foot Norman towers and cast-iron pedestrian gates. A Gothic-revival (rare in Missouri) stone gatehouse sits alongside. Drive right; park by the curb near the soccer field.

Trail

Begin your eastbound walk on the sidewalk that parallels South West Drive, a park loop road. To your right is the Maury Street gate, consisting of four limestone piers at Arsenal Street and two other piers closer to the loop road. (Beyond the Maury Street gate are the white smokestacks of the American National Can Company at Juniata and South Kingshighway.) Proceeding eastward, at a point across from and slightly west of the stone comfort station, an apparent gravestone stands in the grass—it is really a memorial marker planted in 1882 next to a long-gone commemorative red oak tree. It remembers Eliza Hoole, of whom little is known except that she was probably a cousin of Henry Shaw, whose mother's maiden name was Hoole. In 1990, a ceremony was held to plant a replacement oak at the site.

Near the Francis Tunica picnic site, you will spot a bridge constructed of coarse rubble stone along the loop road. Like other bridges in the park, this one fords one of three shallow "watercourses" or rivulets (all draining north into the lake at the Japanese tea garden in neighboring Missouri Botanical Garden). The waterways, some of which were buried to accommodate playing fields, help provide sustenance for the several hundred bald cypress trees that thrive on the grounds. Walk by a grove of bald cypresses mixed with ginkgos, then look left toward the 1914 Roman Pavilion and nearby playground. Some carefully tended grass tennis courts sit near the loop road along the sidewalk to the Roman Pavilion.

Just before Center Cross Drive, on your right, is the the park office, housed in the 1888 limestone south gate lodge that blends Italian villa and Romanesque architectural features. In the lodge lived the gatekeeper who kept chickens in the front yard, opened the gate in the morning, and closed it in the evening. "I don't know what else he did," admits Karel. The south entrance on Arsenal Street is also the spot where pretzel vendors and newspaper sellers have been posted on weekends and holidays for at least 80 years. At the corner of the loop road and Center Cross Drive is the five-sided, now tightly capped wellhouse, one of only three remaining examples in the park of wells dedicated exclusively to the needs of horses. Well water became available when the city laid a pipe in 1872 for its new Asylum for the Insane on Arsenal Road (about a mile west), adding a connecting pipe to the park.

Cross Center Cross Drive. On the left is the Turkish Pavilion, the park's busiest picnic and family gathering shelter. Originally it was intended as a dovecote—pigeons and songbirds would gather around its bulbous, onion-shaped upper level—but this roosting area was soon closed. Next on your right, across from stop 13 on the Parcourse Fitness Circuit, are two aging Shaw-era catalpa trees, unmistakably identified by their hanging, long, thin, beanish seedpods. A near forest of oaks and ginkgos is on your right, roughly between stops 13 and 14 on the fitness course. On your left, you pass the Cypress South shelter, used now for "basket parties," but originally designed as a very elegant wellhouse.

Up ahead you cross a bridge with wooden sides and shortly begin a gradual climb. On your right, the open fields become wider; more ball fields appear, and the land rises in elevation. This part of the park, its highest spot, is known as "The Hill." Directly north of the crest, along the loop road, is one of the park's most distinctive summerhouses: the Chinese Pavilion, its columns fiery red and its decorative dragons staring menacingly from its ribbed roof corners. This shelter exemplified to Henry Shaw the Victorian preoccupation with the Oriental world. Such discoveries as Chinese vases, silks, screens, and architecture were appearing in England when Shaw visited. While there, he most likely viewed the famous red-and-black pagoda, a main attraction of London's Kew Gardens. Shaw's version of the pagoda may be America's most charming example of Anglo-Chinese garden architecture, Karel believes. In 1992, it was restored by the Friends of Tower Grove Park.

After passing the Chinese pavilion, take the first sidewalk to your right and head south to the Spring Avenue gate along Arsenal Street. Once there, notice the row of somber linden trees that lead from the stone gate to a nearby urn with an American holly tree backdrop. The setting looks like something from Calvary Cemetery! Above the Gothic-style gate is a pointed arch made of coarse rubble; it looks cemeterylike. That's why Shaw's workmen in 1870 nick-named the entrance the "cemetery gate." The Friends also helped restore this handsome entrance.

After walking through the gate and back, walk east on the descending path that parallels Arsenal Street inside the park. Once you arrive at the Stupp Memorial Garden on your left, walk through the garden (if its gates are unlocked) or around it, making sure to see its striking amphitheater as well as the Stupp Center itself, a gathering place for senior citizen and neighborhood groups. Turn right on the loop road, which passes (on your left) the formidable Sons of Rest shelter, laid out in the shape of a Greek cross. "Sons of Rest" is a Victorian euphemism for "retired persons."

At Main Drive, look to your right toward the Grand Boulevard entrance, the first in the park to open. Etched into its opposing stone towers are the words "Entrance" and "Exit." Winged griffins and

*Here, beside the Columbus statue in Tower Grove Park, members of the
United Italian Society of St. Louis celebrate Columbus Day in October 1937.
(St. Louis Mercantile Library Collections)*

sleeping lions cast in zinc top the stone side and outer piers. Shaw
personally designed this magnificently ornate baroque entrance so that
its presence might signal to visitors the genteel atmosphere of the park.

Before walking west to start the last half of the hike loop, walk
around the bronze Christopher Columbus statue, thought to have
been the first Columbus statue in America. (Munich sculptor Ferdinand
Von Miller executed the Columbus as well the park's Von Humboldt
and Shakespeare statues.) The 9-foot likeness of the normally clean-
shaven Columbus sports a beard simply because Shaw wanted him to
have one, legend says. An agitated Von Miller protested such artistic
liberty, then finally succumbed, carving a blunt disclaimer somewhere
inside Columbus's toga. Director Karel has used a stepladder and
flashlight to find the disclaimer, but so far, no luck.

After you've seen the Columbus statue, walk straight west on
the north sidewalk along Main Drive, where a now-ancient Kentucky

coffee tree, probably planted by Shaw himself, leans over the sidewalk. At a point roughly opposite the Chinese pavilion, and north of the sidewalk, a solitary stone bridge, designed originally to be an "eye-catcher," sits out in the open. Groundskeepers call it "the bridge to nowhere" since there is little evidence of water nearby. Soon on your left, in the middle of Main Drive, is Cypress Circle, which has, says Karel, the best assemblage of bald cypress trees in the park.

Continue walking west, crossing a blue footbridge. Leave the Main Drive sidewalk at the gold, olive, and pale yellow octagonal North Humboldt shelter, which once doubled as a wellhouse. Walk through a corner of the brick-floored structure to reach the wide sidewalk leading to the similarly octagonal music stand. From the Humboldt shelter, look back over your left shoulder to view Humboldt Circle, fronted with a bronze statue of Alexander von Humboldt, scientist, explorer, philosopher, and father of modern geography. In Shaw's time, he was a universally admired personage.

In the park's early days, Sunday afternoon concerts were held in this Victorian bandstand, ringed by marble busts of the composers Shaw admired: Mozart, Wagner, Beethoven, Gounod, Verdi, and Rossini, whom Shaw once met in Europe. A Shaw rule was that all concerts must offer a medley of tunes by one of the composers. In 1966 vandals tweaked the noses from the composers; the busts were restored in 1992, along with the stand. Two piers on the west side of the stand were planned to accommodate the busts of composers Donizetti and Arthur Sullivan, but Shaw's death precluded the project, so the piers are topped with handsome stone spheres instead.

To the left of the music stand are the artificial ruins and sailboat pond. "I know of no other such ruins in the United States," says Karel. Ruins—"ornamental landscape"—were a part of the 18th-century romantic movement, especially on large English estates. "Shaw saw the opportunity to have some ruins of his own," says Karel. Shaw acquired 10 wagonloads of stone blocks from the burned-down Lindell Hotel at Sixth and Washington in St. Louis, then hauled them to the park, where he personally supervised their rearrangement as a backdrop for the pond. In 1856, when the hotel was built, it was America's largest; fire destroyed it in 1867. The pond fountain is also built on hotel rubble. In warm months, newly married couples join a south St. Louis tradition: being photographed while posing by the stone railings at the south end of the oval pond.

Just west of the ruins are the tropical lily ponds and palm houses, the latter bordered by American holly and ginkgo trees. The ponds, a chain of three miniature lakes, were developed by James Gurney Sr., who became park superintendent in 1889. He was succeeded by his son James Jr., then the son's daughter, Bernice, who retired the dynasty in 1976. About 30 varieties of tropical lilies bloom there, roughly from July 1 through the first hard frost—often not until early November. One massive Victoria lily—"the plant from Mars," as Karel calls it—offers powerfully fragrant blossoms the size of pinkish watermelons. Each of its enormous buds blooms at a different time during the summer, but each bud is in full bloom only at night, and only for two or three days. A rule of thumb is that lilies with green leaves bloom by day; lilies with red leaves by evening and all night.

Across the roadway from the ponds is the south Palm House, opened in 1878. It was a precursor to the 1882 Linnean House at Missouri Botanical Garden; both were designed by architect George I. Barnett. In the winter, St. Louisans could walk through the Palm House to admire its palm trees, which in the summer were taken outdoors and arranged around the ponds. The south Palm House, destined to be the park visitors center, is the oldest standing greenhouse west of the Mississippi River. Its fraternal twin, erected in 1885, is located just behind it and serves as a maintenance shop today. Back in the 1940s, superintendent Bernice Gurney conducted book discussions in the south Palm House, or "conservatory," as she called it.

Just before crossing Center Cross Drive, look to your right to the north gate and to the pair of freestanding stone columns capped by lounging stags. They flank the roadway just inside the Magnolia, or north, park entrance, another strong ensemble of original stone and iron.

Walk west on North West Drive after crossing Center Cross Drive. Across from the tennis courts is the stone stable, the first structure to be built in the park. Next to it is the chief ranger's house.

"It's an intentionally rustic design with sturdy stone walls," observes Karel. About 2 long blocks ahead on your left is the 1924 Stone shelter, a model for much of the rustic park architecture constructed at least 10 years later by Depression-era Civilian Conservation Corps or WPA groups in places like Babler State Park in west St. Louis County and Pere Marquette State Park near Grafton, Illinois.

On your right, beyond a formidable pin oak grove in which we counted hundreds of yellow crocuses in bloom one balmy February 26, is the Robert and Martha Gaddy Wild Bird Garden. Birders by the hundreds ply the garden paths, especially during spring and fall bird migrations. Robert Gaddy has a long list of birds he's spotted in the park: Le Conte's sparrows, winter wrens, yellow-breasted chats, warblers, most species of thrush, shorebirds from Alaska, broad-winged hawks in the thousands, redstarts, even a low-flying lone mature bald eagle. "Birds stop here during migration to refuel and get something to eat," explains Gaddy. "Tower Grove is one of the two best places in St. Louis [the other is Kennedy Forest in Forest Park] to see migrating birds," says David Becher, another serious birder. "Birds usually migrate by night. When morning comes, they look for nice green places such as this to drop down for a rest."

Just past the bird sanctuary the sidewalk bends south. The Kingshighway gatehouse and entrance come back into focus and so, too, does your parked automobile.

South St. Louis County

Hikers descend Cromlech Glen, *a massive earthwork sculpture on the trail at Laumeier Park.*

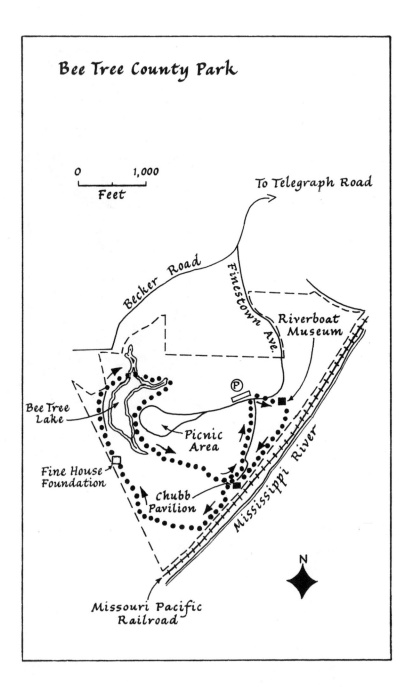

Bee Tree County Park

0   1,000
Feet

To Telegraph Road

Becker Road

Finestown Ave.

Riverboat Museum

Bee Tree Lake

Fine House Foundation

Picnic Area

Chubb Pavilion

Mississippi River

Missouri Pacific Railroad

N

Bee Tree
County Park

Location: St. Louis County, Missouri
Hiking distance: 2¼ miles
Hiking time: 1 hour
Bicycles: permitted

While traveling in England in the 1920s, Eugene D. Nims and his wife, Lotawana, admired an English Tudor mansion so much that they hired its architect and later replicated the home on a Mississippi River bluff in south St. Louis County. The affluent Nimses—he was president of Southwestern Bell Telephone Company—called their property Bee Tree Farm, using it as a weekend retreat. Their main home was an equally imposing mansion at 56 Portland Place in St. Louis's central west end.

When the new sandstone-faced home was completed in 1929, Lotawana planted the gardens, most of which survive today. For awhile, she planted red tulips only. An oval red tulip embedded in lead glass in the mansion front door is a memento of that phase. Lotawana's beautiful white and yellow jonquils and narcissi, which flourish in April, still blanket the grounds on all sides of the mansion. "Mrs. Nims's father was a riverboat captain, so she planted flowers behind her home for the pleasure of people, such as her father, passing by in boats," says Marga Finger of the Golden Eagle River Museum, located within the mansion. "Lotawana dedicated her gardens to her father."

Mrs. Nims had "peacocks, goats, guinea hens, and other animals wandering around the front lawn," recalls Russell J. Hart, former St. Louis Area Boy Scout Council chief executive, who visited the estate when Eugene Nims chaired the council. The Nimses had cows, horses, and mule teams, which they kept in the red barn that remains intact by the mansion parking lot. In the Nimses' time, the property was extensively farmed, says Whitey Schierhoff, who brought in his tractor to help out. "I cultivated for soybeans and corn on the land where Bee Tree Lake is now," says Schierhoff. The mansion itself has distinguishing marks: an Irish chimney with spiral-laid bricks; all-stone interior walls; all-tile stairs and floors. Balconies and patios face the river.

Centerpiece of the free-admission river museum (open from May 1 to October 31) is a collection of relics from the *Golden Eagle,* the last stern-wheel, wooden-hulled, overnight passenger steamer to sail from St. Louis. On a trip to Nashville, Tennessee, in May 1947 it ran aground near Grand Tower, Illinois. All the passengers were safely bused back to St. Louis, Marga Finger among them.

Access

From I-255 in far south St. Louis County, turn south onto Telegraph Road. Drive 4.3 miles to Becker Road and turn left. Drive 1.5 miles to Finestown Avenue and bear left for a short ride into the park. Park on the lot across from the mansion/museum. Your walk begins at the museum.

Trail

Five trails crisscross the park; your walk links several of them.

From behind the museum, take the stone stairs down to an eroding grotto, then walk down a grass path to a narrow dirt trail carved into the bluff edge. Turn right. Hike through weedy woods on the park's Mississippi Trail to the Chubb Pavilion, less than ¼ mile away. From this lookout, named in memory of R. Walston Chubb, who assisted in raising money to make the park a reality in 1973, the American Bottom section—across the river in Illinois— is in full view. About a mile south on the river, near the Meramec River's confluence with the Mississippi, is the spot where, from the 1920s to the 1960s, the excursion boat *Admiral* would turn around on its daytime and evening cruises and head back to its levee mooring in downtown St. Louis.

From the Chubb Pavilion, walk to your left (south) on the wide gravel path until you see the sign that redirects you onto the Missis-

The lake at Bee Tree Park is the ideal stop for a picnic.

sippi Trail. Walk left to get on the trail, then amble along the bluff edge, avoiding paths that lead off the main trail. Be alert for small stumps and snags, especially in the fall and winter when they're hidden by fallen leaves. Shortly, the bluff-edge path heads upward and intersects with Crow's Roost Trail, where you must make a right turn. Here, the path drops down through riches of dogwoods and redbuds to the park lake 1 mile away. Along the way is the foundation of what may have been the home of Philip Fine Sr., who dreamed in the 1780s of creating a river town to rival the larger village of St. Louis. He and his family operated ferries that crossed both the Meramec and Mississippi Rivers. A settlement called Fines-Town materialized, but barely, on land between the two rivers. Philip died in 1819. Almost two decades later his son Benjamin tried unsuccessfully to revive plans for Fines-Town. (*The Western Pilot*, a river gazetteer, reported in 1839 the presence of Fine's Island in the Mississippi near the mouth of the Meramec. Fine was described as "an old settler." The island has since disappeared.) Just beyond the home foundation is a trail intersection; walk straight ahead on the descending path as it narrows and finds its way to the lake.

Bee Tree Lake is worked over by at least two families of beavers, says Ed Hovorka, former park supervisor. "Normally, beavers won't stray more than 5 or 10 feet from the water, but here they go back at least 30 feet. We've lost hundreds of trees due to the beavers. We've often had 20-foot trees standing one day and gone the next after the beavers literally chewed them down, pushed them into the lake, and floated them to their dens."

Take the worn, sometimes overgrown, path around the lake. Just before a footbridge, and up the hill on your left, is a prairie patch recently planted by park naturalists. Protected by chain-link fencing, the footbridge spans the silty, swampy water on the lake's far western end. In the spring, the lake resonates with singing chorus frogs; its banks glow with striking bouquets of wildflowers, including deep purple dwarf larkspur. Once over the footbridge, walk immediately to your right on what is now the Beaver Trail, which hugs the shore and heads to another crossing at the north end of the lake. Just before the north crossing is an elevated, weatherworn birdhouse, dubbed "Fowl-A-Day Inn" by Boy Scouts who installed and named it and other birdhouses in the park.

At the north end of the lake, cross two raised wooden platforms that must do for a footbridge. Walk up the stairs, then bear right on the path, now called the Trillium Trail in honor of the brown trillium that blooms here in the spring. Follow the path southward, with the lake on your right. At a Y, stay to your right until the path emerges onto a sloping, lakeside green where trees are girdled with poultry wire to fend off rascally beavers.

Anglers work from the docks of the 15-foot-deep lake, which has produced a 36-pound catfish and a 9½-pound largemouth bass. "Biologists at the Missouri Department of Conservation, which manages the lake, tell me that it is one of the best for bass within a 20-mile radius," says Hovorka. The park is home to wild turkeys, who trot about at dusk, and a family of around six deer, seen occasionally. "We used to have a family of tame red foxes, but they seem to have died off, maybe due to distemper," says Hovorka. "They would wander up to picnic tables and help themselves to the fried chicken or barbecued beef if the unsuspecting picnicker left the table unguarded."

Walk east along the lake edge until you see a sign for Bee Tree and Paw Paw Trails. Turn right. Just before the first footbridge, take a left onto Paw Paw Trail, which moves you over another footbridge and up the spring wildflower–rich hill to the Chubb Pavilion. Walk from there along the roadway back to the parking lot.

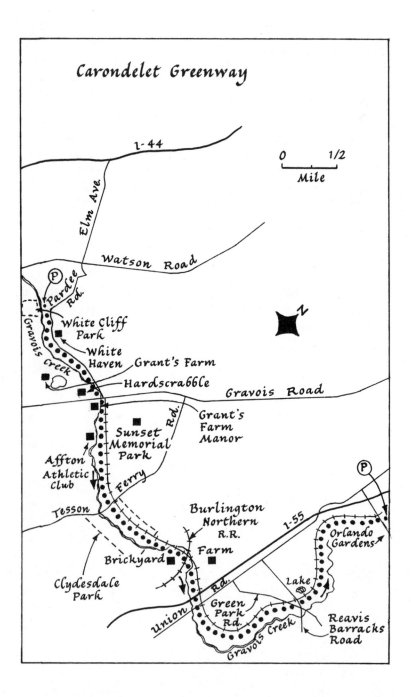

Carondelet Greenway

I-44

Elm Ave.

Watson Road

0   1/2
Mile

Ⓟ

Pardee Rd.

Gravois Creek

White Cliff Park

White Haven

Grant's Farm

Hardscrabble

Gravois Road

Grant's Farm Manor

Sunset Memorial Park

Ferry Rd.

Affton Athletic Club

Tesson

Burlington Northern R.R.

Ⓟ

I-55

Orlando Gardens

Brickyard

Clydesdale Park

Farm

Union Rd.

Green Park Rd.

Lake

Gravois Creek

Reavis Barracks Road

Carondelet Greenway

Location: St. Louis County, Missouri
Hiking distance: 6½ miles one way
Hiking time: 3 hours
Bicycles: permitted

Beginning in 1872 freight trains of the Pacific Railroad, later named the Missouri Pacific, steamed down 13 miles of single tracks from the main line in Kirkwood to the Ivory Street railroad ferry at the Mississippi River. Known as the Kirkwood or Carondelet Branch, the spur haphazardly followed Gravois Creek, providing freight trains a fast alternative to the congested railyards near downtown St. Louis. Once at the river, trains were ferried by sidewheelers to Illinois for connections with major eastern carriers. The last ferry closed in 1940.

When the rail line was abandoned in 1990, Gateway Trailnet, Inc., a nonprofit group focusing on land conservation, and its founder and executive director, Ted Curtis, saw the railbed as an ideal hike/bike path, an urban counterpart to the popular Katy Trail in St. Charles County. Trailnet bought the abandoned corridor from Union Pacific Railroad Company with the intention of converting it into a St. Louis County linear park. Trailnet carried out a program of fundraising, trail development, planting, maintenance, and neighborhood relations. Its volunteers provide continuing cleanup, fixup, and fundraising help.

Gravois Creek comes in and out of view along the rail spur. In the early 1700s, lower sections of the creek were supposedly sprinkled with lodges and settlements of both the Kaskaskia and Tamaron tribes. Along its banks in the 1700s, settlers saw elk, bison, deer, bobcats, bears, and mountain lions, wrote Roger W. Taylor in *Watershed I*. Until earlier in the 20th century the creek was a near perfect place to swim, bathe, and fish, as thousands of old-time southsiders can attest.

Access

Two automobiles are required for this walk, which begins at White Cliff Park, Crestwood. Leave the second vehicle at the trail's south trailhead near the Orlando Gardens parking lot.

Drive to the Elm Avenue exit of I-44 in Webster Groves. Take Elm south; cross Watson Road. At Pardee Road, turn right and drive half a mile to White Cliff Drive. This is the road into the park, where you'll begin your walk.

First, to reach the south trailhead, continue right on Pardee, which becomes Grant Road. At Gravois Road, turn left and drive to Mackenzie Road. Turn right on Mackenzie, which becomes Reavis Barracks Road. Drive to Union Road and turn left (north). Drive 1.3 miles to Hoffmeister Avenue. Turn right; park at Orlando Gardens Banquet Center. The trailhead is at the south side of the lot. Leave one car and drive the other back to White Cliff Park to start the southbound hike. Park in the area near the picnic tables.

Trail

Begin the hike with an optional 1-mile warm-up walk around the old Glendale quarry in the middle of White Cliff Park. From the picnic area cross over the Gravois Creek footbridge and walk through the concrete piers of the former quarry's loading dock. Once past the actual quarry (now a 40-foot-deep lake with tall limestone walls), walk uphill on the path that rims the top of the quarry, then heads back down to the parking area.

From the parking area walk to Pardee Road. Walk left on Pardee for about ⅓ mile to the abandoned railbed. Turn right to start your hike. To your right, by a high-voltage stockade fence, is the Anheuser-Busch, Inc. Clydesdale pasture, once the main breeding site for the company's high-profile feather-legged draft horses—seen in company ads and the annual Tournament of Roses Parade in Pasadena. Since A-B transferred most of its Clydesdale operation to California, only a few animals remain to mingle among the hordes of

Canada geese that have made the place a prime feeding ground. Charles Lindbergh is said to have landed in the pasture in a single-engine plane in the late 1920s, says regional historian Ross Wagner. "I'm told that the entire Sappington School over on Gravois Road was let out to watch Lindbergh land," he adds.

White Haven, where President Ulysses S. Grant resided in the late 1850s, is visible up a driveway on the left. It is now a National Park Service historic site. President Grant signed a bill in 1872 designating Yellowstone as the nation's first national park. (The National Park Service was not to be organized until 1916.)

In 1821 Frederick F. Dent, Grant's father-in-law, bought White Haven, a spacious plantation that included all of present-day Grantwood Village and Grant's Farm. After Grant married Julia Dent in 1848, the new couple lived briefly in the large Dent home at White Haven. Later they built Hardscrabble, a two-story log cabin, at the north end of the plantation on today's St. Paul Cemetery on Rock Hill Road, south of Watson Road. Near Hardscrabble, Grant farmed about 80 acres, sowing wheat, oats, corn, and potatoes. After several months in the cabin, which Julia thought crude and homely, they moved back into the Dent home. During the Civil War, Grant took title to White Haven, intending to move there later to raise horses. Though his plans changed dramatically, he kept the property until 1884, the year before he died.

Before the Dents, White Haven had been owned by Theodore and Anne Lucas Hunt, who moved there from St. Louis because Mrs. Hunt was supposedly frightened of attorney Thomas Hart Benton, later Missouri's first US senator. In an 1817 duel, Benton shot and killed her brother, Charles Lucas, piercing his heart from 10 feet away. In 1888, Luther H. Conn, who fought with the Confederates in Kentucky during the Civil War, bought White Haven and named the surrounding area Grantwood, in memory of the late president. Subdividing in 1903, Conn sold some rolling hillside land to August A. Busch Sr., president of Anheuser-Busch.

On his new property Busch erected a large log hunting lodge with rustic wooden bridges over Gravois Creek. Along Gravois Road, he installed a still-standing fence containing surplus Civil War musket barrels. Later he built a wooden mass observatory shaped like a dirigible, then started collecting wildlife. "August A. bought animals the way other millionaires bought the Old Masters," wrote Peter Hernon and Terry Ganey in *Under the Influence: The Unauthorized Story of the Anheuser-Busch Dynasty* in 1991. Descendents of the original animals roam the grounds today.

In the early 20th century a small railroad siding called Grant's Station stood by the tracks just south of the present roadway into White Haven. "Carloads of manure would regularly be placed on the siding and local farmers and gardeners from Sappington and Affton had 48 hours to haul it away," recalls Wagner. Presumably, Clydesdales purchased in Scotland and shipped to Missouri were also unloaded at the rail siding, says William Vollmar, Anheuser-Busch corporate archivist.

Cross Gravois Road. The remnants of a stone arch and fence that you see, complete with a cannon, are the remains of the Zumstork restaurant, which August A. Busch remodeled in 1907, adding the arch and a screened-in porch overlooking the Gravois. The structure had been a restaurant site since the late 1800s, but its exact lineage cannot be determined. Cattycorner to the restaurant remains, and inside the main gate to Grant's Farm, is Hardscrabble, Grant's log cabin, which Busch purchased and moved to this site. Once open to visitors, it has been closed for years.

South of Gravois Road the Busch animal collection continues. Missouri mules and colorful South American llamas are often seen in the enclosure on your right called Grant's Farm Manor. It abuts the Affton Athletic Club complex. For several years the St. Louis Blues practiced on the club's indoor hockey rink. And when Missouri Pacific freight trains rolled by during club softball games, the play would cease. Up on the hill at your left, beyond Cor Jesu Academy (and out of view to walkers), is the Busch family plot in Sunset Memorial Park. August A. Busch and his son, August A. (Gussie) Busch Jr., as well as other family members lie facing Grant's Farm.

Cross Tesshire Drive, then walk under the Tesson Ferry Road viaduct. Soon you will come to St. Louis County's 120-acre Clydesdale Park (formerly Gravois Creek Park), which straddles both sides of Gravois Creek, though Clydesdale's main walking trail and its beauty spots are south of the creek. A footbridge across the creek from the Carondelet Greenway may soon connect the path with the main part of the park.

Upcoming on your right is the former Alpha Portland Cement Company, originally Continental Brick Company. (The property will soon become a light industrial manufacturing complex.) In the late 1800s a nearby settlement called "Pokertown" housed the Italian immigrants who worked at the brickyards. "The Italians, in particular, scooped clay from the nearby hills and hauled the clay away in horse-drawn wagons," says Wagner. The clay was used to make bricks. The tall timber railroad trestle near the Alpha quarry still supports the busy tracks of Burlington Northern Railroad's main freight line to Memphis.

Beyond the quarry on your left, the Phil Hesch farm—one of two by the trail—stands on a hill near I-55 and Union Road. Established in 1903, the farm has no tractors or trucks, only draft horses to pull Hesch's farm wagon, manure spreader, and harrow. In the summer Hesch uses a pony and wagon to haul produce to his stand on Reavis Barracks Road. He swears that he saw President Harry S Truman ride by the farm on a Missouri Pacific passenger train in the late 1940s.

Cross Union Road. At busy Pro-Am golf driving range on your right, one activity years ago was hitting practice balls off passing freight trains, old-timers recall. An undeveloped 67-acre park lies east of the driving range. Union County Park, mostly open fields and some upland forest, was once a sod farm.

Cross Green Park Road, then walk by spring-fed Grasso Pond located behind the yellow-brick Adco office building, original home of the old Grasso Brothers Coal Company. On a special spur of the Carondelet Branch, freight cars unloaded coal in the Grasso coalyard. "Our company used to haul coal to the Alpha quarry, first with mule teams, then trucks," says real estate entrepreneur Joe Grasso, a grandson of the founder.

Cross Reavis Barracks Road. From here until the end of the walk, just over 1 mile ahead, is the first completed section of the

Carondelet Greenway, with both fine gravel and paved surfaces. To your right, beyond the St. Louis County automobile impounding area, is Hill's Auto Parts, Inc. auto junkyard. "I ride a bike in the yard about 3 miles a day just for exercise," says congenial owner Joe Hill. Behind the fence on the left is "The Island Lake," built in 1945 by the fisherman-owner of the old Taylor Dairy, which operated next door. Once better known as "Pop Taylor's Lake," it is now fenced off.

The final lap of the trail offers a floodplain forest, rows of subdivison homes with tidy gardens, a trestle bridge over a branch of Gravois Creek, and wildflowers and prairie grass plantings, thanks in part to seed donations from the Missouri Department of Conservation. The trail ends (or begins, depending on your hiking plan) by the Orlando Gardens Banquet Center.

Emmenegger Nature Park

Location: Kirkwood, Missouri
Hiking distance: 1½ miles
Hiking time: 1 hour
Bicycles: not permitted

In the early 1900s, Edwin A. Lemp, youngest brother in the family that owned Lemp Brewery, a pre-Prohibition brewing giant in St. Louis, often drove out from the city to hike and camp on a bluff 200 feet above the Meramec River valley. Smitten with the idyllic locale, Lemp built a stone-and-timber residence called Cragwold that some said resembled the home of a Roman senator. Cragwold was surrounded by 95 acres of craggy, hilly, and wholly wildflower-enriched land.

Lemp loved animals, especially hooved mammals and exotic birds. George Vierheller, a close friend who ran the St. Louis Zoo, loaned Lemp Siberian yaks, Japanese Sitka deer, buffalo, sacred cattle from India, antelope, and llamas to roam the grounds, which Lemp licensed as a federal game preserve. Through Lemp, the zoo acquired its first lions, writes Stephen P. Walker in *Lemp—The Haunting History*.

Some say that a descendant of one of the Sitka or fallow deer lives on in the area, particularly in Powder Valley Nature Center next to Emmenegger Park. "We have observed this deer near the bird feeding area behind the Nature Center building," says Glenda Abney, Powder Valley and Emmenegger manager. "He is known around here as the deer who hangs out with the turkeys because we often see him following turkeys on the ground."

Inside Cragwold, Lemp installed a sunken atrium that became "a domestic jungle containing one of the most extensive and valuable

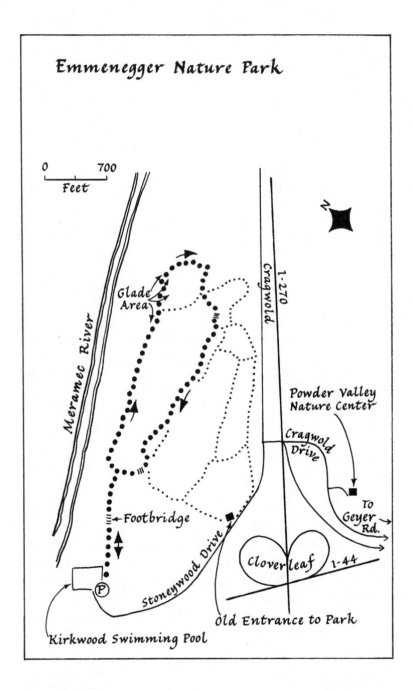

Emmenegger Nature Park

private collections of tropical and semitropical birds in the country," writes Walker. More than 200 birds lived in the atrium, where some trees stretched from floor to ceiling. Twenty-four varieties of parrots and a plenitude of finches had permission to fly free throughout the house. In the Lemp front yard, 60 peafowls strutted about.

In 1971, local homebuilder Russell Emmenegger purchased Cragwold. "They moved the last buffalo out before I bought the place," recalls Emmenegger, who sought unsuccessfully to convert the blufftop grounds around his new home into a 150-unit luxury condominium development named "Cragwold Park." Subsequently, Emmenegger gave the game-farm acreage to the city of Kirkwood, stipulating that it remain in a natural state unfettered by "ball fields and swings" and that it carry the Emmenegger surname. He has since moved away.

Edgar Denison, the late Kirkwood author of *Missouri Wildflowers,* enjoyed the park for its spring wildflower show. "There are Dutchman's-breeches, blue-eyed Mary, and trout lilies in masses here that you can't see anywhere else in the St. Louis area," he said. "I personally planted some extremely rare species in here, but I won't tell you where they are," he said, chuckling.

Butterfly enthusiast Mike Van Voren of Webster Groves says that he has stood for 3 to 4 hours on a thin-soiled glade at the top of the park waiting for swarms of zebra and tiger swallowtails to fly in. In April, he says, "this park fills with black-and-yellow swallowtails, largest of all the butterflies." "I saw more butterflies on the glade in an hour than I had seen in my whole lifetime," says William Mockler of Webster Groves, who has hiked the area since 1960. He calls the place "Nature Park."

Access

Take I-44 West to Lindbergh Boulevard and turn left (south). At Watson Road, turn right and drive 1 mile to Geyer Road. Turn right on Geyer, then turn left onto Cragwold Drive. Follow Cragwold as it curves past the entrance to Powder Valley Nature Center and crosses I-270. Turn left at a dead end and follow Stoneywood Drive west to the Kirkwood swimming pool complex. The trail begins near the bridge behind the pool.

Trail

Begin your walk by crossing the new footbridge installed by the Missouri Department of Conservation, which manages the park for Kirkwood, as well as the popular Powder Valley Nature Center next door. The creek, which empties into the Meramec River on your left, is one of several that course though the floor of Emmenegger Park. Old-timers knew this area years ago as Sylvan Beach Resort. It flourished in the 1930s and 1940s.

Accessible from old US 66, the resort offered a pool, beach, arcade, skeet shooting, and a boat dock on the Meramec. "Sylvan Beach is where the Polar Bear Club took cold swims each New Year's Day," says Francis Scheidegger, a Kirkwood photographer. "I remember shooting a Miss Sylvan Beach contest there in 1939." Mockler remembers "the smoke from their barbecue grill wafting over the old Highway 66 bridge as the road wound down through the wooded hills toward the river." (In later years, the place was known as the Fontainebleau swimming club.)

Cross the bridge, then walk northward among the bottomland cottonwoods and box elders. Gradually begin your ascent to the blufftops through a hard maple forest. Three glades and several limestone shelves that are great for viewing appear in succession on your left, the last being the butterfly glade. These semiarid glades offer magnificent views of the Meramec River basin or "Chrysler Valley," as Mockler calls it, referring to the Chrysler automobile assembly plants. Also in view: St. Louis Soccer Park, Weiss Airport, busy I-44, and perhaps some low-flying wild turkeys. Mockler has counted at least 30 wildlife species at Emmenegger, including deer, flying squirrels, foxes, woodcocks, great horned and screech owls, and coyotes, whose footprints he has seen in the snow.

Mockler likes to tell tales about his solitary ventures at Emmenegger. "I went once [to the park] on December 23, maybe the coldest day of the year," he writes. "I was there when the sun rose. It was -25 degrees in the coldest part of the valley and -17 degrees about halfway up to the river bluff overlook. The rising sun turned the top of the bluff blood red. I was so enveloped in the redness that it seemed that the air was aglow."

On a January 4, when it was also numbingly cold, Mockler stood atop a bluff about 4 PM. "Wave after wave of ducks were flying up and out of the river valley and sweeping low over the ridge. The collective sound of their whistling wings was very unusual. Planes going into Weiss Airport were taking evasive action because of the ducks." Down off the bluffs, "the woods were literally crawling with robins. They were flying everywhere through the trees and were all over the ground."

After viewing the world from above, follow the path north along the rim through an upland woods profuse with red cedars. The trail turns to your right—and downward—near the old Lemp estate, which is off-limits to hikers and not viewable from the trail. The meandering walk down from the glades takes you, at least in the spring, among clusters of wild geraniums and hyacinths, and past large concentrations of paw paw trees (where butterflies come to dine). Deeper into the woods on either side of the rocky path are flowering dogwoods and redbuds.

Once on the valley floor, turn right on a path that crosses several streams and explores the rich urban woods, loaded with spring wildflowers. It's not surprising in early spring to see walkers strolling this part of the park with wildflower books in hand. "This valley is extremely rich in soil; it's sealed in and very shady. Because of this, there is always a surprise waiting for people who walk here," says the Reverend James Sullivan, who leads Thursday botany walks for the Webster Groves Nature Study Society. "On some of the shady slopes we have relatively uncommon waterleaf and often we see goldenseal," says Father Sullivan. "When we see this wildflower, we know it's a sign of extra rich ground." Some goldenseal is viewable near a fallen oak tree you must step over on the valley floor. A colony of wild ginger is usually found next to the log. Most of the wildflowers are to be found near the streams—the blue-eyed Mary, trout lilies, bellworts, toothworts, wild sweet William, bloodroot, and yellow violets, to name but a few. It's not unusual to spend an hour or so in early May, before the leaves make canopies of the trees and block much of the sunlight, to leave the path and search for wildflowers and to swap tales of discovery with other walkers.

As you complete the loop walk within Emmenegger Park, your trail winds back to the footbridge near the trailhead through a forest of large white ash trees—many approaching 100 years of age and showing signs of wear and tear—bitternut hickories, basswoods, northern red oaks, and wild cherries.

Fenton City Park/ River Loop

Location: Fenton, Missouri
Hiking distance: 5½ miles
Hiking time: 2 hours
Bicycles: permitted

In 1818, land speculator William L. Long laid out a settlement on the Meramec River and named it for his grandmother, Elizabeth Fenton. The Meramec, a free-flowing stream filled with clams, mussels, and crawfish, attracted Long; so did the area's rich soil and nearby salt deposits.

Long supposedly lived on a plantation in Fenton. On his land he is said to have discovered some pygmy or dwarf burials, ranging in size from 2 to 4 feet in length. Later, burials of "turtle people with massive jaws" were also found. Members of Major Stephen H. Long's (no relation) expedition from Pittsburgh to the Rocky Mountains stopped in Fenton in 1819 and later reported finding graves containing "bones of a diminutive race of men near the river." Because of the discovery, the alleged gravesite attracted visitors well into the mid-1800s, when the William Long family decided to cultivate the grave area. In 1991, archaeologists from the University of Missouri–St. Louis said that they could find no evidence of the pygmy burials, or of William Long's residence by the river.

Since its founding, Fenton has accommodated the Meramec. In 1855, a covered wooden toll bridge opened; its stone foundation supported a replacement iron bridge just 30 years later. In 1925, another steel bridge replaced the 1855 span: It is now the "old Gravois bridge."

Fenton city attorney Jerome Wallach has boyhood memories of Fenton in the 1940s. He and his family lived on a ridgeside above the river. "On summer evenings, about one car an hour drove down

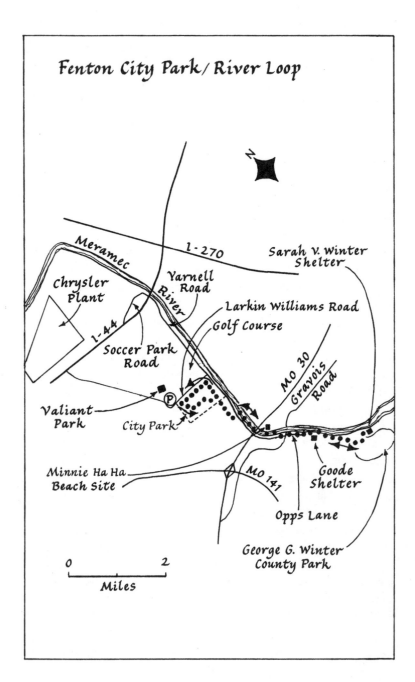

Fenton City Park / River Loop

Larkin Williams Road, which was always called the River Road. If you lived there, you'd pretty well know who was driving. It was often so quiet that you could hear human voices on the river half a mile away." It was the Chrysler Corporation that nudged Fenton back to life when it began automobile assembly operations in 1959.

Access

From the intersection of I-44 and I-270, take I-44 West to exit 275, Soccer Park Road. Follow Soccer Park Road east; at the Meramec River it bends to your right to become Yarnell Road. Follow Yarnell south until you reach Larkin Williams Road. Turn right on Larkin Williams; drive past Fenton City Park (on your left) until the road swings to the right and pint-sized Valiant Park appears on your right. Leave your car at Valiant Park; begin the walk on a path that heads south across Larkin Williams Road into Fenton City Park.

Trail

Valiant Park, the only city park in America named for a Chrysler automobile, abuts the Riverside subdivision, built by Walter Wolfner and his father in the early 1960s. "My dad named many of these streets after Chrysler cars—Fury, Valiant, Dart, Imperial, and so on—so that Chrysler employees might want to buy one of our homes. At least some of them did," says Wolfner.

Once in Fenton City Park, follow the rambling perimeter path through shady groves of aging oaks and sycamores. After about ½ mile, a footbridge on your right fords Yarnell Creek, though the hill beyond is uncomfortably steep, its paths plotted haphazardly. "I'd say there are at least four intact Native American mounds up there," speculates Wallach.

Soon the walkway divides at a triangular planted memorial to James R. Coleman, a Fenton alderman who died while jogging. Bear to your right, passing the UAW Retirement Center complex. "My grandfather owned that land; it's where he kept his hogs," says Wallach. The path continues south, twisting and turning, then reaches Larkin Williams Road. Cross it; turn right on the paved path that parallels the river and is locally called Fenton Meramec Greenway.

Walk under the twin MO 30 bridges. High-water marks that document the damaging floods are on a north bridge-support pier. Pass the Coleman overlook, laden with factual plaques about yesteryear Fenton and the river. At Mound Street are the site of and foundation remnants of the 1855 covered bridge. A plaque at the site says, in part, that the three Fenton bridges that now cross the Meramec carry 120,714 cars each day. "At ten cents per car, we could pay for the original covered bridge (said to have cost $19,000) 4½ times per week," claims the plaque.

Opposite Mound Street, on the other side of the river, was Minnie Ha Ha Beach, Fenton's early-20th-century municipal playground, which also featured slot machines. "Hundreds of people used the beach on weekends," recalls Wallach, who lifeguarded there in the 1950s. "Back then, the Meramec was a meandering stream like the Huzzah and Upper Gasconade Rivers are today. There were even some small islands that we waded to and played on. Now the river is a dredged-out trench."

Follow Water Street to Gravois Road. After crossing Gravois, walk left to American Legion Post 100 at Opps Lane. To your left is the 1925 Meramec bridge.

Walk south on Opps Lane, then access the paved bike path across from the Metropolitan Sewer District Fenton treatment plant sign. The paved path continues into St. Louis County's George G. Winter Park. Once inside the park, the path bears left and begins to parallel the Meramec River. Cross a wooden bridge, then walk left to the Robert L. Goode picnic shelter. (Goode, a farmer who died in 1945, is said to have lived in Hardscrabble, Ulysses S. Grant's abandoned log cabin, in the 1880s.) Continue south to the Sarah V. Winter shelter, situated by a wide bulge in the Meramec, the spot where the Concord Village Lions Club presents its BudLight Championship Grand Prix powerboat races each August.

"This is a world-class event," says Bill Seebold Jr. of the Grand Prix. "It has a reputation of being the Indy 500 of powerboat racing. Racers come to Fenton from all over the world to compete." Seebold's shop in Fenton makes many of the 17-foot, 825-pound, 140 mph racers used by the BudLight team and its competitors. "Our boats are

Hikers view the bulge in the Meramec River at George G. Winter Park on the Fenton walk.

the most agile racing vehicles in the world, including land vehicles," claims Seebold. "They look like Indy cars on water without wheels."

Over three days in August, some 30,000 to 40,000 spectators fill the Meramec's banks to see the races. The course is roughly a 1-mile-long square box in the Meramec. Usually a field of 20 boats races for the championship, won 13 times in 23 years by Seebold and his BudLight teammates, his sons Mike and Tim among them. Nearly $1.3 million has been raised by the Concord Lions and donated to projects related to blindness, and to other charities, says a club founder, Charlie Juengel, who adds, "This may be the biggest project of any Lions Club in the world."

It was the Winter Brothers Material Company that caused the bulge in the Meramec. For years, Winter dredged sand and gravel from the waterway, stretching the river wider and wider. Eventually the company donated the land for the park in 1972 and, more recently, land for a companion Jefferson County Winter Park to the immediate south.

After rambling about the Winter parks, backtrack all the way to Fenton City Park at Larkin Williams Road. Once there, take the perimeter path to the right. Walk to the tennis courts, then continue northwest toward Riverside Golf Club.

"Ours is a flat golf course, the kind you see in Florida," says owner Walter Wolfner. "There are probably as many historic artifacts, such as arrowheads, under our golf course as are under Fenton City Park. When my dad developed Riverside subdivision, a guy wanted to buy a lot sight unseen because he had heard there was a Native American grave in the yard which would yield arrowheads he thought would be unique."

Follow the path past the environmental meadow on your left, a place for wildflowers, prairie grasses, and the many green ash trees that give cover to songbirds and habitat to rabbits, squirrels, and quail. Just ahead, a plaque notes prehistoric activity in the area, possibly as far back as 2000 to 3000 B.C. At least 54 prehistoric sites have been flagged in Fenton by University of Missouri–St. Louis archaeologists. The city park's west end is so loaded with artifacts that it has been made a state "archaeological site."

After leaving the park, the paved path veers to your right and reenters Valiant Park, ending the Fenton walk.

Someday, Fenton's trails may connect to trails at Unger and Buder County Parks, and Powder Valley Nature Center in Kirkwood, says Terry Whaley, parks and recreation director and chairman of the far-seeing Meramec River Recreation Association. Aims of the group are to develop a network of urban, county, and statewide trails near the river, and to bring the Ozark Trail, which extends to Arkansas, up the Meramec River corridor into St. Louis County. Walkers, stay tuned.

Forest 44
Conservation Area
Dogwood Ridge Trail

Location: St. Louis County, Missouri
Hiking distance: 2½ miles
Hiking time: 1½ hours
Bicycles: not permitted

Three years before the Civil War, Ulysses S. Grant, destined to be our 18th president, was a retired US Army captain trying to make a living as a dirt farmer near his estate, White Haven, in St. Louis County. Since his crops of potatoes and wheat yielded thin profits, he looked for extra income. Grant and his servant purchased wood near the present Forest 44 area for resale in downtown St. Louis and at the Jefferson Barracks army post.

"There was no false pride about U.S. Grant," writes Robertus Love in *Reminiscences by Personal Friends of Gen. U.S. Grant.* "Clad in his old blue army overcoat and high army boots . . . he used to haul wood to Jefferson Barracks, where as a young brevet lieutenant he had shone in society." Elmer Weber of Sunset Hills, whose grandfather, Frank Weber, had a farm on a hill in what is now Forest 44, says, "I think that Grant got $3 a cord for his wood. He kept $1 and gave $2 to my grandfather, who did the cutting."

In the late 1800s, the panhandle-shaped 938 acres that make up Forest 44 were part of 10,000 acres known collectively as the Ranken Estate, which comprised four distinct cattle-raising farms: Antire, Crescent, Ranken, and Tyson. Weber's family worked on the Antire farm, now part of Beaumont Boy Scout Reservation, immediately next door to Forest 44. "We would feed 1200 head of cattle over the winter," recalls Weber, now in his 80s.

"As mule breeders, we sold mules to the army in World War I.

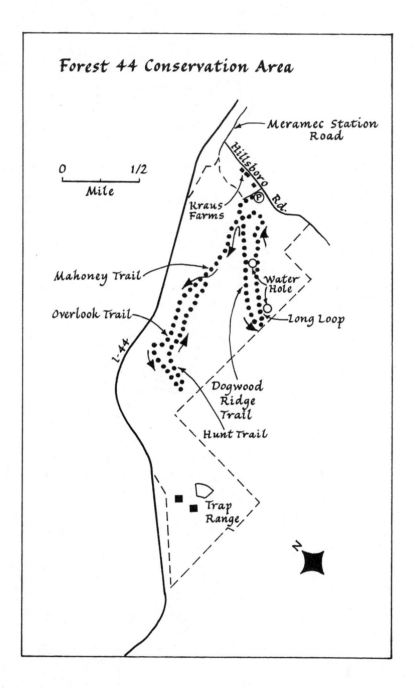

Forest 44 Conservation Area

Meramec Station Road

Hillsboro Rd.

0   1/2
Mile

Kraus Farms

Mahoney Trail

Overlook Trail

I-44

Water Hole

Long Loop

Dogwood Ridge Trail

Hunt Trail

Trap Range

N

After the war, my father decided we needed more mules for the farm—that was long before tractors—so we went to the East St. Louis stockyards to a sale the army was running on surplus mules. My dad bought a dozen mules. When we got home to where Forest 44 is now, one mule made a beeline for Williams Creek [which you cross on your walk]. Strange that the mule knew exactly where to go! That mule turned out to be 'Beck' and it was one of the mules we originally sold to the army. He'd been to the war in Europe and back and now he was home."

Weber remembers David Ranken, one of several brothers who ran the Ranken estate. "David would always appear at two annual events: the longhorn dehorning, where he personally wielded the bloody shears, and the castrations, which he supervised." A cousin, David Ranken Jr., gave $2 million and, later, his entire fortune to endow the Ranken School of Mechanical Trades in St. Louis, an institution still intact. The remaining Ranken land parcels were sold in the mid-1970s.

The Rankens' forests, hills, wetlands, pastures, and meadows are managed today as Forest 44 Conservation Area; St. Louis County Lone Elk and West Tyson Parks; Washington University's Tyson Research Center; and the privately operated Beaumont Reservation. Together, this preserved greenspace has been called "the most scenic approach to any major city in the United States."

In the late 1980s, a local real estate developer was well along with blueprints and schematics for a community of "custom homesites" and commercial buildings on the Forest 44 land. "To achieve such extensive development, the developer would have had to dynamite and level forests, hills, and ridges on the property," says Ellen S. Alton, president of Friends of 44. After nearly four years of public wrangling, plus a statewide citizens' effort by an alliance of 300 individuals and 17 organizations, headed by Alton, the state acquired the land in 1990 for $4.5 million.

Managed by the Missouri Conservation Department, Forest 44 opened its trails to the public in March 1991. Since then, it's been refining the trails and installing wildlife water holes on ridges.

Access

From I-44/I-270, take I-44 West to MO 141 (Valley Park–Fenton exit). Turn left on MO 141, then right on Meramec Station Road. Drive a mile or so and turn left on Hillsboro Road for the short drive to the Forest 44 parking area, trailhead for the Dogwood Ridge Trail.

Trail

The walk through this "last irreplaceable large tract of Ozark forest in St. Louis County," as Alton describes it, begins on a service road that heads west from the parking lot. On your right is the Kraus Farms horse pasture. Mares and geldings usually graze the pasture, underscoring the equestrian appeal of the trail system, which contains not only the Dogwood Ridge Trail but also the Owl and Mahoney Trails for hikers only, and the Hunt, Overlook, Fletcher, Last Chance, Valley, and Buck Trails for both hikers and horses. Most of the trails were once used by Kraus Farms as bridle paths.

"I wanted to change the name of the Buck Trail to the Timberline Trail because it's on a high ridge, but I got a phone call from Mr. Buck himself who talked me out of it," says John Fleming, assistant district forester. He said the Dogwood Ridge Trail was originally named the Hickory Ridge Trail, "but there's only about 2 hickories and 4000 dogwoods on it, so we changed the name. The best time to walk in Forest 44 is in the spring because the dogwoods are blooming everywhere."

Since the Dogwood Ridge Trail sign appears only once, near the parking lot, you must carefully follow the brown-and-white signs that say "Foot Trail" or "Nature Trail" in order to complete the Dogwood Ridge loop. After fording Williams Creek, the trail proceeds to your left by open fields, a streamlet, a "Short Loop" sign—which you should avoid—and another open field. After a footbridge over another stream, the "Long Loop" sign appears. When you see this sign, head uphill onto a ridge covered with mature dogwoods.

On your right and to the south, behind the "End of Public Use" signs, lies Beaumont Reservation, its 2400 acres off-limits to Forest 44 walkers. Too bad, because Beaumont has 47 miles of marked hiking trails, maybe more than any other Boy Scout Council property

Equestrians share some of the trails with walkers at Forest 44 Conservation Area.

in the United States. On its trail system are at least a dozen sites where Native Americans once processed chert for sale or trade. Archaeologists have also found chert sites on Forest 44 ridges.

After rolling along the top of the ridge, the trail descends gradually down the north-facing slope filled with bitternut hickories and autumn olive trees, gooseberry bushes, and more dogwoods. At the bottom of the hill, a footbridge over Williams Creek leads to an open field and the service road back to the parking lot. At this point, you can return to your car or continue walking on the north ridge. Do this by taking a left when you reach the path back to the parking lot. Walk straight ahead until you see the Mahoney Trail sign on your right.

Hike up the Mahoney Trail (named for Bill Mahoney, who once boarded horses at Valley Mount Ranch) in a northwesterly direction. The Mahoney Trail joins the Overlook Trail on the ridgetop and, after a long ridge walk, sometimes within earshot of busy I-44, links with the Hunt Trail. The Hunt takes you down a steep, rocky path to the Forest 44 valley for the walk back to the parking area.

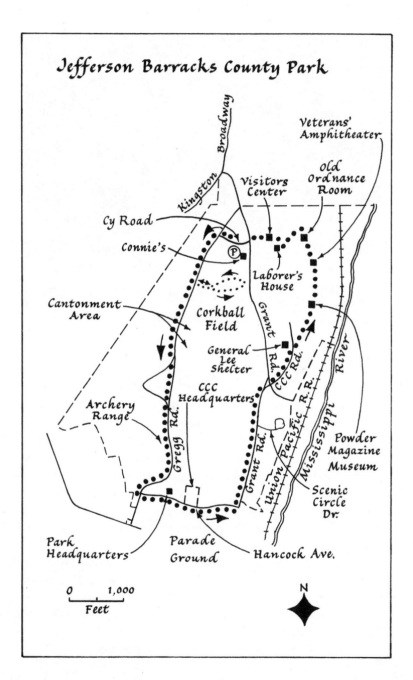

Jefferson Barracks County Park

Broadway

Kingston

Cy Road

Connie's

Cantonment
Area

Archery
Range

Gregg Rd.

Park
Headquarters

Parade
Ground

Visitors
Center

Veterans'
Amphitheater

Old
Ordnance
Room

Laborer's
House

Corkball
Field

Grant Rd.

General
Lee
Shelter

CCC Rd.

CCC
Headquarters

Grant Rd.

Union Pacific R.R.

Mississippi River

Powder
Magazine
Museum

Scenic
Circle
Dr.

Hancock Ave.

0   1,000
Feet

N

Jefferson Barracks County Park

Location: St. Louis County, Missouri
Hiking distance: 4 miles
Hiking time: 1½ hours
Bicycles: permitted

Jefferson Barracks (JB), situated high on a Mississippi River bluff in southern St. Louis County, has been a point of interest since it opened in July 1826. The military post had four different names in its first 4 months: Cantonment Adams, honoring then-president John Quincy Adams; Camp Miller, for Missouri governor John Miller; Camp Barbour, for US Secretary of War James Barbour; and, finally, Jefferson Barracks, for President Thomas Jefferson, who died July 4, 1826. Its initial use was as an infantry school—America's first.

In 1871, the US Army arsenal near downtown St. Louis acquired the north end of the JB property as an auxiliary site for weapons and ammunition storage. The ordnance department built two buildings, both now handsomely preserved, and a home (now razed) for the ordnance commanding officer. St. Louis County purchased the ordnance tract in 1950, four years after JB was declared military surplus and deactivated. At 445 acres, Jefferson Barracks County Park is the "largest historical landmark maintained by a county government in the United States," says the Landmarks Association of St. Louis.

In pre–Civil War days, JB figured in both the Blackhawk and the Seminole wars. In 1832, the JB commandant, General Henry Atkinson, took six companies of the Sixth Infantry on a steamer up the Mississippi River to help defeat Black Hawk's warriors near Rock Island, Illinois. Captured, Black Hawk was brought by steamboat to JB by Lieutenant Jefferson Davis. Author Washington Irving and artist George Catlin visited Black Hawk, Catlin painting him in oil. In

1837, Colonel Zachary Taylor, then acting JB commander and later America's 12th president, left the post after only six months to lead and win the bloody Battle of Lake Okeechobee with troops from JB's Sixth Infantry. It was the only major battle in the first Seminole War, and it helped earn Taylor the nickname "Old Rough and Ready."

In the 1840s, JB was America's largest and westernmost army post. Many of the country's early military heroes were either stationed at JB or passed through it. Only the US Military Academy at West Point, New York, produced more military heroes than JB, writes Ruth Layton in *The Story of Jefferson Barracks*. Civil War–era generals Robert E. Lee, Ulysses S. Grant, Joseph E. Johnston, James Longstreet, Philip Sheridan, Winfield S. Hancock, Don Carlos Buell, Braxton Bragg, John B. Hood, and Albert S. Johnston completed JB assignments. Fifty-six Confederate generals were stationed at JB at one time or another, and at least 11 of them were JB commanding officers, including Lee, Bragg, and both Johnstons, says Marc E. Kollbaum, county park historian at JB.

Grant, a JB infantry lieutenant in the early 1840s, courted Julia Dent, who lived with her parents at White Haven, a plantation home near Gravois Creek in southwestern St. Louis County. "Frequently, he stayed so long [at White Haven] that he was late for dinners taken at Jefferson Barracks," writes Gene Smith in *Lee and Grant*. At one point, Grant was fined three bottles of wine (one for each time he was late) in just 10 days! He and Julia married in 1848. The best man was James Longstreet, who became Lee's "right-hand man" at Gettysburg. After the Civil War, he became a Republican to assist his old friend, Grant, in rebuilding the South.

During the Civil War, JB became a 3000-bed army hospital center. Earlier, Dr. William Beaumont, a pioneer researcher on the human digestive system, was post surgeon. After the war, the small post burial ground acquired a new designation: national military cemetery. With some 3000 interments annually (16 to 20 funerals daily), it now ranks fourth in total burials among the nation's 114 national cemeteries. Although it accepts burials from all across America, it is designated as a regional burial place for service veterans from Missouri and five other states. With nearly 113,000 graves, it is likely that burials will be closed by about the year 2004, when the cemetery runs out of space. Located 0.25 mile southwest of the parade ground via Sheridan Road, the cemetery has a 2.8-mile walking trail designed by Boy Scouts. Trail guides are available in the cemetery office.

During the Spanish-American and both World Wars, JB was a major induction center. In 1941, JB became the first US Army Air Corps replacement and training center. During World War II, it was not only an induction and separation center, but also a basic training camp, technical school, and detention facility for German and Italian war prisoners. Security was so tight then that a milk truck driver who failed to stop at a key checkpoint was fired upon by edgy military police. Throughout the war, reports persisted that POWs were "smuggled out" of JB for nights on the town.

Access

From downtown St. Louis, drive some 7 miles south on I-55 to Germania (exit 202B). Turn left on Germania, which, at Alabama Avenue, becomes Marceau Street. Take Marceau to Broadway; turn right. Take Broadway south for 1.5 miles until you see the brown "Jefferson Barracks Park" sign just before Broadway swings to your right to become Kingston Drive. Follow South Broadway into the park, where you'll pass two stone sentry boxes and a larger stone guard station with the Sixth Infantry alligator crest over the front door. Inside the park, Broadway becomes Grant Road. Follow Grant to Cye Road; turn right on Cye, then park on your left near Connie's concession stand.

Trail

From Connie's stand, near clumps of burr oaks, walk west on Cye Road to Gregg Road. Turn left on Gregg and walk to the first road on your left; take it into the park corkball field complex.

Since 1962, St. Louis Corkball League teams have played here. "We hit upon this site because one of our players worked for Connie's," explains Don Young, known as "Mr. Corkball." "Another player here hit a corkball so far that it landed in the Mississippi, floated to the

Gulf of Mexico, entered the Caribbean Sea, went into the Bermuda Triangle, and disappeared. That's one of the great stories we have in corkball. Have you heard it before?"

Walk back to Gregg, then turn left to continue south on the sidewalk. Natural sinkholes are visible along Gregg. In the 1950s, before the area was a county park, two landfills occupied the center part of the grounds, known as the cantonment area during both world wars. One landfill, just south of the corkball field, permitted daily open burning of debris in an area that a few years before was a huge tent city for Army Air Corps recruits.

"In World War II, the Barracks was expanding so fast that there wasn't enough permanent housing, so canvas-sided huts with wood floors and coal-burning stoves were erected. Up to 1300 recruits, at times, lived in the tent city, which they called 'Pneumonia Gulch' and 'Valley Forge' or something unprintable. Veterans still return to look up the site of the tent city," says Kollbaum.

Animals seem to savor the old cantonment area, now used for battle reenactments, Boy Scout camporees, balloon races, and a new multipurpose trail. Coyotes and wild turkeys reside nearby, as does a standing population of from 9 to 15 deer. Owls and hawks are often seen aloft.

As you walk south on Gregg, the densest oak-hickory forest in the park is on your right. Appropriately for this old military camp, post oak is its dominant tree. The forest extends south from the General Grant shelter to the South County archery range at Hancock Avenue.

Turn left at Hancock. The first redbrick building on your left is park headquarters. It occupies a World War II post office and nurses' dorm. Next door, a former officers' quarters contains the 14,000-member National Association of Civilian Conservation Corps (CCC) Alumni. From 1933 to 1942, the CCC was a Depression-era, New Deal jobs agency. "We put 4 million young men to work," says Amel Burchett, executive director. Why is JB the group's headquarters and museum site? "Thousands and thousands of young CCC enrollees went through JB for their physical exams, which, incidentally, took 3 days to a week to complete," says Burchett.

As you walk east on Hancock, you can view JB's remaining redbrick buildings and the 135-acre parade ground, originally open all the way to the river bluff. In 1912, St. Louisan Albert Berry became the first person to parachute from an airplane, dropping 2000 feet onto the parade ground. Today, the Missouri Air National Guard uses the field as a site for its radar tower, some occasional bivouacs, its annual Family Day for relatives of guard members, and a place to play youth football and baseball. A recent addition to the field is a 1968 McDonnell Douglas F4E Phantom jet fighter. "I'm certain it had missions in Vietnam," says Master Sergeant Mark Groceman. "We trucked it down from Lambert Field where it had been on display at the front gate of the Air National Guard unit out there." Bordering the parade ground on the south are old barracks, a guardhouse, and a recreation hall, all from the 1890s. The former base hospital and post exchange rim the western perimeter.

At Grant Road, walk left. The meadow on your left sits on another landfill, where trash and refuse were once piled into sinkholes that reached 60 feet deep. Periscopish white vent pipes that release underground methane gas are visible reminders. "When we took over the grounds, the County Parks Department built a restroom on the landfill site," says historian Kollbaum. "It was open for only a short time when a county ranger used it, left, and got a short distance when it exploded. The restroom wasn't rebuilt and the land has been posted ever since." (Others have different versions of the story.)

At Scenic Circle Drive, where JB's arsenal commander once had a home, there is a majestic river overlook that is worth a detour. By its entrance at Grant Road is an iron fence made from Civil War–era Springfield rifle barrows. The two entrance cannons by the fence once stood sentinel at the Civil War army arsenal at Second and Arsenal Streets in St. Louis. After checking out the overlook, return to Grant Road and continue north.

At CCC Road, bear right. Hike to the General Lee shelter. From there, look east toward the river, fix your sights on the limestone wall and terrace of the 1857 Powder Magazine Museum, then walk over the lawn directly to the free-admission museum. Museum terraces offer JB's most panoramic views of the river and the American Bottom

High-speed tanks of the army's Sixth Infantry division pass in review on the parade grounds of Jefferson Barracks in 1937. (St. Louis Mercantile Library)

section of nearby Illinois. During the Civil War, rifles, cannons, and ammo were stored in the magazine, another support facility for the main arsenal near downtown St. Louis.

After the museum, take the walkway from the overlook to the Veterans' Memorial Amphitheater, situated in a "natural bowl," actually a king-sized sinkhole that was once part of a landfill. The amphitheater contains a big stage backed by a granite-limestone curtain wall with a small waterfall. Behind the stage, a plaza provides another choice river lookout. Up to 10,000 people can fit comfortably into the amphitheater space, says its designer-architect, William Albinson.

Continue walking north to the 1851 Old Ordnance Room, where powder and weapons were stored after the large St. Louis arsenal was closed in 1871. Now, the place is a museum that charges modest fees to view its rotating exhibits and historical displays. Supposedly, a tunnel running from beneath the building to the river facilitated the delivery of ammunition to JB. From the Old Ordnance Room, take the cinder path west to the 1851 Laborer's House (free admission), restored in 1960 with original blueprints obtained from the National Archives in Washington, D.C. From the Laborer's House, which billeted JB civilian workers, walk past the old stable to the visitors center (another former stable). The center has historical exhibits and a first-rate bookstore with a large selection of history books.

Find your way back to Grant Road, a block or so to the west, and to Connie's stand on Cye Road. Connie's is named for William J. "Connie" Confer, who died in 1982. The stand was opened in 1961 by Confer and his now-retired partner, Augusta "Mac" McNerney. "People come from all over St. Louis to see us," says concessionaire, Dan Todd. Since corkball players like to stop by after games, Connie's has done what is politically correct. It sponsors a team called "The Barbecues."

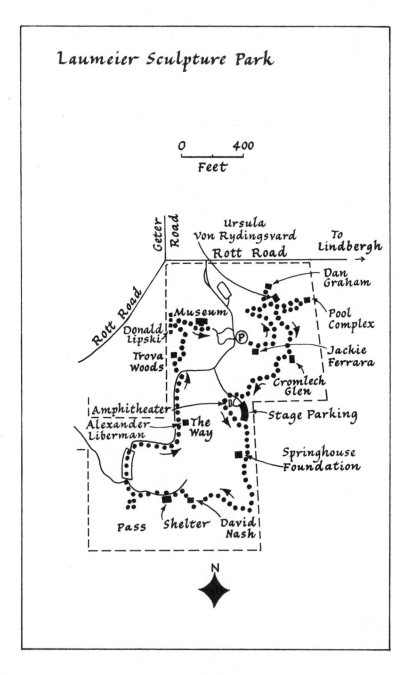

Laumeier Sculpture Park

0 400
Feet

Geter Road

Ursula
von Rydingsvard
Rott Road

To
Lindbergh

Rott Road

Dan
Graham

Museum

Pool
Complex

Donald
Lipski

P

Trova
Woods

Jackie
Ferrara

Cromlech
Glen

Amphitheater

Stage Parking

Alexander
Liberman

The
Way

Springhouse
Foundation

Pass

Shelter

David
Nash

N

Laumeier
Sculpture Park

Location: Sunset Hills, Missouri
Hiking distance: 2⅓ miles
Hiking time: 1½ hours
Bicycles: not permitted

I n 1972, Laumeier Park opened on the arboretumlike grounds near the former home of Matilda and Henry H. Laumeier; Henry was the real estate investor son of a shoe and banking millionaire. The original owner of the Tudor limestone home, erected in 1916 for $20,450, had obtained the architectural plans straight from a magazine article on trendy bungalow designs. Laumeier, who moved into the home in 1941, loved nature, and probably planted most of the mature trees and shrubs surrounding the home. When Matilda died in 1968 (Henry had died in 1959), St. Louis County inherited the property. In its early days, the new county park was a place to take walks, picnic, or cross-country ski. It did not seem to be a park with a purpose.

Then, in 1975, St. Louis sculptor Ernest Trova sought to donate some 40 of his larger sculptures to create a park with an internationally acclaimed collection. After a tour of county parks, Trova picked Laumeier as the perfect site: It had sloping grassy sections, dense woods, and a varying topography. The Trova decision gave birth to the Laumeier Sculpture Park.

Access

Take US 40/I-64 or I-44 to Lindbergh Boulevard South. From either intersection, take Lindbergh south to Rott Road, which is 5.8 miles from US 40/I-64 and 0.6 mile from I-44. Drive west on Rott Road for less than a mile to the main park entrance. Park in the southernmost part of the lot, near the four red poles. The trail begins to the left of the poles, down the stairs.

Trail

As the winding walk begins its descent into the forest, you quickly discover the reason a friend calls Laumeier "an idyllic place where modern art really works with nature. There is truly a sense of discovery in walking Laumeier. Besides finding beautiful trees and wildflowers in the woods, you find art," such as in the first stop along the way, *Laumeier Project.*

Nestled in the woods, *Laumeier Project* was the park's first sculpture to be specifically designed for its site. Its creator, Jackie Ferrara, says it reflects her fondness for games and puzzles and isn't necessarily the pyramidal Mayan tower some see it as. With the 1981 installation of the red cedar–stepped structure, the park began to encourage other internationally famous artists to plan specific sculptures for Laumeier. The results have been so stunning that Laumeier is touted as owning "the world's foremost program of site sculpture."

Resume your walk through the upland forest. The trail takes you downhill and around a curve or two to Dan Graham's *Triangular Bridge Over Water,* an aluminum, steel, and reflective glass bridge that mirrors the nearby trees and flowers, and the clouds above, so well that the structure just about disappears into the woods. Once across the bridge, turn right and walk to an untitled work by sculptor Ursula von Rydingsvard. These rubber-accented cedar tubs stand in rows of nine opposite a grove of redbuds.

Continue walking south. At a seeming trail dead end, walk left, then take a quick right on the path to *Pool Complex: Orchard Valley,* designed by sculptor Mary Miss. This huge work envelops a 1920s swimming pool owned by the Hedenkamp family, whose home fronted on Rott Road where the present firehouse stands. Cedar-lined paths led from the home to the swimming pool where owner Dietrich Hedenkamp, a founder of St. Louis Bank Building and Equipment Company, was said to lavishly entertain business and political friends on weekends. The Hedenkamp home was built in 1910, six years before the Laumeier home. (The 20-acre Hedenkamp estate was purchased by the county in 1980.)

"The sides of the pool are built of rock found on the Hedenkamp estate," said the *St. Louis Globe-Democrat* in 1934. The 12-foot-deep pool was so large that the generous Hedenkamps invited both the Kirkwood YMCA and area Boy Scouts to share it with them. The home and grounds were called Orchard Valley. Walk around this elaborate kidney-shaped structure on the pine boardwalk, as well as its adjoining stairs, decks, pavilions, twists, and turns. The pavilions were built over what was once the swimming pool bathhouse. The elaborate construction "is about time, memory, and kinds of space," theorized art critic Patricia Degener.

Once you've walked around the complex, return to the main trail near the exit sign. Take the trail down the hill to *Cromlech Glen,* a massive earthwork designed by Beverly Pepper.

"Someone coming on [*Cromlech Glen*] unaware . . . might take it for the weathered remains of a Civil War fortification," wrote Degener in the *St. Louis Post-Dispatch* in 1987. "It reminds me of a very primitive prehistoric mound," observes my wife. Laumeier literature notes that *Cromlech Glen,* a land form, is "a sodded basin with high walls built by excavating machines to enclose an isolated space" entered through a narrow gap. Inside the rounded bowl is an amphitheater intended by the artist as a place for poetry readings and theatrical performances. For a better perspective, hike up and around the flagstone walk that rims the amphitheater.

Across from *Cromlech Glen*'s entrance, walk over the plank bridge and up through the woods to the large outdoor stage, which is at the base of a spacious natural amphitheater. Appearing here in the late 1970s and early 1980s were composers Aaron Copland and Morton Gould, and pianist Lorin Hollander, all performing with the St. Louis Symphony Orchestra, among whose conductors were Sarah Caldwell and Leonard Slatkin. Actor Paul Winfield recited Shakespeare on the stage. In the last decade or so, the stage has been used for nonsymphony concerts and festivals.

From the south end of the stage, reenter the forest through a stand of shortleaf pine trees. Walk left onto the hiking path, then shortly turn right and head downhill. Halfway down are the remains of a stone structure. "It looks like a little shrine in the forest," a passing hiker says of what was most probably a springhouse, origin unknown.

In the bottomland forest at the foot of the hill, with the stream on your left, walk under the park's tallest oaks, cottonwoods, hickories, and sycamores. This is the section of Laumeier where the most wildlife can be found. "Nobody knows much about animals in urban settings such as this," says county ranger Dennis Hogan. "For instance, a pileated woodpecker thrives on our sycamores. But a pileated usually needs 400 acres of mature hardwood forest. We're about 300 acres shy of that at Laumeier, but they still come here. We don't know why."

Follow the bottomland trail over two wooden bridges, then climb a set of 25 charred logs that takes you to the educational pavilion. The log stairs constitute a work of art, David Nash's *Black Through Green,* installed in 1993. Nash says that, over the years, as the stairs are walked on and worn by weather, they will deteriorate and turn back to earth. This process of decay, he indicates, means that nature is not just background for his art, but a part of the environmental sculpture itself.

Continue west past the educational pavilion and into the adjoining meadow. Ahead is the rustic cor-ten steel configuration called *Crete,* which consists of six "bent parallelograms, tips touching corner-to-corner." To the left of *Crete* is Meg Webster's *Pass,* a 1½-acre ecological sculpture. Walk around, then through this dazzling collection of Missouri habitat—from shade and herb gardens to prairie grasses and berry bushes. "*Pass* will change with the seasons," writes Beej Nierengarten-Smith, Laumeier director. "It will wither in the winter and bloom once again in the spring. In its divergent approach to appreciation of aesthetics and nature, it truly demonstrates the integration of art and nature." *Pass* is in the vanguard of what promises to be a heavy emphasis by Laumeier on environmental art and sculpture, says Debra Reinhardt, director of public relations.

Walk up the hill on the grass to Dennis Oppenheim's *Rolling Explosion,* a pair of "flanged 10-foot steel wheels joined by a rectangular frame" positioned midway along 60-foot tracks. Walk straight over to Beverly Pepper's orange-plated steel creation, *Alpha,* then turn right and head for *The Way,* the park's monumental red signature piece. Sculptor Alexander Liberman took six years to construct it from oil drums welded end-to-end. He says his piece somewhat resembles a classical ruin.

Walkers examine Ball? Ball! Wall? Wall!, *a string of 55 salvaged marine buoys, each weighing 650 pounds, west of the Laumeier Park museum.*

After pondering *The Way,* return to the blacktop path and continue north past the restroom facility. Enter "The Trova Woods" through a clearing in the trees on the left. Trova's *Poet Series*—four black-painted cor-ten steel figures of walking, sitting, and standing poets—is installed at intervals in the medium-thick woods.

From the Trova Woods, walk up the sidewalk and over the footbridge by the George Rickey reflecting pond, where a stainless steel kinetic sculpture resembling needles swaying in the wind occupies center space. From here, head for the western boundary of the park for a look at artist Donald Lipski's *Ball? Ball! Wall? Wall!,* a wavy, 300-foot-long line of 55 hooked-together salvaged marine buoys weighing 650 pounds each. It resembles—according to a park flyer—"a gigantic string of pop-in necklace beads or pearls." You can next examine the sculpture behind the Laumeier Museum, then the pair of cast-bronze sculptures on the museum's terrace lawn—the 1927 Carl Milles equestrian *Folke Filbyter,* and Fernando Botero's *Roman Soldier.* One of Trova's popular *Falling Man* works is on display in the reflecting pool. Besides major exhibits, the museum has a shop that sells unusual art objects and unique jewelry, ceramics, fiber, and glass. It's open Tuesday through Saturday from 10 AM to 5 PM and Sunday from noon to 5.

The parking lot is located just east of the museum.

West St. Louis County and Beyond

Walkers relax before taking the stepping-stones across Brush Creek on the Brush Creek Trail at Shaw Arboretum.

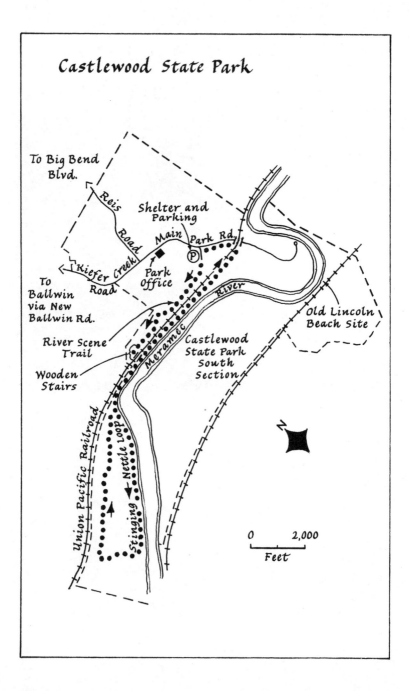

Castlewood State Park

To Big Bend Blvd.

Reis Road

Shelter and Parking

Main Park Rd.

Kiefer Creek

To Ballwin via New Ballwin Rd.

Kiefer Road

Park Office

River Scene Trail

Wooden Stairs

Meramec River

Castlewood State Park South Section

Old Lincoln Beach Site

Union Pacific Railroad

Stinging Nettle Loop

N

0   2,000
Feet

Castlewood State Park

River Scene and Stinging Nettle Trails

Location: St. Louis County, Missouri
Hiking distance: 5 miles
Hiking time: 2 hours
Bicycles: not permitted on bluff
portion of River Scene Trail

Castlewood State Park is bisected by the ancient Meramec River, which, writes Charles B. Little in *Greenways for America,* "slides in long curves beneath towering rock-faced bluffs" as it flows downstream to its mouth at the Mississippi River. Some of those towering bluffs resemble turrets of medieval castles and may have inspired the name Castlewood.

Though not as old as the Meramec, the Castlewood park grounds are traceable to 3690 B.C., according to archaeologists at University of Missouri–St. Louis (UMSL). They found 32 prehistoric living, camping, and work sites in or near the park and figure that the quarrying, production, and trading (mainly for fur) of chert, the flinty stone used in tools and weapons, was the main livelihood of the primitive tribes.

Just after the Civil War, investors from the St. Louis Vine and Fruit Growers Association had a grandiose plan to convert land near the present park into "The St. Louis Park of Fruits," which had a division named Castlewoods. The "Park" plan included a hotel, 20 miles of dirt avenues, and a mile-long row of bushy grapevines by the tracks of the Pacific Railroad, later renamed Missouri Pacific. Financial problems aborted a plan for resort homes on the land; by 1900, every hint of the "Park" had vanished.

In the 20th century, St. Louisans tested the recreational waters of the Meramec River. Valley Park was the Meramec's key resort town, but there were other settlements such as Times Beach, Drake, Fern Glen, and a reincarnated Castlewood. The latter (some called it Castlewood Camp), with its weekend clubhouses, saloons, and beach, was chic from about 1915 to 1950 when post–World War II vacationers found affordable destinations well beyond St. Louis.

In peak years, Castlewood attracted up to 10,000 visitors each summer weekend; they arrived mainly in automobiles and trains. The Frisco Railroad line to Springfield, Missouri, maintained a few shelters on the south bank. Enterprising farmers served lunches in their homes to weekend canoeists who paddled by on their way to Castlewood and its centerpiece, Lincoln Beach, whose heyday came during the Prohibition years.

Lincoln Beach lay about 75 yards to the south across the Meramec from Castlewood. It offered fine white sand, good swimming, sunbathing, picnicking, badminton, and vaudeville and gymnastic acts direct from St. Louis. To get to the beach from Castlewood, one either paddled a canoe, paid a nickel to ride a 12-passenger motorized flatboat, or swam.

Then, as now, the 12-foot-deep Meramec could be choppy. A volunteer Red Cross lifesaving unit, the Meramec River Patrol, operated in canoes near Lincoln Beach to warn off or to rescue swimmers and waders in trouble. (In 1950, the patrol reported that it had made 725 rescues in 22 years.) There were many drownings among people "who wanted to hurry to Lincoln Beach by swimming across," says Ethel Wilder, who spent childhood summers in a clubhouse east of the beach. By 1945, the beach was gone, submerged by a switch in the river's course.

Lincoln Lodge faced the beach on the north bank. In the two-story brown frame building (its foundation is still visible) were a tavern, restaurant, dance hall, and sleeping rooms, recalls Joseph McFarland, who managed clubhouses on the grounds in the early 1940s. A next-door canoe storage barn held 200 canoes; on most Saturday nights, canoe parking space was precious.

Until about 1970, the land that comprises the 1800-acre state

*Lincoln Beach, across from what is now Castlewood State Park,
was a busy place in the 1920s. (Castlewood State Park files)*

park, including 600 acres the park owns on the south side of the
river, supported about 130 clubhouses. It was McFarland's job to
collect annual clubhouse lease fees, which ranged from $90 to $300.
On the bluffs overlooking the river, Castlewood-on-the-Meramec
resort, distinct from the clubhouses near the riverbank, contained
some 250 additional clubhouses. Some survive today in altered shapes
and sizes and can be seen from the bottomland River Scene Trail,
especially in winter.

Aside from clubhouses near the river and up in the bluffs, a
small community existed in the area immediately south of the junction
of Kiefer Creek Road and New Ballwin Road. Known as the village
of Castlewood, it had churches, stores, saloons, and year-round homes.
In the village's glory days toward the end of Prohibition, at least 10
taverns lined the main streets, writes historian Cathy French Nagel,
including The Lone Wolf Club (where Harry Truman once guested
on the piano). The Castlewood Pool, a half-moon-shaped, 18,000-

square-foot, spring-fed pool opened in the early 1940s; it first rivaled Lincoln Beach, and then replaced it as a recreational destination. Long abandoned, the pool stands behind a chain-link fence off Sontag Road in the village.

After decades of clubhouse decay and public dumping on the bottomland along the north bank, the state converted the acreage to a park, opening it in late 1979. "Before the park was opened, this place was one big trash heap. People came from everywhere to dump things," says John Hearst, retired park maintenance supervisor. "Much of the trash and bulldozed clubhouse debris is still buried beneath the park grounds." Park superintendent Richard Love says that about 300,000 visitors use the park annually. "At least two-thirds of them walk our 17 miles of trails," he reports.

Access

From I-270 and Manchester Road in west St. Louis County, drive west on Manchester Road 6 miles to New Ballwin Road. Turn left. Drive 3 miles to Castlewood Road in the old village of Castlewood. Turn left on Castlewood Road, then right on Kiefer Creek Road, which takes you into the park. Drive past the park office to the trailhead parking lot on your right. Once parked, hike up the steep hill by the park bulletin board to reach the River Scene Trail on the blufftop. The walk begins to your right.

Trail

The gravelly trail edges westward along the rim overlooking the Meramec. In this area, red and gray foxes are often seen around sunup. Scattered among cedars and wildflowers are relics of the area's past: clubhouse foundations, fireplaces, water pipes, chunks of concrete stairs that now lead nowhere. In the woods to your right is the hulk of the 100,000-gallon reservoir to which water was pumped uphill 2400 feet from a deep well near Lincoln Lodge. A grid of pipes from the reservoir supplied water to the clubhouses.

The best river views are about ¾ mile along the rim, just before the first trail bench and a major westward bend in the river. Waterbirds, such as ospreys and great blue herons, often float the thermals over the river. And you can often see deer roaming the wide open spaces on the south side of the Meramec.

In its gradual descent, the River Scene Trail connects with a new yellow pine boardwalk with three overlooks and 90 steps. Replacing the dirt path in an erosion-prone part of the blufftop, the boardwalk was built over 19 months by "The Statewide Trail Crew," three skilled carpenter-welders who travel the state for the park's owner, the Department of Natural Resources, developing trails, bridges, and boardwalks. "The toughest part of building this boardwalk was hauling the boards from flat land up here on our backs," says Edward Barnhart, a crew member. Toward the end of the boardwalk, the dangerously eroded concrete staircase that once rose from the Castlewood rail shelter to the hotels in the bluffs comes into view. Once you reach the railroad tracks, walk through the 1930 underpass, then turn right to start the 3-mile loop of the Stinging Nettle Trail.

The Stinging Nettle Trail tends to stay by the water's edge. At places it is very narrow, and, after rain, very muddy and slippery. Besides the foreboding presence of hundreds of tall, dark cottonwood and box elder trees, the floor of the woods is seasonally blanketed by dark green stinging nettle plants, which are common floodplain plants and, around here, frequently flooded out. (Be wary of brushing against a stinging nettle. The plant's downy hairs are really hollow tubes that release irritating fluid when touched. Old-timers say that if they're boiled to remove the poison, nettles can be great in soups or as stand-alone vegetables. In fact, Britons still make nettle purée, a thick soup of young nettle leaves; it tastes like it's been made with lettuce.) The turnaround point in the loop, marked by signs, is about ¼ mile beyond an abandoned bus. The return path takes you slightly deeper into the bottomland forest, but the river is almost always in view. (Love says the park's master plan calls for eventually extending the Stinging Nettle Trail along the river to Glencoe, about 6 or 7 miles beyond the present turnaround point.)

After completing the loop, and with the railroad underpass on your left, continue walking straight east along the riverbank through more bottomland forest where giant arching sycamores and cottonwoods reach out over the water. During the spring, colonies of bluebells and marsh buttercups lighten the way along the trail. From the forest, you emerge onto Lincoln Field, which, in the spring, is reminiscent of a village Green where people run dogs, fly kites, or spread a blanket to get some sun. Around dusk, deer may wander down from the hills to graze and or to claim sleeping sites.

From Lincoln Field, follow the path to the main park road. Walk left on the road, under the rail viaduct, to the trailhead parking area.

Edgar M. Queeny County Park

Location: St. Louis County, Missouri
Hiking distance: 4 miles
Hiking time: 1½ hours
Bicycles: permitted

Queeny County Park, which debuted in 1974, is named after its last owner, Edgar Monsanto Queeny, president and chairman of Monsanto, Inc., between 1928 and 1960. (Monsanto is America's fourth largest chemical company, says *Fortune* magazine.) He and his wife, Ethel, occupied their Greek-Revival "country cottage," Jarville, from 1931 to 1962, then sold the home and grounds. Since Queeny was board chairman of Barnes Hospital in St. Louis at the time, he gave most of the Jarville sale proceeds to the hospital to construct the 17-floor patient tower that bears his name.

Queeny was a horseman early in his life, but after a riding accident he used the paths on his Jarville estate sparingly. He allowed only one neighbor to use the grounds for riding, says Rich Koester, a maintenance staffer from that period and, later, a supervisor at Queeny Park. Many of the trails in the north end of the estate were in place in Queeny's day, but the roads and paths on the south end are new. The Queenys used the trails more frequently after Mrs. Queeny acquired a golf cart in 1955, says Koester. Queeny himself liked to drive the grounds in a station wagon or his early-model Buick Riviera. "He once drove by with a high-ranking general when we were out cutting silage," recalls Koester. "Mr. Queeny often got stuck in the mud with his cars out in the fields."

As a sportsman and naturalist, Queeny led African safaris, filmed seven documentaries on African subjects, made a documentary on Atlantic salmon, and wrote one book on hunting and fishing in

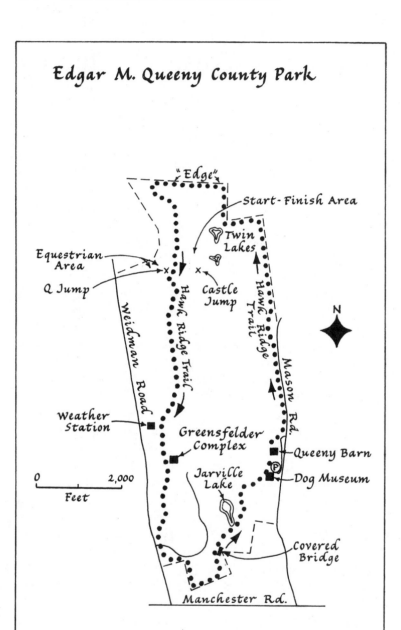

Edgar M. Queeny County Park

Alaska, and another, *Prairie Wings,* on wild ducks. For the latter, he took all the duck photos himself, mostly at Wingmead, his rice plantation and duck-hunting preserve near Stuttgart, Arkansas. "That was his real farm," says Koester, "although he raised cattle and hogs at Jarville until he sold the place."

In 1986, a plan to sink an 18-hole golf course into some of Queeny's 570 acres was voted down by St. Louis County voters, thus preserving the hills and valleys, meadows and woodlots—"the best piece of open space we have in St. Louis County," says environmental activist Kay Drey. The park has fishing lakes, equestrian and hiking trails, and the impressive Greensfelder Recreational Complex, which offers sports facilities to thousands of nearby residents as well as a summer home to the St. Louis Symphony Orchestra for some of its Pops concerts. The annual St. Louis National Charity Horse Show is held indoors at Greensfelder in the early fall, followed by the outdoor Queeny Park Horse Trials.

Jarville, named after a village near Nancy, France, was a plantation home in pre–Civil War days and changed little until the Queenys converted it to an elegant 20th-century estate in the 1930s. Today Jarville has been reconverted into headquarters for the Dog Museum, an organization that moved here in 1987 from midtown Manhattan in New York. The Dog Museum added 14,000 square feet to Jarville, linking it to Queeny's brick carriage house/garage, now the museum shop and office. The museum is said to contain "every artistic depiction of canines possible." There are dog paintings, ceramics, figurines, books, videos, and special exhibits on dog collars and houses among its offerings. On most Sunday afternoons, the public is invited to meet owners and fanciers of rare or special breeds. Once dogs were welcomed as museum guests if accompanied by their owners. No more. "Adverse things began to happen," a museum staffer tells me. "The dogs brought in fleas. We had to tear up our carpeting as a result."

Access

From I-270 in western St. Louis County, take Manchester Road west for 1.7 miles to Mason Road. Turn right on Mason; drive 1.3

miles to the park entrance sign. Turn left, then left again into the parking area.

Trail

From the parking lot, follow the path north to Queeny's white barn and stables (which originally contained eight horse stalls); a polo-players weather vane sits atop its copper roof. Queeny liked polo, and is said to have played here frequently in his early Jarville years. His polo field was in the valley northwest of the Dog Museum. The barn is now the park office and ranger station.

In the years around 1950, the barn served a double purpose: It held four dairy cows, which provided milk for the Queeny breakfast table, and it served as a studio for Queeny's filmmaking hobby. One of Queeny's African documentaries was shown in 1951 at two packed St. Louis movie houses. His request for national distribution soured, however, when the Legion of Decency censored the film for its nude shots.

Continue north on the paved path by the barn. Pass the park entrance on your right and, on your left, a small grove of honey locust trees, as well as an equestrian practice jump area used mainly to train mounted park rangers.

As it moves northward, the path parallels Mason Road for awhile and officially becomes the Hawk Ridge Trail. As the pavement stops and a wide dirt path takes over, multiflora roses and honeysuckle bushes appear, then oak-hickory forest. The terrain becomes hilly, and redbud, dogwood, serviceberry, and elm trees come into view. Contemporary luxury homes on the park's northern boundaries appear on your right. Some neighbors have planted magnificent gardens, almost natural extensions of the park itself.

After 1 mile you'll cross Owl Creek. Walk up the hill; follow the Hawk Ridge Trail, which bends sharply to your right, heading north. To your left is Twin Lakes, where fishing is permitted if you're 12 or under, or 64 or over, and carry a fishing pole. Canada geese, mallards, and wood ducks nest near the lakes. (Queeny, in contrast, raised only quail when he lived here, says Koester.) During daylight hours, the park's deer often loiter near the lakes. As you hike the north end of the trail, clover and alfalfa fields abound. Hay from the fields is shipped to the county's Greensfelder and Suson Parks to feed the horses that the county owns and uses to patrol its larger parks.

To your right on the northern border is "the edge," a tangle of wild cherry, sassafras, redbud, hackberry, and elm trees and saplings that attracts the birds and rabbits and other animals that feed here year-round. Queeny's herd of between 40 and 50 deer enjoy the edge as much as they do the clover and alfalfa. Soon the trail swings left and aims south through open meadows.

In one of the widest open spaces in the park, a clustering of equestrian cross-country obstacles, including the Q jump to the right of the trail, is in evidence. All are part of the Queeny Park Horse Trials, held each October since 1982. The Q jump is often the last jump on the course for competing equestrians. "It's our photo-op jump," says Dick Wessel, who constructed all 30 or so jumps and is a co-organizer of the trials. Near the Q jump are the whiskey barrel jump (which still held some whisky when first installed) and the stone fence jump. On your left, and down the hill 900 feet, is the castle turret jump, which Wessel fashioned from plywood and based on a photo of a German castle he admired.

Just past the righthand jump area is the animal pasture where county park horses graze. After 2½ miles of walking, perhaps the best vista in the park is off to your left: an eastward scan across the valley to the old Queeny barn and homestead, about 1½ miles away. This open field, which slopes eastward into a valley, becomes the stadium jump area during the horse trials. "All of our stadium obstacles are collapsible; we store them off site," says Wessel.

Soon pavement reappears on the trail. On your right is a St. Louis County continuous air monitoring station loaded with computerized loggers that provide data to ensure the county complies with federal clean air standards. Its tall tower measures wind speed and direction; the white tower probe records air temperature. For more than 20 years, the station has been checked daily by instrumentation specialist Larry Eilbott, who knows the park well. "One day as I was standing on the porch, I saw a fellow riding an elephant north on the trail. The elephant turned out to be Flora, star of Circus Flora, which was putting on a show in the park."

After passing the old park supervisor's home (it had been a Queeny caretaker's home), the paved path becomes a two-lane road for about half a mile until it reaches the main road near the park's Weidman Road entrance. Walk on the shoulder on the right side of the road. Parking areas and open fields are on your left, as is the Greensfelder Recreation Complex. On your right, as you proceed, is Towne and Country Stables on Weidman Road (where many Queeny equestrians board their horses); later on, you reach the new Islamic Center of Greater St. Louis, which, true to Islamic law, faces toward Mecca. The white mosque, with its 40-foot, copper-colored dome and towering minaret, opened in 1994.

After crossing the main entrance road, walk straight ahead on the grass to the forest edge, then head left on a dirt path that borders the woods. Cross a wooden footbridge, then bear right on a paved path that takes you across a 1982 cedar, covered bridge erected by county park employees.

Jarville Lake, once the pride of Mr. Queeny, will soon appear on your left. Parklike, the lake is surrounded by youthful crab-apple trees, memorial benches, Canada geese (in-season), and a striking pine grove. Next door is a marsh pond favored by ducks and kingfishers; cattails and sedge fill out its borders. Now walk uphill to your right toward the Dog Museum. Ironically, Queeny's long-empty dog kennel sits on the hillside to the right. (Queeny once made a documentary film about his favorite Labrador, Mike, and employed the St. Louis Symphony Orchestra to help record the live soundtrack in what is now Powell Symphony Hall.) After the trail passes the park department greenhouse, the next point of interest should be your automobile waiting in the parking area by Mason Road.

Edmund A. Babler Memorial State Park

Woodbine and Hawthorn Trails

Location: St. Louis County, Missouri
Hiking distance: 5½ miles
Hiking time: 2 hours
Bicycles: on paved bike paths only

L ate on January 27, 1930, Dr. Edmund A. Babler, 54, had just left the monthly Deaconess Home and Hospital medical and surgical staff meeting when he was felled by a stroke that left him severely paralyzed. Thirteen days later, he died. A reconstructive surgeon, Babler was respected by colleagues and patients alike. His funeral drew what a newspaper described as one of the largest crowds in St. Louis history.

One of Edmund's surviving siblings, Jacob, a lawyer and former Republican national committeeman from Missouri, led efforts to preserve Edmund's memory. He and his brother Henry gave to the state the 868 acres they owned in west St. Louis County, accompanied by a $1.5 million check for perpetual park upkeep. "I never heard a million five hundred thousand dollars talk louder than that," said US Secretary of the Interior Harold L. Ickes in dedicating the park in October 1938. The Ickes radio speech was beamed nationally by the Mutual Broadcasting System. "For an automobile age public, Babler Park can easily develop into much of what Forest Park was for St. Louis during the World's Fair years," the *St. Louis Post-Dispatch* commented. Pleased by the public's initial response, the Bablers gave the park 800 more acres. The Bablers' original upkeep endowment still pays for nearly 60 percent of park maintenance expenses, says Dale Kannewurf, park naturalist.

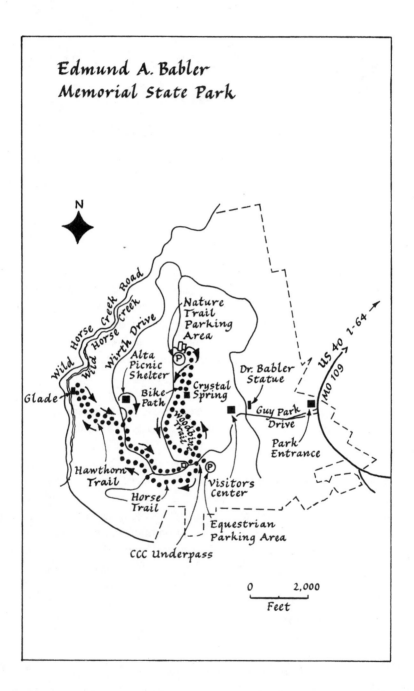

Edmund A. Babler
Memorial State Park

Babler State Park claims to have more limestone buildings and structures built by the Depression-era Civilian Conservation Corps than all other Missouri state parks. Twenty-two of the buildings are listed on the National Register of Historic Places. The park's massive stone entranceway off MO 109, as well as the gutters and curbing along Guy Park Drive, bespeak the limestone dexterity of the 400 CCC members and 300 WPA relief workers who developed the park. Most of the stone was quarried within the park grounds or close by. Perhaps the most imposing artistry in the park is the 80-ton, 25-foot bronze statue of Dr. Babler, rising above a grassy knoll west of the main entrance.

In 1942, the US Army commandeered much of Babler. It used the CCC barracks to house World War II German and Italian prisoners of war captured in North Africa and to billet military police recruits. Some barracks were made into a fresh-air convalescent center for military patients from the Jefferson Barracks Army Hospital in south St. Louis County. After the war, the state offered 100 acres of Babler to St. Louis County for a $15 million, 1000-bed navy hospital and medical research center, but the deal fell through.

In the mid-1850s, the land that is now Babler Park held several corn, wheat, and hemp plantations, staffed by dozens of slaves, wrote the late Alfred Kerth Jr., a park volunteer and area historian. In the 1890s, he added, the Centaur Lime Company quarried limestone in the future park's hills, reducing it to lime in kilns that still exist. CCC volunteers doubtlessly used the old quarry to find limestone for park buildings and roadways in the 1930s.

Access

From the intersection of I-270 and I-44, take I-44 West to exit 264 at MO 109 in Eureka, about 12 miles. Turn right on MO 109. Drive north 10 miles to the park entrance.

From the intersection of I-170 and I-64/US 40, take I-64/US 40 West 10 miles to the Chesterfield Airport Road turnoff. Exit; drive south on Long Road, which intersects Chesterfield Airport Road. Keep driving south on Long Road until it dead-ends at Wild Horse Creek Road. Turn right. Follow Wild Horse Creek Road about 3 miles to County Highway C. Turn left on C (at the Amoco station). Drive south to MO 109 and turn right. Drive 1.5 miles to the park entrance.

Once inside the park, follow Guy Park Drive past the new visitors center (a recommended stop) for 2.2 miles until you reach the Nature Trail parking area. Park by the bulletin board near the far east end of the lot. The trailhead is south of the bulletin board.

Trail

At the trailhead, turn right onto the Woodbine Trail. After crossing a small footbridge, you encounter some 75 sweet gum trees rising in a nearly straight line and probably planted about 100 years ago as a homestead boundary. When the Woodbine Trail reaches the paved bike path, turn left on the path. As you walk straight ahead, you'll see some of the open green areas that characterize Babler, as do its wooded hills and broad roadways. Crystal Spring, one of the park's four small springs, appears along the left side of the path. Although springs suggest possible underground caves, none has been found at Babler.

Beyond Crystal Spring, on the right side of the bike path, is a CCC-built limestone comfort station with a reddish hip roof, stone sills, and vandal-marred decorative art over the windows. Across the path, a ravine rich in northern red oaks, basswoods, redbuds, dogwoods, and paw paws resembles "a northern forest, one you'd expect to see in Michigan or Wisconsin," says David Bradford, a former naturalist at Babler. Continuing uphill on the bike path, one of the park's largest fields of ferns, mostly Christmas ferns, covers much of the hillside on your right.

The bike path proceeds through a CCC underpass whose flat segmental arch ceiling may accommodate the moss-and-mud nest of an eastern phoebe in the spring and summer. Once through the underpass, turn right on a wide gravel path that takes you across the equestrian parking area and through a clutch of cedar trees. You can continue your walk on a horse trail, which takes you to the Hawthorn Trail loop, 1¼ miles ahead. The horse trail straddles some old ridges that naturalists think were used by Native Americans. Their local

It's playtime near the 80-ton statue of Dr. Edmund Babler at Babler State Park.

encampments may have been satellites of the early Woodland and late Mississippian Indians who inhabited Cahokia Mounds in nearby Illinois. Along this rocky, bumpy, and slippery-when-wet trail section, hikers have seen more deer and wild turkey than anywhere else in the park. A healthy herd of some 100 deer resides at Babler.

Once at the Hawthorn Trail, walk left, following the left leg of the 1¾-mile loop. Flanked by red maples, the Hawthorn loop bends to your right and eventually reaches a glade—the Missouri equivalent of a desert. Whorled milkweed, prairie parsley, orange puccoon, dwarf hackberry, and other flora thrive here, as do several gnarled, sun-fried chinquapin oaks and a large gum-bumelia tree that once tied for the honor of the state's largest, until someone discovered a bigger one downstate.

Soon after the glade, the path slowly rounds a bend that overlooks Wild Horse Creek (you must walk cautiously to the bluff edge to actually see the blue-green creek). In this area, the relatively uncommon spring wildflower white trillium often appears. In summer, ant mounds are numerous. Entomologist James Trager says

Babler may have the most ant species in the metropolitan area. As he hikes, Trager lifts rocks and uncovers small dirt mounds to reveal hundreds of thousands of red and black ants that tenaciously work their communities. Trager claims to have found 60 to 65 ant species on the Hawthorn Trail, plus some species not previously identified scientifically.

Beyond the point where the creek can be seen (the larger Missouri River lies about a mile to the north but can't be viewed from the path), the Hawthorn is mostly uphill through a stunning oak-maple forest whose summer canopy of green leaves is so thick that sunlight barely slips through. Because of the dense canopy, the forest floor here is nearly devoid of understory trees and bushes.

After completing the Hawthorn loop, walk straight ahead and cross Wirth Drive. Walk left to the Alta picnic shelter. A classic CCC project, the cross-shaped picnic place has a four-sided central fireplace, thick stone walls, heavy natural oak timber posts and struts, and a flagstone floor set in concrete with built-in wooden picnic benches. In keeping with the Depression-era philosophy of the National Park Service, whose ideas influenced Babler's design, the structure has a strong rustic cast.

Now it's time to return to the original trailhead near the Woodbine Trail. From the Alta shelter, walk east along Wirth Drive until you come to a stop sign. Walk straight ahead through the intersection, rejoining Guy Park Drive, which takes you to the equestrian parking area about one city block ahead on your right. From the parking lot, walk east to find the CCC underpass once again. Walk down through the underpass, then take a long footbridge on your right to get back on the Woodbine Trail. Eventually, the Woodbine Trail reaches the bottom of a long hill. Turn right on the dirt path (avoiding the nearby blacktop path). Cross over the footbridge, then turn left on the road that leads to the parking lot and your automobile.

Rockwoods Reservation

Lime Kiln Trail

Location: Glencoe, Missouri
Hiking distance: 3 miles
Hiking time: 1½ hours
Bicycles: not permitted

Lime Kiln Trail is the longest of six trails in 1900-acre Rockwoods Reservation. The tract was purchased by the Missouri Department of Conservation in 1938 from stockholders of the Cobb, Wright, Case Mining Company, which mined limestone in the vicinity from 1876 to about 1930, and may have operated as many as 11 lime kilns. When the state bought the land in the late 1930s, a post office, school, boardinghouse, weathered saltbox houses, and the mining company store were all that remained of an old mining settlement called "Rockwoods." The company store (its foundation survives, about ¼ mile north of Rockwoods headquarters on Glencoe Road) was projected to become "the main wildlife exhibit center for Missouri." The building, which had animals tethered out front, was then known as "The Letterman Museum," dedicated to George W. Letterman, botanist and naturalist who lived in Allenton, Missouri, from 1870 to 1913, and whose knowledge of trees and plants was nationally known. He reportedly discovered, near his home in the Rockwoods area, the largest-ever box elder.

In limestone mining's heyday, a freight spur of the Missouri-Pacific Railroad Company ran "up the valley" from the main tracks at Glencoe, Missouri, north along what is now MO 109, and turned into the present Rockwoods Reservation to run along Hamilton Creek to the turnaround point near the quarry. Rockwoods workers still find railroad ties from that period.

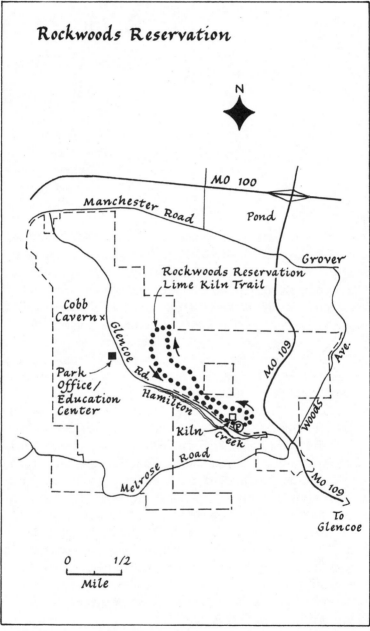

Park archives indicate that most of the kilns in the valley burned native limestone into usable lime, mostly for construction projects around St. Louis. One towering lime kiln near Glencoe Road survives; its long-abandoned, relatively small limestone quarry lies on the hillside directly behind it. Records indicate that this surviving firebrick-lined, 40-foot-tall kiln, which stands sentinel by the trailhead, produced powdered lime used solely for the foundation of a two-story frame country home in nearby Glencoe for St. Louis banker-philanthropist James E. Yeatman. Only the foundation of the 1856 home, which burned in 1920, remains; it is situated behind the LaSalle Institute buildings about 1.5 miles south on MO 109. Apparently the kiln served no other purpose.

Yeatman's presence glamorized the bucolic Meramec valley during the pre–Civil War period. He had been an incorporator, in 1849, of the Pacific Railroad Company (the first rail line west of the Mississippi River); and the first president of both the St. Louis Philharmonic Society and the St. Louis Mercantile Library. The latter institution is the counterpart of the famous Boston Athenaeum, and is now the oldest cultural institution in the St. Louis area.

In 1950 a new limestone educational building was erected to replace the company store museum. Following tradition, animal display pens were installed next to the new building. Each year, thousands of visitors came to see the penned deer, coyotes, foxes, and other animals that were orphaned or unwanted pets that could not be released. But, following reports of animal bites and escapes and also a change in public attitude, the pens were gradually removed. By January 1994, the Rockwoods "zoo" was no more. (Near the building is the north trailhead of the well-known Greenrock Trail, a 10-mile woodland path that ends at Rockwoods Range. The Boy Scouts of America maintain the trail.)

George Moore was park naturalist in the 1940s and 1950s; he probably laid out or at least redefined the Lime Kiln and other trails. His St. Louis radio show, "Along Rockwoods Trails," was popular for years. Moore's comments usually received broad coverage. He once unashamedly told the *Post-Dispatch* that "deer, particularly fawns, are the most dangerous animals in Missouri, potentially." He cited examples of hunters who had been killed by deer (the animals' methodology wasn't described), and recalled two hunters who were "treed by an infuriated doe."

Rockwoods Reservation currently includes—in addition to its splendid trail system—an educational museum building; springs and caves, particularly Cobb Cavern, a spacious, abandoned quarry; and clear, bubbling streams, all with one generic name, Hamilton Creek, a tribute to the farming family of Ninian Hamilton, who lived nearby, courtesy of a Spanish land grant received around 1803.

Access

From the intersection of I-270 and I-44, take I-44 West to MO 109 (exit 264) at Eureka, nearly 12 miles. Take MO 109 North for 3.8 miles, to the Rockwoods Reservation sign. Turn left off MO 109, then right on Glencoe Road for a 0.5-mile ride to the Lime Kiln Trail parking area.

(Near the MO 109 turnoff you will see house and building foundations from Rockland, another turn-of-the-century mining settlement.)

Trail

Walk southeast on the path to the right of the kiln, along a forest edge where deer, opossum, and foxes like to dine. Undisturbed shrubs, sun-fed ground cover, vines, and an abundance of sunflowers render this edge a special retreat for wildlife. Past the edge, the rock-bound trail gradually heads uphill on a sunny south slope that offers flashy springtime displays of green violets. Naturalists believe that the rich limestone content of the soil in this area is partially responsible for many of the crooked, double-trunked trees that appear along the way. Visible on the first ridgetop is the rich black soil of the more fertile north slope, where white oaks and hickories flourish.

Continuing on the ridge, you will see on your left the site of the quarry that supplied limestone for the Yeatman kiln down below. Later appear what seem to be sinkholes, but may not be. Assistant St. Louis district forester and former Rockwoods naturalist Cathy deJong believes these may be test holes dug by miners 75 years ago to probe

Mule-drawn carts around 1900 haul limestone from the quarry to the lime kiln located on land now part of Rockwoods Reservation.

for limestone. Nearby are shadbush or serviceberry trees. "Back in the early days, people held religious services under serviceberry trees, whose white blossoms came out early in the spring," says Ramon Gass, a forest entomologist. "Arbors of serviceberry trees substituted for the physical presence of a church."

On the trail's highest point—nearly ⅔ mile into the walk—the north and south slopes intersect, producing a habitat edge where wildlife prospers. Rockwoods's last major fire, in 1942, scourged this part of the forest; surviving trees contain fire scars on their lower trunks.

As the ridgetop trail flattens (this stretch may have once been part of the Old Glencoe Road, theorizes Mike Korte, resource assistant at Rockwoods), great thickets of sassafras trees appear, as do dogwoods and one of Missouri's largest persimmon groves. Cathy deJong points out that trees that grow high on a ridge suffer the most lightning and storm damage; a look around supports her statement.

As you walk, the trail switches to and fro from north to south slopes, then, before the descent begins in earnest, reveals a remnant of an old logging road. Where the trail is covered with chert, there is an arid, open area where nothing seems to grow, except perhaps wild huckleberry, which thrives in the gladelike soil. "Even the leaves blow away from here," comments Gass on an autumn walk. If you look closely, some areas that appear to be banked earth may be railroad rights-of-way from the days of ridgetop quarrying.

The trail descends steeply into a dark cove or ravine through which ubiquitous Hamilton Creek flows. As if you had crossed an imaginary line in the forest, the hum of speeding automobiles and trucks on I-44, five miles to the south, becomes joltingly obvious. After descending natural stone steps amid heavy rocks and an open, gladelike area, the trail leaves the central forest and points southward beside Glencoe Road. Bright green watercress is found most of the year in the spring branch alongside, where the water is clear, cold, and highly undrinkable.

Appearing on the last ½ mile of the walk are stinging nettle plants and clutches of wild forget-me-nots. "If you rub the juice of a forget-me-not on your skin, you can reduce the severity of pain from a stinging nettle," says Gass. A grove of buckeye trees, a patch of paw paws, and a cluster of spicebushes are natural landmarks as you near the giant lime kiln and the parking area just beyond.

Shaw Arboretum

Location: Gray Summit, Missouri
Hiking distance: 3½ miles
Hiking time: 2 hours
Bicycles: not permitted on trails

Shaw Arboretum was purchased in 1925, when the Missouri Botanical Garden (known informally as Shaw's Garden) in midtown St. Louis faced major environmental problems: Smoke-borne industrial toxins were ruining many of its plants, trees, and shrubs. The new rural outpost in Franklin County, first called "The Gray Summit Extension," offered many natural features: glades, flood-plain and upland forests, a creek, open fields, the nearby Meramec River, gravel bars, and measurably more sunlight, and fewer factory pollutants, than midtown St. Louis.

Affluent neighbors—the Wohls, the Desloges, and the Stratford Lee Mortons—lived nearby. In 1925 Morton wished aloud that "this community (with the arboretum as centerpiece) would become an-other Huntleigh Village [an upscale suburb in southwestern St. Louis County] with its great estates." The wish never materialized, though the David Wohl estate has now become the Adlyne Freund Education Center at the Arboretum.

In the late 1920s, the arboretum, then nearly half a day's drive from St. Louis over gravelly Manchester Road, was open sparingly to the public. Mainly, the arboretum grew plants, especially orchids, for Shaw's Garden; but it also sold plants to local nurseries and florists. Hundreds of St. Louisans were nevertheless soon driving out on weekends to see the impressive orchid displays.

In the late 1930s, assistant superintendent Louis Brenner almost singlehandedly laid out a network of walking trails, which now totals about 12 miles. "I carried a double bit ax, scythe, a long-handled fork, a gallon jug of water, and a lunch box. I never saw a soul all day. I did that for quite a number of years," Brenner recalled later. Once the

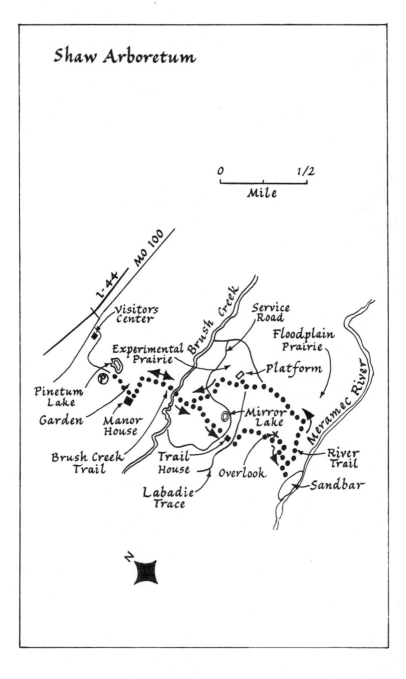

Shaw Arboretum

0 ⊢——┴——⊣ 1/2

Mile

I-44 / MO 100

Visitors Center

Brush Creek

Service Road

Floodplain Prairie

Experimental Prairie

Platform

Pinetum Lake

Mirror Lake

Garden

Manor House

Meramec River

Brush Creek Trail

Trail House

Overlook

River Trail

Labadie Trace

Sandbar

N

trails were down and the bridges over Brush Creek completed, the arboretum staff invited in the public.

Overall master planner for the arboretum was John Noyes, who had gained some celebrity as landscape architect for St. Louis–area streets and institutions such as Wydown Terrace in Clayton; and Dromara Lane, the St. Louis Country Day School, and the John Burroughs School, all in Ladue.

Access

From the intersection of I-270 and I-44, drive 22 miles west on I-44 to MO 100 (exit 233) at Gray Summit. Turn left, cross the highway bridge, then turn right onto MO 100 West. Drive to the nearby arboretum gatehouse entrance on your left. Register at the gatehouse, where maps and brochures are available; there is a small admission fee for nonmembers of Missouri Botanical Garden. Take the drive to your right for about 0.5 mile until you reach the parking area near the Pinetum, and the Brush Creek trailhead.

Trail

Begin your walk at the Pinetum, arranged around human-made Pinetum Lake. Early arboretum managers boasted that "the most extensive collection of conifers in the Middle West" was to be found near the lake. White pines dominate the Pinetum now, but there are impressive stands of spruce, bald cypress, and juniper. In the spring, bright daffodils bejewel the adjacent meadows. "We plant 3000 new daffodil bulbs each year," says John Behrer, arboretum manager.

From the Pinetum, walk south to access the gravel path to the Whitmire Wildflower Garden, which nestles in a shady hillside below the 1879 brick manor house. Former Confederate Army Lieutenant Colonel T.W.B. Crews, a lawyer who commuted to St. Louis by train, built the five-bedroom "English-Georgian" redbrick structure for his wife, Virginia, and their children. Since Crews's time, the home has had many occupants, including past arboretum superintendents. Now the refurbished and expanded former residence contains interpretive natural history and environmental exhibits in cooperation with the Missouri Department of Conservation.

Take time to walk around the Whitmire Wildflower Garden, parceled into five distinct habitats: glade; tallgrass prairie; pine and hardwood savannah; wet meadow; and woodland. "Most of the plants are from Missouri and surrounding states," says arboretum naturalist James Trager. Within the garden are the woodland pond, which favors shade-tolerant flowers; a gazebo made from cedar logs felled on the arboretum grounds; and the boardwalk pond, which reflects the sun at marvelous angles and supports an array of cardinal flowers and blue lobelias along its margins. Large numbers of bluebirds and finches, among other songbirds, inhabit the garden.

One anomaly in the garden is the gravestone of Mary Isabelle Davis, who died in 1884. "She may have been a niece of Mrs. Crews who died, probably of cholera, while visiting her aunt and uncle," speculates librarian/historian Sue Reed, who wrote a book on the history of eastern Franklin County. Three other graves found during the garden's development are unmarked. "They're probably graves of Crews's servants; back then servants' graves were never marked," says Reed, who believes others may be nearby. None of the graves was disturbed during development of the Whitmire Garden.

Near the boardwalk pond, find the path that heads east to the Brush Creek Trail. Take a right onto the trail, then walk south into the heart of the arboretum. The winding, descending Brush Creek Trail contains at least 23 tree species, all described in a booklet for sale at the gatehouse. Along the trail, you must pass a deer exclusion fence, which keeps the arboretum's deer herd in the main part of the woods, away from the main horticultural area that holds the Pinetum and the Whitmire Garden.

After a stepping-stone crossing of Brush Creek, the path rises through a scrubby, second-growth forest of shingle oaks and nonnative shrubs and reaches an intersection. Take the path to the right and head toward the Trail House. Once through a cedar forest, the path emerges into a meadow that is being converted into a tallgrass prairie. Follow the wide, undulating grass path to a service road, then to stairs descending to the limestone-and-log Trail House, built in 1942 as a picnic shelter with rest rooms. A thicket of deciduous holly shrubs is a canopy for the stairs. "Cedar waxwings [birds crested like cardinals,

On the lookout deck at the 1980 "Experimental Prairie" at Shaw Arboretum.

and silky gray with flecks of red and yellow] love those berries," the late Edgar Denison, author of *Missouri Wildflowers,* told me as we hiked one day. "Our deer like to eat the lower ivy leaves on the Trail House," adds Behrer.

From the Trail House, walk east on the "Labadie Trace," carefully following the green arrows to the Overlook Trail. "Labadie Trace is only an honorary title," says historian Reed. "The real Labadie Trace was a wagon road that started at the Missouri River in nearby Labadie, then swung around to follow what is now Highway 100. It went all the way into St. Louis hauling goods that couldn't be shipped by river. It was used from around 1819 to 1855; after that, steamboats handled the bigger loads." Chinquapin oaks, hickories, cedar trees, and flowering dogwoods crowd the woods along the trace.

Turn right at the Overlook Trail sign, then make two more sharp right turns to reach the overlook on a gradually descending path. "The farther down you go on this walk, the more wildflowers you see," said Denison, pointing out a trout lily and a shooting star. The overlook is on a bluff above the Meramec River floodplain and valley. You can see the tops of the sycamore trees that grow in the bottomland forest where the trail will soon take you. They are the arboretum's tallest trees. Much of the pastoral land across the Meramec—650 acres of it—is owned by the arboretum; this includes a farmhouse and two log cabins, used for educational programs.

On either side of the steep, rocky path as it drops from the overlook are, from April through June, showy yellow celandine poppies. "The sight of these poppies is almost beyond anything else in Missouri," proclaimed Denison. Just ahead, a split-rail fence borders a hillside glade filled seasonally with shooting stars, pale purple coneflowers, and Missouri evening primroses. Denison said he saw shrublike green violets along the rocky path one April. "Nobody recognizes them," he said.

Once on the bottomland, take the first path to your right and walk to the gravel bar on the Meramec River. En route is a sycamore tree that's over 19 feet around and could be 150 years old. Near the gravel bar is "an endless variety of chert, sandstone, and limestone rocks, piles of driftwood, animal tracks, and frogs by the hundreds," says an arboretum pamphlet. Major flooding in 1993 and 1994 injured or destroyed countless trees and shrubs near the gravel bar. Backtrack to the main bottomland trail, more formally known as "River Trail." Continue walking east.

Stinging nettle and wild rye grass are abundant in the understory of this floodplain forest, as are huge poison ivy and wild grape vines, which seem to strangle some of the younger trees. This linear stretch is topped by arching, cathedrallike elms, sycamores, and cottonwoods. In the spring, Virginia bluebells bloom by the thousands on the forest floor.

The trail makes an abrupt left turn and heads uphill at a cornfield that Denison believed was a World War I–era emergency landing strip, though the fact is hard to verify. Now part of the field is being changed into floodplain prairie. (The path to your right led to a Meramec River ferry used in the 1940s when the arboretum had a farm and cattle operation on the south side of the river. It was not a public ferry.)

Old cedars, Carolina buckthorns, and red oaks line the uphill service road that intersects Labadie Trace. Turn left at the trace. Walk along this path, partially bedrock, to its junction with the Prairie

Trail. Take a right and walk up to "The Experimental Prairie," a land restoration project begun in 1980. Climb the nearby observation deck for a better view of the majestic tallgrass prairie, where 200 native prairie plant species, including 80 wildflower species, are found. (More than a third of Missouri's 15 million acres was once covered with tallgrass prairie; less than 1 percent remains.)

As recently as 1970, the land that is now prairie was used to graze cattle from the Missouri Baptist Children's Home. "That stopped in 1974 and the land lay fallow until 1980, when we planted four kinds of grasses and four wildflowers, two of which remain: the Maximilian sunflower and blue prairie sage," recalls former arboretum naturalist William Davit.

"We also grew plants in our greenhouse and put them in small plots in the prairie. We hand-planted most seedlings; the most was 11,000 in 1982. We started with 48 acres and now there are nearly 80 acres of prairie." Trager, the current naturalist, adds, "We want to expand to three times that. We want the prairie integrated with other plant communities such as open woodland, the glades, streamsides, and the riparian forests." From April through October, there are always some prairie species in full bloom.

Leave the observation deck and take a right on the mowed grass path flanked by big bluestem (one of the predominant prairie grasses), goldenrod, Maximilian sunflower, Indian grass, and other species. After passing a lone oak tree, cross the road at the bottom of the hill. Continue straight ahead through the newer prairie, planted since 1983, considerably richer in colorful wildflowers, and, says Trager, "closer to the natural diversity of the real prairies."

Pass a demonstration plot—an area not mowed or burned since 1972, which will become a mature hardwood forest if left continually undisturbed—of New England asters, clumps of goldenrod, and other species that attract migrating monarch butterflies by the thousands each fall. Once you're through the prairie, turn right on Brush Creek Trail to return to the parking area by the Pinetum.

North St. Louis and St. Charles County

*This wooded trail leads down to a marsh at
Marais Temps Clair Wildlife Area.*

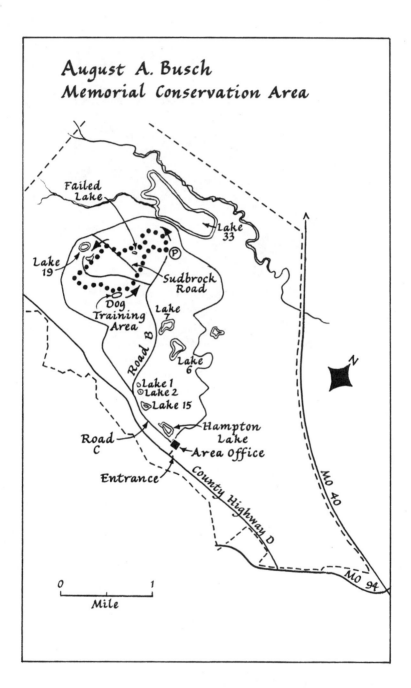

August A. Busch
Memorial Conservation Area

Failed
Lake

Lake
33

Lake
19

Ⓟ

Sudbrock
Road

Dog
Training
Area

Lake
7

Road B

Lake
6

Lake 1
Lake 2
Lake 15

N

Hampton
Lake

Road
C

Area Office

Entrance

County Highway D

MO 40

MO 94

0   1

Mile

August A. Busch Memorial Conservation Area

Busch Hiking Trail

Location: Weldon Spring, Missouri
Hiking distance: 3 miles
Hiking time: 1 hour
Bicycles: permitted

I n 1941, what is now the Busch Conservation Area (BCA) contained a $65 million World War II TNT plant, officially called "Weldon Spring Ordnance Works." It was probably the largest such operation in America. From December 1941 to August 1945, with the exception of a 6-month production shutdown starting in January 1944, nearly 5000 workers produced up to a million pounds of TNT a day for bombs and shells. One specialty was TNT to be used in large "blockbuster" bombs targeted at Nazi submarine pens. More than 1030 buildings, 50 to 60 miles of roads, and 26 miles of railroad tracks were part of the complex.

The plant was erected on approximately 18,000 acres, mostly consisting of farmland and three rural hamlets: Howell, Hamburg, and Toonerville. Under the guise of emergency war preparedness, the federal government seized, then razed, the towns. For their property, the nearly 250 stunned and enraged landowners were compensated about $159 an acre. In his book, *The Rape of Howell and Hamburg,* Don K. Muschany calls the War Department takeover "an American tragedy."

Managers from the Missouri-Kansas-Texas Railroad (M-K-T or "Katy") were responsible for the powder plant's location. Army Ordnance Department records reveal that the M-K-T contacted government officials in late 1940 and suggested the site, conveniently located near the Katy Railroad's tracks by the Missouri River, less than a mile away. The government agreed and ordered the plant built, with a spur line leading directly to the Katy tracks.

The three hamlets sat on green, rolling acreage known as Howell's Prairie. Many residents could trace their ancestry to Daniel Boone and his children, as well as to Francis Howell Sr. and Captain James Callaway, emigrants from Kentucky and Virginia, who arrived during the original American settlement from 1799 to 1840. Many of the Howells and Callaways are buried in six small cemeteries that remain within BCA; none is viewable from the Busch Hiking Trail.

After World War II, the federal government sold 6987 surplus acres to the Missouri Department of Conservation. A $70,000 gift from Mrs. August A. Busch, widow of a former president of Anheuser-Busch, Inc., sped the purchase. Excepting 100 reinforced concrete TNT powder storage bunkers, most of the BCA land is now clear of war artifacts, although it's possible that residual, contaminating chemicals from the TNT production remain in some areas.

Each bunker, designed to store up to 250,000 pounds of TNT and DNT, was 61 feet long and 27 feet wide, with a 6-inch concrete floor. Bunker foundations reached 4 feet below ground. Usually bonneting their roofs were 2 feet of black earth, Mother Nature's antidote to the enemy planes that army officials thought might bomb the place.

To further confuse the enemy, the army constructed the bunkers at different angles and locations on roads that twisted and turned through old farmland and hamlet streets. "The theory was that if one bunker blew up, the one nearby would survive because it wasn't located right next door," explains Karl J. Daubel, environmental coordinator of the Weldon Spring Training Area, a sub-post of the army's Fort Leonard Wood. He is the site's invaluable historian.

"We now have only traces of information of what this place was like during World War II. Much of it comes from Army Corps of Engineers records and drawings and from what I could find in the National Archives in Washington, D.C.," Daubel says. "One thing is peculiar to me," he adds. "Even though the place was huge, it never rated a general to run things; it always had a major or lieutenant colonel in command."

Access

From the intersection of I-270 and I-64/US 40, drive west on US 40 to M0 94, about 15 miles. Turn left on MO 94. Drive to Highway D; turn right. Drive 1.5 miles to the BCA turnoff. (During the TNT years, the production plant was located completely on the south side of present Highway D, with the storage area completely on the north side, where BCA is now situated. Back then, both MO 94 and Highway D were plant roads with grass medians.)

Once inside the BCA enclosure, drive past the redbrick office (in World War II, the storage facility manager's office) and through the usually open gate into the wildlife area. After the stop sign, bear left at the fork and get on Road C. Pass Ahden Knight Hampton Memorial Lake, also called Refuge Lake; then Lakes 15 and 2. At a Y, drive right on Road B, known as Howell Road prior to 1941. Follow Road B until you see a brown-and-white trail sign at the bottom of a hill, just before Road B turns sharply to your right. (The distance from the gate to the trail is 2.4 miles.) Park your car and begin your walk.

Trail

Start your walk on the service road along a brushy ravine. This land was once part of a Spanish land grant given to Francis Howell Sr. in 1800. He died in 1829 and is buried with his family in the Howell Cemetery, about a mile east of the trailhead. Bunker 62 soon appears. On its roof is a mantle of cedars, oaks, and hickories; their long roots cuddle the sides of the igloolike bunker. Its great steel door is welded shut. The building is decontaminated and empty, save for trespassing bees and wasps that enter the vents. It remains a cool 65 degrees all year. Bunker 62 typifies most of the remaining bunkers at BCA.

"The bunkers were protected like the White House in Washington is protected," observes John Miller, a BCA naturalist. "There was usually a semicircular concrete loading dock sticking out like a lip in front of the bunker door as well as a raised circular concrete rampart in the center of which stood a light pole to illuminate the bunker. The concrete in front of the bunkers was supposed to hold off 'advancing enemy tanks.'" Miller says that the bunkers are being considered for use as bat caves but that the ceilings might be too slick to support sleeping bats.

Farther along the trail, heavy with spring-blooming dogwoods and redbuds, a cleared viewing area looks toward Lake 33, off to your right. It is the largest of BCA's lakes and ponds; all were put in by the Department of Conservation, which manages BCA. From late February through fall, goose nesting tubs are placed on the lake and many of its small islands so that some of the area's 500 Canada geese can roost there before hatching their eggs. Half the resident geese wear leg bands (left for female; right for male) or neck collars to help chart where the big birds fly, if anywhere, says James E. Garr III, wildlife management biologist for the Department of Conservation. "Most of them won't go anywhere so long as we have open water and enough food for them."

After Bunkers 64 and 65, a lone brown trail marker at a road crossing signals a sharp right turn onto a trail section that passes what BCA people call a "failed lake."

In the 1950s, engineers tried to develop the site (on your left) into a lake, but the natural geography said no. Now it's both a swampy lake remnant and a good spot to study reptiles, amphibians, and the wood ducks that float on the darkish water. "There are four species of spring peepers [frogs] in here," says Miller. "And there are chorus frogs, hundreds of them. When they sing it sounds like what happens when you run your thumb down a plastic comb."

Next, the trail winds through a forest in which deer, wild turkeys, coyotes, and foxes thrive. "We're in the business of feeding wildlife like these at BCA," says Garr. "Our habitat includes cropland, bedding areas, water, timberland, old fields, and grassy spots that all contribute to the animals' nourishment." BCA may have the most deer in the area. Its population—several thousand—is so large that it must be thinned occasionally through archery and muzzle-loader hunts strictly controlled by the conservation department.

Once through the forest, turn right on a road that you must share briefly with automobiles. Before World War II, this road was

A passerby tests the door of a World War II TNT powder storage bunker on the walk at Busch Conservation Area.

called Sudbrock Road, honoring a pioneer family. After a short distance, turn left onto a service road that follows a dry upland woods of cedar, oak, and black cherry trees. (If you had continued straight ahead on Sudbrock Road, you would pass—in half a mile or so—the possible site of a War of 1812 fort once used to defend against Native Americans, says Ken Kamper, a Daniel Boone historian and member of the Daniel Boone and Frontier Families Research Association. Kamper says there were two forts on the present BCA land, Howell's and Castlio's, but "the exact sites need more study.")

Lake 19, seen from a levee on the trail, is loaded with catfish, bass, and green sunfish. Herons and wood ducks are frequent visitors. An impressive colony of yellow American lotus plants (water lilies) occupies a corner of the lake from June through September. Wildlife feast on seeds found in the waxy blossoms of the lilies, wrote the late Edgar Denison in *Missouri Wildflowers*. Some lotus seeds, he said, remain edible for up to 200 years. Just past Lake 19, and near the road on which you're walking southward, John Chapman, better known as

Johnny Appleseed, may have planted some apple trees in the early 1800s, says Kamper. "There are solid reports that Johnny Appleseed was in the eastern Missouri frontier during Daniel Boone's time."

From the lake, walk straight ahead. Pass an intersection, a field latrine, and Bunker 81 before dead-ending at a service road. Turn left on the narrow dirt road. Near Bunker 82 are timber-free fields that Garr says are "critical nesting areas for quail, turkeys, and rabbits." Up to 4000 hunters annually bring their hunting dogs to this area for wild game training and trialing. Pistols with blanks are used.

On the last mile of the walk, you might see a sizable gathering of white-tailed deer, mainly at dusk. If you don't spot deer, there's a small chance that you might see a wild turkey returning to roost after a day on the wing.

The brown trail signs will guide you back to your automobile. You will pass a bench, more bunkers, and a large wheat field, one of many at BCA leased to farmers, who leave part of their harvest to feed the wildlife. "This is not a totally serene and peaceful walk," says my wife, "because you can't block out those funereal wartime bunkers." That, of course, is what makes this walk over old Howell's Prairie so historically special.

Howell Island
Conservation Area

Location: St. Charles County, Missouri
Hiking distance: 2¾ miles
Hiking time: 1½ hours
Bicycles: not permitted

The explorers Lewis and Clark saw Howell Island on their way to the Great Northwest in 1804. "Except for flooding, farming, and timber harvesting, this island hasn't changed much," says naturalist John Miller. "Everything on the island reflects what a floodplain is supposed to be. Whatever can and should happen, including major flooding, has been happening here for centuries. It's a perfect floodplain model."

Howell Island is named for farmer Thomas Howell, its first owner of record, in 1853, and a nephew of Francis Howell Sr., who settled in St. Charles County in 1800. In the early 1800s, pioneers from the East drove their wagons over Old Bonhomme Road (now Old Olive Street Road) to a settlement on the Missouri River known as Howell's Ferry Landing, next to the present Howell Island. From there, they ferried across the river to another landing at Weldon Spring. This was when the river's main course was south of the island instead of north of it, as it is today.

One of the larger islands (2548 acres) on the lower Missouri River, Howell is about 100 acres larger than Lambert St. Louis International Airport. Because of its size, it was recommended by the 1960 St. Louis County Supervisor, James McNary, to be the site of a second major airport to serve the St. Louis area, a backup for Lambert.

The airport proposal drew little opposition until a sharp *St. Louis Globe-Democrat* reporter visited the island, which happened to be almost totally flooded. News reports and editorials sealed the fate of the site, immediately dubbed "McNary's Folly."

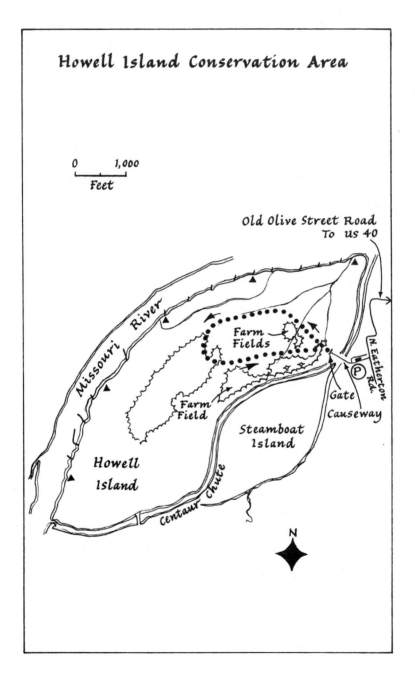

Howell Island Conservation Area

0   1,000
Feet

Old Olive Street Road
To US 40

Missouri River

Farm Fields

Farm Field

Howell Island

Steamboat Island

Centaur Chute

Gate

Causeway

N. Eatherton Rd.

P

N

Floods have taken a heavy toll on the island, even in the face of improvements such as wing dikes and channel dredging by the U.S. Army Corps of Engineers. In 1939, a writer for a local newspaper, *The Watchman Advocate*, thought the problem of flooding rivers was past. "The old river has been subdued by modern day engineering skill and now rushes harmlessly by."

In 1978, the Missouri Department of Conservation purchased the island for $1 million from a New York businessman who had wanted to build a huge "industrial complex" on Howell, but couldn't muster the resources. The department found an abundance of deer, coyotes, wild turkeys, foxes, beavers, and muskrats on Howell, open to hunters in-season. In the great flood of 1993, water from the river rolled over the island, crashed through the nearby Monarch Levee, and flooded 10,000 acres of the Chesterfield valley, some sections with up to 15 feet of water. With the flood came tons of silt, improving fertility throughout the island, particularly for giant ragweed, which grew huge central stems and towered 10 feet, or more, by 1994.

The rock causeway to Howell Island crosses Centaur Chute, which 100 years ago was the main channel of the Missouri River for steamboats passing on their way into St. Louis. The village of Centaur was located south of the island on the St. Louis County side. It was a steamboat landing spot and headquarters of a successful limestone quarry.

Access

From the intersection of I-270 and I-64/US 40, drive 10 miles west on I-64/US 40 to the Chesterfield Airport Road exit. After exiting, follow the ramp road to its intersection with Chesterfield Airport Road; turn right. At a Y in the road by a Phillips 66 station, bear left on Old Olive Street Road, which soon becomes North Eatherton Road. Drive straight ahead until you see the sign to Howell Island. Turn right; park in the lot and then walk over the levee and across the causeway. Please exercise caution when following the causeway, since the river is known to rise suddenly. Don't use the causeway if water is running over it. The walk begins 300 feet beyond the orange gate on a path that leads to your right into the floodplain forest.

Trail

At times, this walk through the flat bottomland can be very muddy, almost impassable, so be prepared with mud shoes or protective hiking boots.

Be aware that hunters share the island at certain times of the year. Archery deer hunters are present from October 1 to December 31. Muzzle-loading firearms deer season occurs in early December. Spring turkey hunting occurs the last week in April and the first week in May. There are also fall turkey and small game (squirrel) hunting seasons. No hunting acidents have been recorded at Howell, but caution should be your guide; wear bright colors.

Essentially, your trail is an established service road that loops around the island. Large concentrations of water-tolerant cottonwood trees appear along the way, as do box elders and other floodplain trees. Due to soil types and hydrology, there are no oak trees on Howell. Unfortunately, many of the box elders, weakened by the major flood of 1993, were blown down in heavy windstorms in 1994. A look into the forest reveals that most of the trees were severed at the flood line, the high-water point on their trunks at which they were the most vulnerable.

It's not the tall cottonwoods that predominate at Howell. It's the common horsetail plant, or as Native Americans called it, "scouring rush," used because of its abrasive qualities to scour cooking utensils. The first colonies of leafless, green-stemmed horsetail appear on your left in the forest about 200 feet from where the path officially begins. Look carefully to see how deer and other animals have created paths through fields of horsetail, a favorite snack food for the deer. Speaking of food, morel mushrooms grow on Howell; they're removable if you can find them.

In years when there is no major flooding, several hundred acres of the island are leased to farmers who grow corn and soybeans. Some of these fields are seen along the trail, which, for the most part, is endless bottomland forest, filled with colorful wildflowers in warm months and tinted dull brown in winter. In some sections of the woods, slightly off the trail, walkers may see trees that have been rigged with portable deer stands, elevated platforms about 10 to 12 feet high, where hunters with bows and arrows wait for deer to pass nearby. "Deer rarely look up, unless alerted by movement, smell, or noise," says Miller.

As the trail continues, there are more horsetail colonies, and more giant sycamores and cottonwoods, some 80 to 100 years old. At 4:30 one sunny mid-March afternoon, Miller and I spotted a great horned owl roosting on a cottonwood branch about 30 feet away. Waiting nonchalantly for dusk and the protective cover of darkness, the owl was surprised by us. He flew away silently through the trees and was quickly out of view. The great horned, Miller explains, is the one owl that crows like to harass or "mob," although it is twice the size of the average crow.

As it loops leftward, the path passes strangulating grapevines and some native pecan trees, which, says Howell's wildlife management biologist, Dan Crigler, appear to have survived the 1993 flood. In the center of the island, where the path turns sharply to your left and heads straight back to the orange gate, is a spot that once supposedly contained a small-plane landing strip.

Adventurous hikers and bow-and-arrow hunters like to take off to the west for the Missouri River banks, about ¼ mile away. (If you go, take a compass to chart your direction.) Across the river are the limestone bluffs of Weldon Spring Wildlife Area that John James Audubon observed and sketched as he floated by. When you reach the river, you may see sandbars with willow trees alongside as well as wing dikes that were constructed by German and Italian prisoners of war housed in Chesterfield valley in 1944 and 1945. In the winter, it is not unusual to stand on the riverbank and see bald eagles fly over. Many of them roost near the bluffs. If you don't walk to the river— and most hikers don't—follow the trail past more farming fields and horsetail clumps back to the trailhead.

Howell Island is probably the most primitive walking place in the metropolitan area. Buried by floods, mutated by a river whose silt deposits have expanded it many times over, depleted of many of its major trees, the island, which seems to heal fast, is always intriguing.

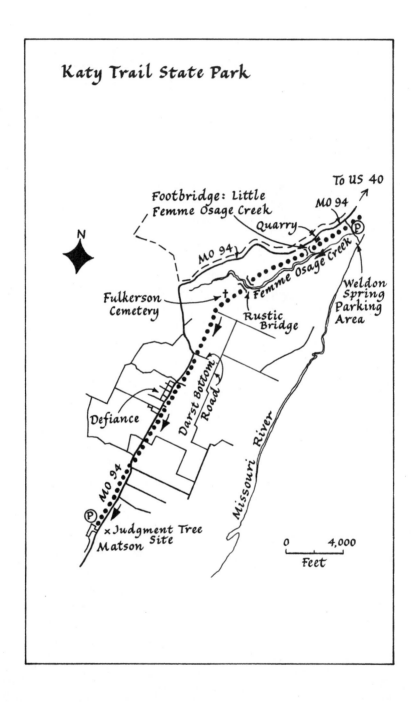

Katy Trail State Park

N

To US 40

MO 94

Footbridge: Little
Femme Osage Creek

Quarry

Femme Osage Creek

Fulkerson
Cemetery

Rustic
Bridge

Weldon
Spring
Parking
Area

Darst Bottom Road

Defiance

MO 94

Missouri River

P

Judgment Tree
Site

Matson

0   4,000
Feet

24

Katy Trail State Park

Location: Weldon Spring to Matson, Missouri
Hiking distance: 4½ miles one way
Hiking time: 2 hours
Bicycles: permitted

This walk along the Missouri River bottomland is saturated with the history and lore of explorers Lewis and Clark and, especially, Daniel Boone, who lived near the present town of Matson in his last years. The whole walk takes place on Spanish land grants given from 1797 to 1803 to the earliest American settlers, in particular Boone's son, daughter, and three grandchildren.

When Boone arrived from Kentucky in 1799, he found himself in a wilderness known mostly to French fur traders and local Native Americans. He had been told that the Missouri River area in Spanish Louisiana was rich in wild game, buffalo, prairie, and timber such as pecan, walnut, and oak. He also understood that Missouri was known for its absence of lawyers and lawsuits! Back in Kentucky, he had been hounded by lawsuits over debts. In Missouri, he trapped so many beavers, writes Cecil Hartley in *The Life of Daniel Boone,* that he was able to discharge all his old debts with income from the sale of pelts.

The present Katy Trail lies on the bed of the old Missouri-Kansas-Texas Railway (M-K-T or "Katy"), which laid the tracks in 1892. By the very next year it was operating four daily steam-powered passenger trains on the line. At Franklin, Missouri, these trains made connections with a Hannibal-to-Texas train that also carried through cars to and from Chicago. By 1915, the "Katy Flyer" and "Katy Limited" passenger trains whizzed through St. Charles and Warren Counties headed for San Antonio. In the railroad's prime, the Flyer and Limited, along with Katy livestock, mail, and freight trains, all used the nearly gradeless, gently curving tracks. In 1986, the railroad removed its tracks, abandoning a route that had become unprofitable.

Access

From the intersection of I-64/US 40 and I-270, take I-64/US 40 West to MO 94, 15 miles. Turn left onto MO 94; drive 5.3 miles south to the Katy Trail Weldon Spring River access turnoff on your left. Turn left; drive down to the parking area.

Since this is a one-way walk, you'll want a second car awaiting you at your end point. To leave the second car, exit the Weldon Spring parking area and turn left onto MO 94. Drive through Defiance and continue to Matson, 5½ miles west. Park in the Matson Katy Trail lot.

Trail

The walk begins at the Weldon Spring parking lot by historic Femme Osage Creek. In May 1804, the 34-man Lewis and Clark expedition poled up the Missouri River, stopping at the nearby mouth of the creek, says Ken Kamper, a longtime Daniel Boone scholar, and editor of the *Boone and Frontier Research Letter*. At the time, says Kamper, a settlement of 30 to 40 families lived in the area; many stood on the shore, gawking at the strange flotilla. This settlement was the start of a 25-mile stretch along the river that encompassed the colony of Boone frontiersmen from Kentucky.

Early along the trail, which is bounded in places by steep, vine-heavy limestone walls, is the Weldon Spring wastewater treatment plant, set off by a chain-link fence. The United States Department of Energy is trying to clean up an adjacent quarry filled with the radioactive water, chemical contaminants, and sludge that remain from a World War II TNT plant and a postwar uranium-processing facility, both of which occupied sites in the Weldon Spring area. The quarry dumping occurred between 1942 and 1969. The cleanup will involve pumping up to 20 million gallons of treated water into the Missouri River by the year 2000. Opponents say that since all contaminants can't be removed from the river, the drinking water of St. Charles and St. Louis County residents is threatened.

Stop at the footbridge over the Little Femme Osage Creek. All the bottomland you see on your left, between the trail and the Missouri River, once belonged to Daniel Boone's daughter, Susannah, and her husband, Captain William Hays. Somewhere out there the pair lies buried; no one knows exactly where.

Next stop on the trail is a rusty M-K-T truss bridge over Femme Osage Creek, usually very low. In a flood, however, the swollen waterway acquires the coloring of rich chocolate. "We're keeping the bridge as it is, in a controlled rust condition," the trail superintendent tells me. "When it's running with water," observes Kamper, "the creek probably looks the same as it did in Boone's time, when it could have been traveled in small boats."

Nearly ½ mile straight ahead on the trail, and up on a hill to your right, is the private Fulkerson Cemetery, where several Boone settlement people are buried, says Kamper. Soon the trail crosses Darst Bottom Road, which may have been an old Native American trail; it later served as the first American trail from the Boone settlement north to St. Charles. In a field on your far left is the almost wholly collapsed two-story log house of Major Zachariah Moore, a Revolutionary War soldier who built it in 1810.

Enter Defiance, whose citizens beamed in October 1992 when NBC-TV news anchor Tom Brokaw came into town and rented a bicycle to ride the Katy Trail. Two landmarks up on the hill to your right overlook Defiance (and can be seen more easily in the winter). One is the Thomas Parsons seven-room, three-story Federal-style 1842 home faced with red bricks fired in the backyard kiln. The other is the Pleasant Hill Memorial Methodist Church, erected in 1922.

Defiance's main street, MO 94, is called Missouri Avenue, as a tribute not to the state but to Missouri, wife of James Craig, who secured a railroad depot for the town in 1894. Missouri Craig died after being struck by lightning while seated at her sewing machine. Defiance got its name after defiant townspeople rebelled when the new M-K-T railroad put a depot in nearby Matson. When town leaders, urged on by Craig, persuaded M-K-T to recognize their town, too, they marked their victory by naming the hamlet Defiance, changing it from Bluff City.

In the early 1900s, Henry Schneider was the Defiance depot agent. His routine was described in a 1941 history of the area, written anonymously and published in the *St. Charles Journal:* "It was exciting to watch the mail being packed carefully in each end of the mail pouch, buckled securely in the middle and carried to the depot where . . . Schneider hung the pouch to upper and lower rings of the crane in precisely the right manner. Soon the high speed train thundered by. The pouch was grabbed by a hook; from an open side door of the mail car, incoming mail pouches were kicked onto the depot platform by the train's mail clerk as he waved a passing greeting to the agent."

Slightly beyond Defiance, on another hill off to your right, is a striking two-story white frame home trimmed in green. It was erected in 1889 by Charles Knapel, a German immigrant who later headed the local school board. David Darst Sr., who arrived in 1797, is said to have lived in a log home on the cedar-lined private lane west of the Knapel home. Darst once owned all the land between here and the end of the hike in Matson, Kamper says.

Just before the trail enters Matson, look to your left at the Stelzer pumpkin farm. To the right of the farmhouse is a stone structure that used to support a two-story house with walnut-paneled walls. Kamper states that the house is said to have been built by Boone's son, Daniel Morgan Boone. "The present site of the structure was never owned by the Boones, though it is somehow connected with Boone history."

Between the Matson Katy Trail parking area and the Missouri River are the 850 acres that Daniel Boone once held under his Spanish land grant—the only land Boone ever owned. "See the lone tree standing in the field to the east of the parking lot?" Kamper asks. "The site of the original Judgment Tree [an elm], under which Boone, as the Spanish-appointed syndic or justice of the peace, made his decisions from 1800 to 1804, is about 150 feet in front of that lone tree, halfway between Highway 94 and the tree."

The vanished hamlet of Missouriton, which the Boone family founded around 1818 and wanted as the capital of the Missouri Territory, was directly beyond the Judgment Tree on the Matson side of the river, facing the distant bluffs. A course change in the river,

A rustic railroad bridge spans Femme Osage Creek on the Katy Trail.

coupled with disastrous floods, has removed the physical evidence of Missouriton's existence. In its brief heyday, mail was delivered to Missouriton by ferry from Labadie. In the winter, when the river was frozen, the postal carrier simply walked across the ice with his mail pouch. One distant bluff, across from the site of Missouriton, towers over Tavern Rock Cave where explorer Meriwether Lewis slipped and fell 20 feet down the bluff, apparently uninjured, in 1804. The incident was described by William Clark in the *Lewis and Clark Journals.*

Off Alice Drive, which connects with MO 94 in Matson, is the nine-room 1848 Colonial Abraham Matson home, with an 8-acre lake and two family cemeteries. On this land—private and off limits to trail users—Boone's son, Daniel Morgan, built a double-room log cabin in which his father lived from 1800 to 1804. It is also the site of Boone Fort, which the son erected to ward off Native Americans during the War of 1812. The cabin was razed in 1854. Another log house on this property, built in 1817 by Isaac Darst, son of David Darst Sr., still stands.

Abraham Matson's son, Richard, inherited the property and occupied it when the M-K-T line came into Matson, named because Matson farm holdings were on both sides of the new railroad tracks. Matson was a water stop for Katy's steam-locomotive-powered trains. Richard traveled to nearby Augusta during the Christmas season to buy a few gallons of whiskey, a local historian wrote. "Before every meal during Christmas week, [Richard] would give everyone at the table a full glass of whiskey."

Two blocks south of Matson's Katy Trail parking lot is the Sugar Creek Winery. Since it's up on a hill, it offers a spectacular view of the whole river valley, says Kamper. "The winery is in the heart of Daniel Morgan Boone's Spanish land grant." Viewable toward the river are Daniel Boone's land grant holdings in their entirety.

Little Creek Nature Area

Location: Florissant, Missouri
Hiking distance: 2 miles
Hiking time: 1 hour
Bicycles: not permitted

This "little island of urban wilderness," as some call it, is boxed in by a Venture store, a condominium complex, I-270, and Florissant's Dunegant Park. Little Creek Nature Area is a 98-acre outdoor classroom operated since 1972 by the Ferguson-Florissant school district. A fifth-grade student won a contest to name the place; there were hundreds of entries.

Other area school districts—Hazelwood, Parkway, St. Peters, and Frances Howell, to name a few—have outdoor classroom programs, but none matches the scope of this one. "Nearly every student in the district uses Little Creek at one time or another," says Judy Huck, a Little Creek elementary teacher. Little Creek is thought to be among the largest outdoor classrooms owned by an American school district. Dozens of other districts query Ferguson-Florissant about starting little Little Creeks.

Little Creek contains an office/museum, a barn and adjoining barnyard, a caretaker's home, and a classroom for field biology and other subjects. The two-story, redbrick office/museum was once home to dentist Clarence Albin, who built it in 1936 on land that had been part of St. Ferdinand Commons in the early 19th century.

"I could walk in the woods and fields all day in the 1930s and early 1940s without seeing another house," recalls John Albin, the dentist's son. "Traffic was so sparse on Dunn Road [then MO 77] that we could sleigh ride on it when there was snow. When the horses had to be shod, we would ride them to the old town section of Florissant where there was a blacksmith."

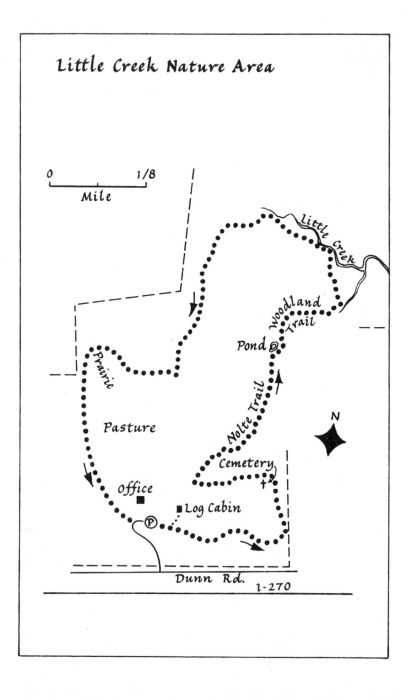

Little Creek Nature Area

The Ferguson-Florissant school district bought the Albin property to convert it to a bus garage site. Science teachers and district consultants began using the old Albin home for meetings. One day, someone said, "I wonder what's behind the house out there in the woods?" The next day, a small group of teachers discovered the treasures of Little Creek. "We used corn knives to cut out the vines and tall grasses and to blaze a makeshift path," recalls Ethel Nolte, a retired science consultant who taught for 10 years at Little Creek. "We came back from the woods tired but excited about what we had found." As a consequence, the school buses had to be parked elsewhere.

Over the next few years, the district bought more land, added new learning programs, fixed up the buildings, and opened Little Creek to the public. "It is unique in Missouri with its gentle slopes, open fields, heavy woods, and small stream—all in a primitive natural state," the Missouri Department of Conservation says in a report.

Access

From the intersection of I-270 and North Lindbergh, drive east on I-270 for 2.9 miles to exit 28 (Washington-Elizabeth). Turn left; drive over the I-270 bridge. Make a sharp, careful right onto Dunn Road. Follow Dunn for nearly a mile to the Little Creek entrance on your left.

From the intersection of I-270 and MO 367 North, take I-270 west 2.4 miles to the West Florissant exit. Upon exiting, take Dunn Road west (left) for about half a mile to the Little Creek entrance on your right. Park in the lot. Stop at the office to pick up a trail map; it's indispensable.

Trail

East of the parking lot, a yellow-blazed trail (the Log Cabin loop) marks the beginning of your walk. Take the wide path to the restored log cabin, once the home of the pioneering August H. Trampe family of Florissant. "When I was a boy, old-timers around here said that gold was buried near the log cabin," says John Albin, "but we never found any."

Continue on the path that leads east from the cabin's front yard. Walk through an understory of small maples and dogwoods and past patches of strangling kudzu vines and a split-rail fence near the property's eastern boundary. Soon you will reach Pohlman Cemetery, tucked in by a white fence. Six persons were buried in the plot, from roughly 1837 to 1917. County records show that Friedrich Pohlman paid $82 in 1846 for the 40 acres, all now part of the Little Creek Nature Area.

When the Albin estate was eventually sold, real estate agents had the cemetery bulldozed into a ditch so prospective buyers might have a clearer view of the land. Later, persevering members of a local women's club found the tombstones under several feet of dirt and began overseeing the cemetery restoration.

After leaving the cemetery, follow the trail to an intersection dominated by a large shingle oak tree and a "Nolte Trail" sign. Turn right onto the Nolte Trail, which heads downhill on a mulched path through a tangle of honeysuckle and poison ivy vines, copious hackberry trees, and the preserve's only known witch hazel shrub colony. Cross the Rabbit Bridge, one of ten Little Creek Nature Area bridges, all named for resident wildlife.

At the bottom of the hill, some steps to your left lead to a student-built woodland pond, where water lilies are usually in full flower from April to June. A breeding spot for amphibians, the pond is a source of water for Little Creek critters. Continue straight ahead on the trail, now called "Woodland Trail," following it as it bends left, passes the Opossum Bridge (don't cross this bridge), and parallels Little Creek, on your right. Near the Raccoon Bridge (don't cross this bridge, either), the Woodland Trail swings west to begin its climb to the prairie. Little Creek is a tributary of Coldwater Creek, a very familiar north county waterway.

Little Creek flows through what Chris Brown, the area's supervisor, calls a "classic lowland forest—a riparian corridor." Look for tall sycamores and box elders, which flank the creek, and for creekside limestone formations that shelter foxes, raccoons, opossum, and other animals. About five foxes live on the grounds. "Quite often, they break into the barnyard and steal some of our chickens," reports Mary Delaney, office secretary. Deer have been seen grazing on the front lawn near the Dunn Road gate. "The deer come and go; we don't

A walk around Little Creek Nature Area might include a stop at the log cabin.

know where since we're really surrounded on all four sides by concrete," says Vernon LeClaire, botanist and field biology teacher for the project.

Once up the hill, look for the "Prairie Loop Trail" sign, which points the way to the 2-acre prairie. "It's really a small plot of ground, a sort of garden or restoration," says LeClaire, who supervised the initial 1982 hand sowing of 800 prairie plants by high school students, assisted by first and second graders. On view are five classic prairie grasses: big and little bluestem, Indian and switch grass, and side oats grama. Dozens of wildflower species bring the recreated prairie to life, especially in July and August.

It's taken about 10 years, but songbirds associated with the American prairie are beginning to visit Little Creek, says LeClaire, who's waited patiently. Indigo buntings, American goldfinches, and several warbler species call the place home. More and more, migratory birds are dropping by the prairie and other spots in Little Creek on their spring and fall journeys.

A student-planted windbreak, located on the north edge of the prairie, consists of seven rows of trees, each 300 feet long. Short trees, such as hollies and autumn olives, dominate the front rows, while walnuts, pines, and tall oaks are found in the middle. The planting is designed to protect the prairie and create a buffer zone for the prairie plants and small mammals and birds.

After wandering through the prairie and the windbreak, walk south on the mowed grass path on Little Creek's western border. Along the way, on your left, is the pasture, enclosed by a wooden fence. In it are goats, sheep, and an active apiary. A sheep-shearing program for first graders is held each spring. Mary Delaney, the secretary, cards the wool. On the office spinning wheel, she produces yarn for shawls, sweaters, and other items.

Farther along on your left is the black walnut grove consisting of 25 trees planted by Boy Scouts about 25 years ago. "In 1992, the trees started producing walnuts," beams LeClaire. South of the grove is the student-planted orchard, with eight kinds of fruit represented. From the orchard, continue south to the fledgling memorial forest (your own gift can buy a tree to plant in someone's memory) and to the old apple tree, circa 1941. Near it, Eagle Scouts have crafted a marker that highlights the area's role in history, starting in 1682, when the Shawnee tribe supposedly camped nearby.

Before you leave Little Creek, visit the barnyard, whose major residents are chickens. "When their eggs drop, we incubate them; when they hatch, we put them into the barnyard with the rest of the chickens," says caretaker Steve Harris.

Our walk doesn't formally include the fifth trail at Little Creek, the Northside Trail. Plagued by frequently out-of-order bridges and vegetation overgrowth in the warm months, the Northside, rich with black locusts and northern red oaks, is probably best hiked in the winter.

Marais Temps Clair
Wildlife Area

Location: St. Charles County, Missouri
Hiking distance: 3¾ miles
Hiking time: 1½ hours
Bicycles: permitted

Marais Temps Clair (MTC) means "fair weather marsh." The French named this ancient river oxbow; they explored the area in the 1700s. Undoubtedly, Native Americans had found the place previously. Managed by the Missouri Department of Conservation, it is said to be the largest marsh in eastern Missouri. Situated 8 miles south of the Mississippi River and 8 miles northeast of the Missouri River, it lies smack in the middle of the Mississippi River flyway, the country's busiest navigation route for migrating waterbirds.

MTC's 918 acres are split between 200 acres of fields planted with corn, wheat, soybeans, clovers, and sunflowers, which provide forage for geese, deer, and other animals; and 700-plus acres containing moist soil plants, such as bulrush and millet, that are apportioned into 10 pools, all controlled by pumps to add or withdraw water. Running south to north are a center ditch and a drainage ditch, both joining at the north end of MTC to continue through other wetlands to the Mississippi River. Filled with buffalo fish, crappie, catfish, carp, and gar, the center ditch is popular with fishers. Nine hundred additional acres of MTC are owned by its neighbor to the north, a private gun club.

Marais Temps Clair isn't well known. From 1920 until around 1935, part of the area was the private home of an elite no-name club of St. Louis intellectuals, many of them college professors and *St. Louis Post-Dispatch* editorial writers and columnists. The clubhouse was located in the north end of MTC on land now owned by the gun club; the kitchen was its focus.

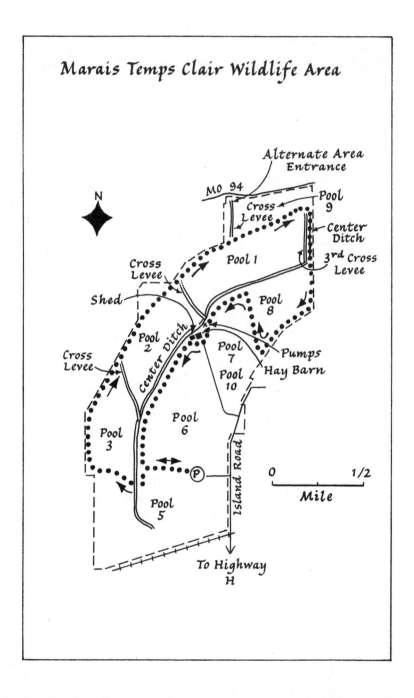

Marais Temps Clair Wildlife Area

"No steak was ever more delicious than the large thick ones cooked brown and crisp and juicy on the old range in that kitchen of pleasant memories; and surely no ducks were ever more tasty than the ones the old oven turned out for us on those cold nights when we gathered about the table at Marais Clair—a group made merry with cocktails and clamoring for food," wrote the *Post-Dispatch* columnist, Clark McAdams, who turned out the "Just a Minute" column in the 1930s.

Among the more bizarre entrées served to club members—and even to visiting dignitaries—were red-winged blackbirds that members had shot near the marsh and taken to the kitchen for broiling. "We sat down to many a platter of these succulent little birds," wrote McAdams. Both the president of the National Audubon Society and the chairman of the federal advisory committee on migratory birds shared broiled blackbird as guests of the club.

Club members were keen on the center ditch, which in the early 1920s was bordered with beautiful white lotus plants. In those days, members paddled through the ditch on moonlight canoe rides. They nicknamed the ditch "The Grand Canal."

Nearly 60 years later, red-winged blackbirds still crowd the marsh; along with grackles, they are its most plenteous birds. "One winter, not too long ago, we saw 60,000 grackles at MTC," estimates Paul Bauer, who conducts bird walks in and around the marsh for the St. Louis Audubon Society.

One day in mid-March, our Audubon group of novice birders counted 18 species at MTC, including ruddy ducks, shovelers, coots, pied-billed grebes, lesser yellowlegs, blue-winged teals, and the hardest bird of all to follow with binoculars, the sparrow—any species of sparrow. "They fly so fast and they're so darting that they are almost impossible to track," comments Bauer. "We occasionally see a tundra swan in here; we used to call them whistling swans," says David Jones of Ladue, a serious MTC birder. "Recently, we had a rare yellow-headed blackbird, which is very uncommon for this area."

MTC was said to be near the center of the great flood of 1993. Covered with 14 feet of water, MTC lost most of its buildings, its rabbit population, many of its bottomland trees, many species of wildflowers, a good many of its snakes and frogs, and its trail system. It wasn't until November 1994 that the levees were cleared for walking and the deer and coyotes that live nearby began wandering back.

Access

From the I-70/I-270 interchange in north St. Louis County, drive 2 miles north on I-270 to I-370 West (exit 22). Bear left on I-370 West; drive 5 miles west to MO 94 in St. Charles County. Turn right on MO 94; drive 3.5 miles to County Highway H, bearing right. Take Highway H east for 2.5 miles to Island Road. Turn left, and drive on Island Road for 1.7 miles to the Marais Temps Clair parking lot turnoff on your left. Drive 600 feet to the parking area.

During waterfowl season, approximately October 15 to January 10, you may hike after 1 PM Friday through Monday, and all day Tuesday, Wednesday, and Thursday.

Trail

From the parking area, follow the gravel road west, past corn, wheat, and sunflower fields, to the orange gate. Turn left onto the levee; the 6-foot-deep center ditch is on your right. On your left is pool 5, usually planted in corn and later flooded. Continue hiking as the levee bends to your right and flanks pool 3 on your right. "This is the one pool where we let nature take its course, so we don't disturb the natural plant community," says Floyd Ficken, MTC wildlife management biologist. The pool is loaded with black willow trees, bulrush, and millet—just the right nourishment for common gallinules, Canada geese, and egrets. Pool 3 is "the best marsh in Missouri," affirms birding enthusiast Paul Bauer.

As you walk past pool 3, the trail swings to your right and continues north for more than 2 miles on what is called the MTC west levee. To your left is the northbound MTC drainage ditch, which, like the center ditch, absorbs water drained from the area's pools. Beyond the drainage ditch is a long line of cottonwoods, soft maples, box elders, and mulberry trees (the latter two species all but ruined by the 1993 flood); the trees serve as roosting spots for the copious red-winged blackbirds and grackles. On one occasion, we spotted a family of 15 or 20 cedar waxwings parked atop some cottonwoods.

Proceed northward. About 1⅓ miles into your walk a grass cross levee separates pool 3 from pool 2 and allows you, if you wish, to make a short loop of MTC, since it heads back toward the parking area. Pool 2, like pool 3, contains a dozen muskrat mounds, which support about 100 muskrats, according to Ficken. In early spring, Canada geese nest atop the mounds. Pool 2 is occasionally drained, mowed, burned, and seeded with plants favorable to the birds that use it. Among them are snipes, egrets, kildeers, sora rails, herons, and least bitterns.

After the second cross levee, pool 1, the largest at MTC, appears on your right. Dominated by smartweed and other reedy plants, it attracts shorebirds such as yellowlegs, dowitchers, and snipes. And it is filled with beavers that often trespass into the drainage ditch on your left. "We're continually unblocking dams the beavers have made," says Ficken. At the north end of the trail, pass the third cross levee, then turn right onto the fourth levee near "Big Number 5," the heavy-duty pump that draws water out of the pools; the other four MTC pumps put water in. Walk east on the cross levee, which defines the northern boundary of the property, with the center ditch on your right. Leaving the levee, the trail turns right by pool 8 (on your right) and proceeds to a cross levee between pools 7 and 8, where you turn right. (Pool 8 is similar in composition to pools 1 and 2; pool 7 is planted with Japanese millet, milo, and corn.) When you arrive once again at the center ditch, turn left and follow the trail as it changes temporarily into a gravelly path and swings right past two enclosed pumps, and, set back between them, the rusty retired pump that thrummed so noisily in the 1930s.

"During a dry summer the pump ran day and night for weeks at a time . . . and the deep throb of its engines could be heard far away at the club, the only noise you could hear through the night, so quiet was Marais Temps Clair and so remote from all that disturbs our sleep in the city," wrote McAdams.

Immediately after the pumps, on your right, is the hay barn, said to shelter barn owls and possibly Eurasian tree sparrows, the unusual species that is seen only in and around St. Louis, and that attracts binocular-armed birders from all over the world. At the hay barn, the path becomes grassy and possibly muddy; it veers to your right, then swings to your left to follow the center ditch west all the way back to the orange gate. On your left is pool 6, thick with soft-stem bulrush and black willow, where ducks scoot and splash over the water and least bitterns, egrets, and herons fly in and out. At the orange gate, turn left for the short jaunt to the parking lot.

"If they [the Missouri Department of Conservation] manage this place right," says Bauer, "Marais Temps Clair will become a showplace for shorebirds." The department's aggressive 5-year plan calls for more observation and interpretive sites, more handicapped access spots, and "10 basking logs for turtles."

27

Old Town Florissant

Location: Florissant, Missouri
Hiking distance: 2½ miles
Hiking time: 2 hours
Bicycles: permitted

Since its founding in the 1760s, the community originally laid out in a 16-block grid pattern on Coldwater Creek's right bank has been called "Fleurissant" (flowering), "San Fernando," "St. Ferdinand," and, since 1939, "Florissant." Much of the original grid remains, comprising streets named for Catholic saints and prominent early Americans. The French trappers who settled the area were enamored of its fertile black soil and its proximity to the Missouri River to the near north. Until 1803, the area was ruled by the Spanish.

Florissant cherishes its connections with Mother Rose Philippine Duchesne, sainted in 1988, and Old St. Ferdinand's Shrine, the oldest Catholic church building in Missouri. Surviving French- and Spanish-influenced homes in Old Florissant were impressive enough to warrant its designation as the state's first historic district in 1965. And, in some quarters, the local topsoil—fertile, black, alluvial, deep— is called the richest in the state. "We had the richest topsoil in the country until after World War II, when subdivisions took over our farms," recalls retired farmer Ambrose Knobbe. "This was also the greatest horseradish-growing place in America. We peaked in the 1920s, then a disease hit the horseradish plants, and the industry shifted to Illinois."

French and German settlers put their stamp on Florissant. An anonymous writer in 1892 described the town: "Both languages (French and German) are spoken fluently by the inhabitants, who cling with great tenacity to their foreign ideas. The result is an

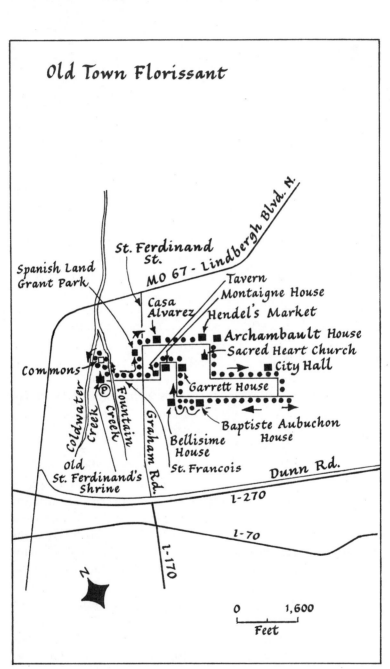

Old Town Florissant

exclusive community, differing materially in language, customs, appearance, and manners from their neighbors. Even the houses and streets partake of this foreign atmosphere. The narrow streets and cabins and cottages, half-hidden by a half-century's growth of vines, remind one vividly of the villages of France."

Today, "Old Town Florissant is better known in outstate Missouri than it is in the St. Louis area," says Rosemary Davison, founder and past president of the Florissant Historical Society. "People in Kirkwood or Webster Groves think Florissant is at the other end of the world. Few people are aware of our history. All of the original buildings in St. Louis are gone. Now we have the oldest buildings in St. Louis County."

Access

In northeast St. Louis County, take I-270 to the Graham Road exit. Drive north on Graham Road, which becomes St. Ferdinand Street. Take St. Ferdinand to St. Francois, turning left. Drive into the parking area in front of Old St. Ferdinand's Shrine, where the walk begins.

Trail

Begin your walk by exploring Old St. Ferdinand's Shrine and its adjacent grounds. The church was built in 1820. It's where Jesuit Father Pierre Jean De Smet was ordained to the priesthood in 1827. A friend of Abraham Lincoln and Kit Carson, De Smet was an influential missionary and peacemaker to Native Americans in the American West, who knew De Smet simply as "Blackrobe." Two tribes, the Sauk and Fox, were led by Chief Keokuk, whose friendship with De Smet often brought him to the Florissant area. Explorer William Clark of the Lewis and Clark expedition once attended a wedding in the church. Of Italian Romanesque Revival design, the building was last used as a parish in 1958. Most of the original pews remain; when first used, they rented for 25 cents a month. (You can tour the church on Sundays from April through December, 1 to 4 PM. No admission fee.)

Next to the old church is the first American convent of the Sisters of the Sacred Heart. Erected in 1819, the Federal-style brick structure is said to look about the same today as it did the day it opened. Mother Rose Philippine Duchesne, its superior, lived in the convent from 1819 to 1827 and from 1834 to 1840. Here, she started a school for immigrant girls, both Catholic and Protestant, as well as Native American girls. It may have been history's first Catholic school for Native American girls and it was the first Sacred Heart novitiate in the United States. Perhaps the most sacred place in the convent is the small white closet under the stairs to the second floor. Legend says that St. Philippine frequently slept under a buffalo robe and a blanket in the closet so she could remain close to the nearby chapel.

Walk north from the shrine complex on a paved path around St. Ferdinand Commons (also called Coldwater Commons Park), part of a 1790s Spanish land grant. Early villagers gathered wood and grazed their cows on the Common by Coldwater Creek. Nowadays, residents pursue an exercise regimen of hiking the Common several times in a row; some residents use the center gazebo for wedding photos.

After looping the Common, take the narrow bridge over Fountain Creek, where Rue St. Francois, the main artery of Old Florissant, begins. From St. Francois, turn left at St. Ferdinand; walk one block to St. Denis. Spanish Land Grant Park (on the southwest corner) is where the first St. Ferdinand's Church, a log structure, stood around 1789. When fire destroyed the church, the nearby grounds continued as a cemetery and parade field. In the early 1900s, the cemetery was moved, though many bodies remained interred. "Some of Florissant's pioneers are still buried there," says Davison. Assisted by St. Louis County, the city purchased the land in 1976, declaring it a "passive park."

Turn right on St. Denis. At 289 is the weathered frame cottage erected around 1790 by Eugenio Alvarez, a military storekeeper for the territory's last Spanish governor. Casa Alvarez, originally a one-room structure that's now been radically altered, is probably the oldest building left in the St. Louis area, says the Landmarks Association of St. Louis. Three blocks straight ahead, at 599 St. Denis, is the former Hendel's Market, now a café. Until recently, the Federal-style

A statue of St. Ferdinand stands at the convent wing of Old St. Ferdinand's Shrine in historic Florissant.

1873 building, with a prominent front porch, had always been a grocery operation, says Davison. Across Jefferson Street, at 603 St. Denis, is the 1850s Federal-style brick townhouse attributed to farmer-hunter-trapper August Archambault, a companion and guide to Kit Carson, Jim Bridger, and John C. Fremont on their trips to the western frontier.

Walk south on Jefferson to examine the Sacred Heart building complex that served German immigrants starting in the 1860s. Since then, the site has seen three Sacred Heart church buildings and four Sacred Heart church schools. Along with the convent, the three present structures exemplify Missouri German architecture, identified in part by segmentally arched windows and ornate cornices. Sacred Heart's German parishioners resented giving confession to a French-speaking priest down the road at St. Ferdinand's Church, says Davison. "The schools of Sacred Heart and St. Ferdinand kept different hours because it was dangerous, parents said, to have both the French and German children on the street at the same time for fear of fistfights or brawls."

At St. Francois, take a left. At 619 St. Francois is the first city hall, an 1890s structure now part of a senior citizen center; in front of it is Florissant's second city hall, wrapped in the corpus of the Buchholz Valley of the Flowers Mortuary. At 646 is a classic-style 1890s steepled building that housed the first Protestant church in town; early Baptist and Methodist congregations shared the facility. Two blocks east is Florissant's third city hall, an appealing French Colonial building that opened in 1970. It's sited on land once owned by a botanist, who planted an entire block of unusual and ornamental trees including some striking copper beeches. Many of the trees survive, protected by their civic landmark status.

Turn right at Brown, then left on St. Catherine for a quick side trip to the restored 1878 Westend Narrow Gauge Railroad station at 1060 (the Florissant Chamber of Commerce office). The building was moved here from elsewhere in town. The 16-mile steam line, which started near Grand and Olive in St. Louis, offered wealthy St. Louisans a quick way to reach their summer homes. For several years locals could brag that the West End was the longest such line in the world. The same line, all electrified by 1892, generated the first trolley railway post office in America.

Walk west on St. Catherine for 5 blocks, then turn left at St. Jacques, where, at 450, the Federal-style Baptiste Aubuchon house has been situated since around 1832. One of its line of owners supposedly arrived home one night to find furniture moved and lights twinkling. Unexplainable footsteps were heard on several occasions. Was old Baptiste sending a message? Return to St. Catherine, then turn left. Walk for a block and turn left again at St. Jean. At 359 St. Jean is the 1820 Bellisime home, Old Florissant's only brick French Colonial residence.

Walk north on St. Jean to St. Louis. Take a right and walk to the Garrett House (406), an 1890 Victorian structure with an Ionic-columned front porch. The porch came originally from a St. Louis home razed to make way for the 1904 World's Fair. Turn around and head west on St. Louis, crossing St. Jean. At 305 St. Louis is the 1845 home once owned by Edward Bates, attorney general in President Abraham Lincoln's first cabinet. At 306 is the white frame 1857 Montaigne house, whose original owners' gambling profits helped finance its second story, says historian Davison. Ghost stories are plentiful about homes in Old Florissant, but Davison's favorite relates to the historic district's Mottin house at 111 St. Catherine: A neighbor was driving her children to school. Somehow, she looked at an upstairs window and saw the figure of a little old woman with something white on her head. Several years later she drove East, visiting the family who had once lived in the home. "Do you have any pictures of your grandmother?" she asked. The host brought out the family album. One photo was of the woman the neighbor had seen in the window, the same white covering on her head.

At St. Pierre, walk left one block until you reach St. Francois again. Take a right and begin the return walk to the parking lot at Old St. Ferdinand's Shrine. Take a peek inside Weidinger's Tavern, dating from 1900. You're safe! No ghosts have been reported here.

Across the River in Illinois

This was once the great stone overlook where visitors to John Olin's estate could view the mighty Mississippi.

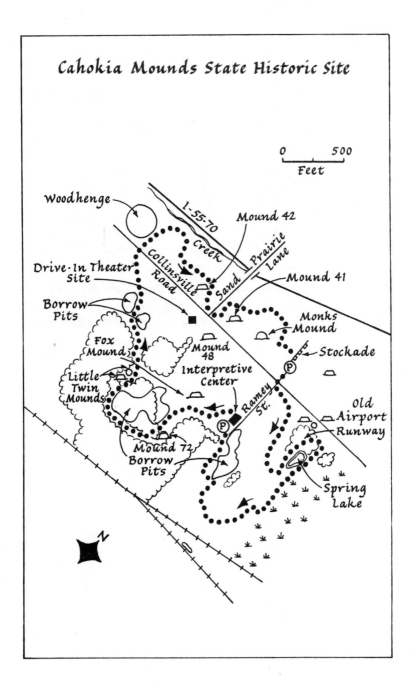

Cahokia Mounds State Historic Site

Cahokia Mounds State Historic Site

Location: Collinsville, Illinois
Hiking distance: 5 miles
Hiking time: 2½ hours
Bicycles: permitted

From A.D. 1000 to 1200, the 6-square-mile area known as Cahokia Mounds State Historic Site supported somewhere between 10,000 and 20,000 people. The Cahokia community was situated on the rich black-earth banks of Cahokia Creek, the waterway that Native Americans of the Mississippian culture used to reach the Mississippi River and the chain of lakes and marshes in the fertile lowlands known as the American Bottom.

The Cahokia site holds the largest collection of earthen mounds in the country. Sixty-eight out of a possible 120 original mounds remain on the site, as do 8 or 10 mounds in neighboring fields and subdivisions. Monks Mound, a 100-foot structure covering 14 acres at its base, is the largest human-made earthen mound in North America. Radiocarbon sampling by archaeologists suggests that it took 250 years to build Monks Mound, from A.D. 900 to 1150, and that it was built mainly with baskets of dirt (at least 22 million cubic feet of it) hauled on human backs. So significant is Cahokia that it has been designated a United Nations World Heritage Site along with the pyramids of Egypt, Independence Hall in Philadelphia, and the Palace at Versailles, France. Each year, visitors come to Cahokia Mounds from every American state and 80 foreign countries, with Germans leading the way.

"Cahokia developed into the largest city in the ancient Midwest—a political, cultural, economic, and religious center," writes William R. Iseminger, Cahokia's resident archaeologist. The ancient city was well planned, says Iseminger. "It included ceremonial mounds, open plazas, market places, ranked residential districts, workshop areas, and cemeteries." Everyone from laborers to aristocrats lived in the community, which was ringed with satellite towns with their own mounds. These include present-day Lebanon and Dupo, Illinois, as well as the largest satellite, the present city of St. Louis, where 26 mounds were reported to have once been located on the city's near north, and 17 low mounds in what is now Forest Park.

The mounds have always been captivating. In 1911, the Monks of Cahokia organized themselves to preserve the mounds. "Members included business and professional men who dressed in hooded monks' robes to hold secret meetings and rituals atop Monks Mound," one newspaper said. The group wanted a national park at Cahokia, but settled for state park status as of 1925. Since 1976, it has been a state historic site.

Access

From downtown St. Louis, take I-55 North/I-70 East over the Poplar Street Bridge. Drive 6 miles to exit 6 (IL 111). Turn right, to reach Collinsville Road. Turn left onto Collinsville Road and drive 2 miles east to Ramey Street. Turn right; drive into the parking area by the Cahokia Mounds Museum and Interpretive Center.

Park and walk to the museum, which contains displays, murals, and an authentic site model to orient you for the walk. An award-winning presentation of Cahokia's history is shown throughout the day in the theater. The museum was designed to blend with mound forms and not specifically to resemble an ancient mound, says Iseminger.

Trail

Leave the museum through the west door to access the trail, marked all the way by white posts with green tops; directional arrows are found on the cement bases of the marker posts.

Early along your walk, a display plot of prairie plants and grasses, many on view elsewhere on the historic site, appears on your left. Continue walking west, disregarding a service road on your left. Pass marker 2, then turn right on a gravel driveway. At marker 3, look to your immediate right to see 46-foot-high Fox Mound, which

Washington University archaeologists examine the top terrace of Monks Mound in 1971. (State of Illinois Department of Conservation)

may have supported an ancient charnel house on its oblong top. At marker 4, bear left and walk to Mound 72, just ahead.

Of all the mounds, 72 is the most thoroughly excavated. Within it are three smaller mounds; underneath *those* mounds archaeologists have found 300 human remains, many of them parts of unexplainable mass burials. One high-status grave contained a 40-year-old male laid over 20,000 marine shell disk beads, and surrounded by six male and female servants apparently sacrificed for the occasion. Although archaeologists suspect more burial sites lie under the ridgetop structure, one-third of Mound 72 remains unexplored.

Continue walking in a southerly direction beyond Mound 72. Marker 7 points to your right to indicate Cahokia's largest borrow pit, a 17-acre depression from which Native Americans borrowed dirt to build their mounds. Residing among tall bottomland trees, it is situated about 50 yards in from the path. In wet periods, the pit fills with water.

Beyond the borrow pit, the trail continues for about a mile on the old service road that parallels the southern fringe of the site—not too far from the railroad tracks there. At an intersection on the trail, turn left, following directions on an unnumbered marker just before marker 8. To the left of marker 8 are the Little Twin Mounds. Passing another unnumbered marker, continue west through bottomland forest rich in green ash and box elder. When the open field comes into view, bear left on the mowed grass path for a walk past two clearly defined borrow pits (one abuts the trail) and some small mounds. Follow the path as it swings to the north to face Collinsville Road. Carefully cross four-lane Collinsville Road to Woodhenge.

Woodhenge is a reproduction of a structure that may have been an astronomical observatory or sun calendar for the Mississippian culture around A.D. 1000. "From the center of Woodhenge," Iseminger has written, "priests could see how the rising or setting sun aligned with the posts. Thereby they calculated changes of season . . . planting and harvest time, and special ceremonial periods." (Cahokia sponsors solstice and equinox sunrise observations four times a year. Check the site's special events calendars for details.)

Passing Woodhenge on its right (and spurning the self-guided tour sign on your right), follow the grass path north by the old bed of Cahokia Creek. From here, the mowed path rambles through a meadow that attracts kildeer, meadowlarks, American goldfinches, and other songbirds. Located above these creek bed flats is Mound 42 (by marker 15), a 25- to 30-foot-tall platform mound that, in contemporary times, had a farmhouse on top and a barn nearby, as well as some mounds so subtle in appearance that they make no more than a gentle wave on the landscape.

Follow the path to Sand Prairie Lane, then cross it to resume the walk on the mowed path on the other side. Stop and look toward your right across Collinsville Road—at the point where Sand Prairie Lane dead-ends. This is the approximate site of the now demolished Falcon Drive-In Theater (1950s to late 1970s). Two small mounds were removed to build the drive-in, says Iseminger. "Everyone in East St. Louis came to play at Cahokia Mounds," comments a middle-aged volunteer in the interpretive museum coffee shop. "The drive-in was very popular. When we were out of money, we'd simply climb Mound 48, next to the theater, and see the whole movie free from up

One-hundred-foot-tall Monks Mound, the largest prehistoric earthwork in the Americas, dwarfs the smaller mounds in the foreground.

there. The mound was real crowded when the more raunchy films were shown." The theater is remembered today by the presence of the Falcon Picnic Area, and by the white trail marker posts, formerly the drive-in's speaker stands.

Resume your walk; pass Mound 41—Moorehead Mound— named for Warren K. Moorehead, an archaeologist who dug here in the 1920s, and was the ramrod who persuaded the Illinois legislature to approve the area as a state park. It was Moorehead who confirmed that the mounds were human-made; previously, it was held that they were probably erosional remnants. Continue straight ahead to Monks Mound, the flat-topped pyramid that supported a 50-foot-tall imperial temple and is the centerpiece of the site's treasures. Take time to explore its base, then walk around to the front of the mound. Climb the 140 or so stairs that pass through three terraces on their way to the top. On high there are impressive views of downtown St. Louis, as well as the horseradish fields to the northeast. Collinsville, with about 1500 acres planted in horseradish crops, bills itself as horseradish capital of the world. Also across the interstate are seven or eight more mounds that belong to the Cahokia site. Monks Mound was named for the French Trappist monks who grew fruit trees and vegetables on the terraces and wheat at the summit between 1809 and 1813, but who lived on Mound 48, long before drive-in theaters.

After Monks Mound, the path continues east through more open fields to a reproduction of the stockade wall that archaeologists believe was part of a larger, nearly 2-mile-long, wall encircling the central core of Cahokia. The wall was part social barrier, part defense. "Who the enemy was is unknown, and there is no direct evidence of attack in the areas excavated," states the official trail guidebook. After viewing the stockade remnants, you have the option of either following the white posts on a short east loop by a half-dozen, mostly conical mounds on the floodplain that edges the residential community, State Park Place; or immediately turning right and walking south through the Monks Mound parking area to recross Collinsville Road, and pick up the white posts in the fescue field on your left, just off Ramey Street. From here you begin the last leg of the walk, slightly less than 2 miles long.

Walk through the grassy field for nearly ½ mile—you may spot a deer or two loping in the distance—to the faded 3300-foot runway of the long-abandoned St. Louis Downtown Airport. Turn left, pass the unnumbered directional marker, and begin a ½-mile loop around Spring Lake, a 2800-year-old freshwater marsh that is tempting to shorebirds such as herons, egrets, and kingfishers. Operating as a private facility from 1955 to 1972, the airport that sat by the side of the spring boarded about 40 to 50 small planes daily.

Once you've looped the lake, the trail changes back to a mowed path. With a large marsh area on your left, and Black Lane Gardens—another residential settlement—in the eastern background, the trail now proceeds south almost to the railroad tracks (about ½ mile). It then meanders through two windbreaks, past a borrow pit (near marker 34), and past more modest mound sites on its final lap to the museum. Within the parking area are three mounds that were unknown until the archaeological excavation for the new buildings. "We had to reshape the parking lot to avoid a burial mound," says Iseminger.

Calhoun Point Wildlife Management Area

Location: Calhoun County, Illinois
Hiking distance: 1½ miles
Hiking time: 1 hour
Bicycles: not permitted

T he Kingdom of Calhoun," a narrow peninsula between the Illinois and Mississippi Rivers ending at the point where the rivers merge, has existed since 1825, when it was split off from larger Pike County, Illinois, which stretched to the Wisconsin border.

Among the first Europeans to see the confluence of the two great rivers were Louis Joliet and Father Jacques Marquette in 1673, followed by Father Louis Hennepin in 1680, and, later that year, Sieur de La Salle, the French explorer. La Salle apparently arrived in the wake of a massacre of 700 local Native Americans, mostly women and children, by Iroquois and Miami warriors. In 1802, Illinois governor Richard Yates called the massacre "one of the greatest tragedies of early American life." (The massacre site is about a mile upstream from the present Brussels Ferry, Army Corps of Engineers archaeologists believe.)

Calhoun County has long been known for its apples; several decades ago it was said to be the nation's third largest apple producer. Although apples and peaches still draw tourists at harvest time, it is the presence of the two rivers that attracts sightseers.

"Here in Calhoun County we are big on river ferries," says George Carpenter of Hardin, Illinois, author of *Calhoun Is My Kingdom.* "There are only six river ferries in all of Illinois; in Calhoun County, we have four of them, including the *Golden Eagle* over on the Mississippi River. It is the only paddlewheel ferry operating anywhere on the Mississippi."

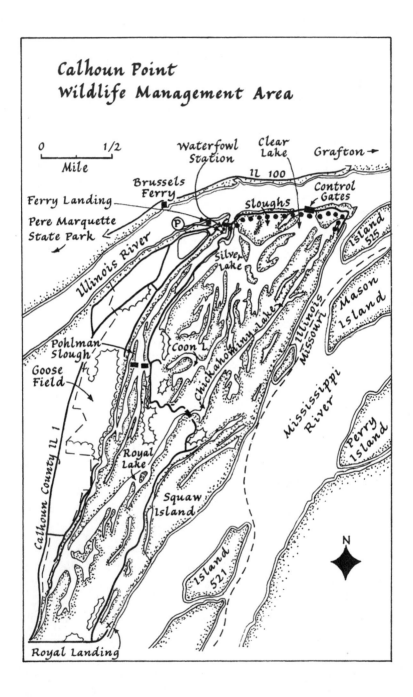

"Nobody moves away from Calhoun County," says school-teacher Robert Kirn of Golden Eagle, a founder of the county historical society. "People leave their farms to their kids and you almost never see 'For Sale' signs. The place is so special that some of the older adults in the county have never left it to visit St. Louis. They have no desire to travel that far."

Until recently, says Kirn, there were no street or road signs in the county. "Every time I went out for a walk," says Kirn's wife, Mary Kay, "visitors would stop me to ask directions." "Before the signs," says Greg Gansz of the county highway department, "visitors would drive up from St. Louis, take the Brussels Ferry across, and wonder what part of Missouri they were in. There were no signs to tell them they were still in Illinois."

Few local residents can say precisely where the true confluence of the two great rivers is, or how to reach it on foot. And few call the place by its formal name, Calhoun Point. "To me, it's simply 'the Point' and the best place to see it is to stand on the Illinois River bank in downtown Grafton and look across," says Carpenter.

Access

From Grafton, Illinois, drive west on IL 100 to the Brussels Ferry landing. Take the free ferry across the Illinois River. Leave the ferry and immediately turn left onto a gravel road. Take the road east until you reach a parking area by a waterfowl check station, then continue ahead to the next parking area. Leave your car. Walk back toward the river until you see an "Authorized Vehicles Only" sign on a maintenance access road. Turn right on the road to begin your hike beside the Illinois River.

It's best to avoid the Calhoun Point walk during waterfowl and deer season (roughly from mid-October to early December) and during wild turkey hunting season in April and early May.

Trail

The flat, narrow maintenance road that parallels the Illinois River on this southernmost tip of Calhoun County is rich in arresting sights. "This place is a mature river bottom, rich in honey locust, pecans, pin oaks, ash, silver maples, hackberries, and American elm trees," observes Ramon Gass, author of *Missouri Hiking Trails.* "The persimmon trees are extra large; the cottonwoods are healthy and tall, and the poison ivy bushes are thick, which means that the soil is rich and gets lots of sunlight." Stinging nettle plants and mosquitoes are both found in multiples along the path in warm months, so be prepared.

A gathering of river birch trees off to the right of the path, some 50 yards into the forest, delights Gass. At least 150 birches, their bark orangy, shaggy, and peeling, rest silently in the woods. "They're the most river birches I've ever seen in one place," Gass says.

Later, Gass points out that beavers have been busy along the trail: The chips from a nearby ash tree are very fresh on the ground. He spies a beaver trail leading from the ash tree near the shore back into the forest sloughs. "Look at their travel lanes," he says. "They're well worn. The beavers have dragged them clean. They must be all over this area."

As we walk, a great blue heron, stopped by the riverbank, rises and flies off, its 6-foot wings pushing it slowly up the Illinois in search of a more private roost. A lone Caspian tern, out fishing, flies low over the river, its wings flapping continuously, its beak pointed at the water. Red cardinal flowers, bunched along the bank, add a touch of crimson on a mid-August day. On our right, ancient sloughs begin to appear. The first one is part of Clear Lake, which supports about 40 duck blinds.

A pair of black double-crested cormorants, grunting like airborne pigs, fly over as we approach the Fish and Wildlife Area water-control gates on Clear Lake. The gates drain the lake during high water and raise it during low water so that resident ducks and migrant waterfowl can have a year-round aquatic food source. "What we are learning from small lakes such as this one is that they provide good food and rest areas for migrating birds," says Kim Postlewait, assistant superintendent in the Rosedale, Illinois, office of the Conservation Department.

As you walk farther east, the trail swings hard to your right, moving deeper into the forest and the sloughs. At the first wide open space on the left after the turn is Chickahominy Slough. "If you look

A walker examines the water-control gates on Clear Lake on the Calhoun Point walk. (Lynn Rubright)

way over to the left toward the far side of this slough, you are looking at the site of the real confluence of the two rivers," says Postlewait. "You can't actually walk to it, but it's right there."

The path terminates on the bank of the Mississippi River. If you face the river, you'll see two islands ahead of you. Island 525 on your left is in Illinois water. Mason Island, on your right, is in Missouri water. Heron rookeries in tall cottonwoods and sycamores are found on both islands. The main Mississippi channel is on the far side of Mason Island. Mason, with a long sandbar that attracts sunbathers from passing cruisers, is named for James Mason, founder of Grafton in 1830. Grafton is in turn named after Mason's hometown, Grafton, Massachusetts. Back in 1849, gazetteers ranked Grafton as the fourth largest steamboat landing between Chicago and St. Louis. Earlier, Grafton was thought to be the largest freshwater fishing port on the Mississippi.

Turn around and return on the same route to the parking area. As you walk, you might see a pileated woodpecker or a wild turkey.

"Our turkey population has steadily increased along with a rise in turkey hunters, who consider this a quality place to hunt," says Ranger Neil Waters. Nearly 250 bird species have been identified in the area, including rare loggerhead shrikes, mourning warblers, upland sandpipers, red-necked phalaropes, and black-billed cuckoos. Brown pelicans are frequently spotted over the rivers.

In the winter months, American bald eagles are seen quite often. Sometimes they are seen roosting in trees by the river or soaring and swooping to pluck dead or dying fish from the water. One longtime fisherman at Calhoun Point, Charles Eberlin, says, "There are 50 times as many eagles around here as there were when I was a boy almost 75 years ago."

Postlewait often hears rumors of panthers in the area. "Every year someone says somebody's seen a big cat or a panther. When they see it, it is usually late at night on the way home from many hours in the tavern." "And Jack Daniels was usually riding as a passenger in the car," adds Gene Stumpf, a Conservation Department policeman assigned to the county.

Heartland Prairie

Location: Alton, Illinois
Hiking distance: less than 1 mile
Hiking time: 30 minutes
Bicycles: not permitted

This 30-acre plot of land once contained a cornfield, hay barn, tractor shed, and farm supervisor's cottage for the 2300-bed Alton State Hospital next door—now known as Alton Mental Health and Development Center. By 1977, the land had been sold to the city of Alton as part of the Gordon F. Moore Community Park, the bulk of which is just across the street. It was then that Mark Hall, a Godfrey resident and earth science teacher at Mehlville Senior High School in St. Louis County, sowed the first seeds in a fledgling prairie on the new park land. His work is sponsored by the Nature Institute in Alton.

"I had no idea where to find seed or how to re-create a prairie," Hall says. "I talked to an expert in Chicago, then I bought some seeds and planted about 10,000 square feet. In 1978, I drove back roads in a 75-mile radius of Alton, searching for small scraps of prairie. I monitored those scraps all summer to see what they looked like when they went to seed. When they were ripe, I collected them and brought them here."

In the early days, Hall worked closely with naturalists who had just started a prairie at Shaw Arboretum in Gray Summit, Missouri. "We reciprocated with the arboretum people," says Hall. "We supplied them forb seeds (prairie wildflowers) that they had difficulty locating and they let us grow some of our seedlings in their greenhouses."

Heartland Prairie, now a bona fide American tallgrass prairie and one of the largest of its kind in southwestern Illinois, is much

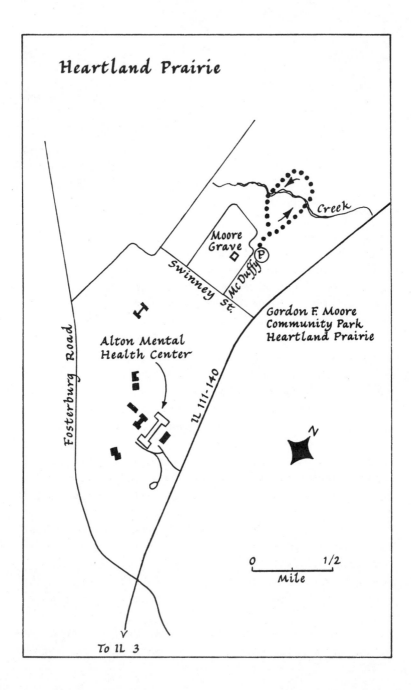

more floristically diverse than other newly started prairies. This prairie has nine prairie grasses and about 140 wildflower species. Hall and colleagues from the Nature Institute, whose focus is on nature education and native plant and animal preservation, continue to plow new ground at the prairie. "Last year, we discovered dozens of ladies' tresses, one of the few prairie orchids," says Hall.

"If you didn't know any better, you'd think that this prairie had been here for 500 years," says photographer Frank Oberle, whose photos adorn The Nature Conservancy's book *Tallgrass Prairie.* "I've seen nearly 400 prairies; this one emulates the best I've seen."

The best time to visit the prairie is anytime between April and October, but Hall recommends some special occasions:

- Mid-May. "This is when the wild hyacinth, prairie phlox, heartleaf golden Alexander, creamy wild indigo, and shooting stars are in bloom."
- Mid-June. "This is the time to see the purple coneflower and the wild white indigo."
- Early July. "Thousands of yellow coneflowers, horsemint, and purple blazing stars are waiting to be seen."
- Mid-September. "Not only are the goldenrods and purple asters at full bloom, but you are also likely to see thousands of migrating monarch and swallowtail butterflies stopping by."

Birds on the prairie are a bonus, says Hall. "As you know, grassland birds had all but disappeared from this part of Illinois because of diminishing habitat. But now many birds have discovered our prairie. Small colonies of dickcissels, Bell's vireos, yellowthroats, goldfinches, and sedge wrens have appeared. In fact, we have one of the few nesting populations of sedge wrens that I know of around here." In winter, large numbers of sparrows, juncos, and goldfinches are seen. Also in evidence are box turtles, grassland snakes, rabbits, deer, coyotes, foxes, woodchucks, groundhogs, and weasels.

During the first weekend of March, the prairie is set abaze to replenish and invigorate it, eliminate exotic plants and dead thatch that have encroached in the preceding year, and discourage unwanted trees. "We'd be filled with cherry and mock orange saplings in five years if we didn't burn the prairie annually," says Hall.

A solitary grave along McDuffy Street on the way to the trailhead belongs to Revolutionary War captain Abel Moore and his wife, Mary, who both died in 1846. Nearby, on July 10, 1814, two of the Moores' children, four other children, and one woman, Rachel Reagan, were slain by attacking Kickapoo tribe members in what is known as the "Wood River Massacre."

In recent times, before it was state hospital property, the prairie land was owned by Eben Rogers, grandfather of the late Alton surgeon Mather Pfeiffenberger Jr. "When I was a boy," Pfeiffenberger recalled, "this was country, the place to come for family picnics." It was Pfeiffenberger, once a Nature Institute board member, who named the prairie "Heartland."

Access

From I-270 East in north St. Louis County, take MO 367 North into Alton, Illinois. From the bridge, turn right on East Broadway. Drive 3 miles east to IL 3 North; turn left on IL 3. Drive 1.7 miles to IL 111-140 (College Avenue). Turn right. Stay in the left lane. Drive 1.3 miles to the traffic light opposite the entrance to Gordon F. Moore Community Park. Turn left onto Swinney Street, then right onto McDuffy. Park near the trailhead, which is to the right of the sign-board. Trail brochures, found behind the sign, are indispensable, but should be returned after your hike.

Trail

A buffer area of small trees and bushes—"Eurasian weeds and gold-enrod," Hall terms it—lies south of the grass lane leading into the prairie. In April and May, migrating bobolinks dart in and out of this maze, as do grasshopper sparrows, meadowlarks, and yellowthroats. "We spotted two dozen migrating bobolinks one spring," says an enthusiastic Hall.

Most walkers follow the trail arrows and usually stop at all 14 cedar markers described in the trail brochure. Other hikers who already know the prairie choose to ramble aimlessly in the labyrinth of paths. This you can do for hours if you supplement the trail guide with a bird book and perhaps one on butterflies and insects.

Tall grasses reign over the forepart of the prairie. In August 1989, citing the power of tall grasses, then-Governor James Thompson of Illinois helicoptered into the area to sign a law designating big bluestem as the official Illinois prairie grass. The late Alton author John Madson wrote in *Where the Sky Began: Land of the Tallgrass Prairie* that "the singular community of grasses and flowers commanded by big bluestem has been called 'the true prairie, *the* prairie.' " There are accounts of big bluestem so dense and deep, wrote Madson, "that cattle vanished in them and could be found only if a herdsman went to high ground and sat in his saddle to watch for telltale movement in the sea of towering grasses." In August, big bluestems, at least 7 feet tall, seem to overpower the trail and dwarf most hikers.

Botanist Vernon LeClaire, who lives nearby, likes to stand and listen to the "sounds of the prairie," which the brochure describes as rippling wind, buzzing grasshoppers, humming bees, and singing birds. "When the sun is above the trees and dew is on the ground, there's nothing prettier than the prairie on a summer morning," observes LeClaire.

Toward the back (eastern) end of the prairie, where the land drops off, the path curls through low, damp ground populated by wild indigo and more big bluestem. Sedge wrens nest near here. Farther into the northeast quadrant and still on low ground, embedded fire-resistant cedar pallets make the path more tractable. Traces of a tributary of Wood River Creek, which Hall calls a "swale," are visible, but only after rain.

A small grove of willow trees has been allowed to stand because of its good looks and character, says Hall. It is near here, lowest point in the prairie and the place where bright blazing stars shine in late July, that LeClaire likes to bring his thermos of coffee and his binoculars. By the willows, he sits quietly, looking and listening. It's a particularly good place to watch the flight of yellowthroats throughout the summer, he adds.

From this far point you can follow the cedar markers back to the trailhead or continue to stroll the other trails randomly. Wherever you are, you are constantly reminded of the rarity and fragility of the place.

"This prairie facsimile was not created just for the recreation and joy of man," writes Alton attorney and conservationist L. James Struif, editor of a detailed prairie field guide that is also available at the trailhead signboard. "We did it partly because prairie is a resource that God put here, and that man has almost destroyed. This facsimile, however, can never become a real prairie. It will always need our help . . . We now realize that humankind cannot control everything in nature but must work with it, and preserve it for our own benefit."

Horseshoe Lake
State Park/
Walker Island

Location: Granite City, Illinois
Hiking distance: 4 miles
Hiking time: 2 hours
Bicycles: not permitted

Horseshoe Lake, once called "the largest natural body of water in Illinois," is an oxbow lake formed centuries ago by the Mississippi River. The area was part of the American Bottom section of Illinois, which was saturated with oxbows and swampy areas when historians first began to describe it around 1800. "Horseshoe Lake was interconnected with others so that a canoeist could travel continuously from Wood River to East St. Louis on water separated entirely from the Mississippi River," wrote botanist Richard C. Keating a few years ago.

Artifacts found near the lake suggest Native American activity as early as 8000 B.C. Recent archaeological findings imply that Native Americans had settled by the lake at least 50 to 100 years before the rise of neighboring Cahokia Mounds. "The Horseshoe Lake Indian population broke down after Cahokia Mounds was founded," says Tim Pauketat, a University of Oklahoma anthropology professor who, with five students, found 25 to 30 archaeological sites during a survey of Walker Island. The sites are mostly near small ridges that were laid down by the river. One large ridge, about 1½ miles long, reaches diagonally across the island. Time has changed the area little—especially its natural attraction for waterfowl, songbirds, and critters of the woods and wetlands.

In more recent times, Horseshoe Lake's northeast shore was the site of Bircher and Young's hotel and dance pavilion (later called

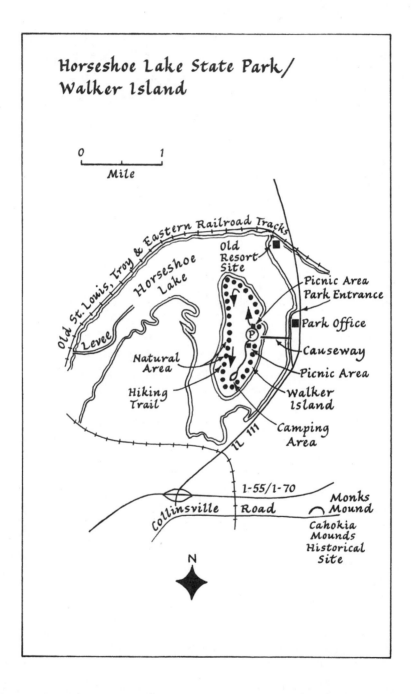

Horseshoe Lake State Park/ Walker Island

0 _____ 1
Mile

Old St. Louis, Troy & Eastern Railroad Tracks

Horseshoe Lake

Levee

Old Resort Site

Picnic Area
Park Entrance

Park Office

Causeway

Natural Area

Picnic Area

Hiking Trail

Walker Island

P

Camping Area

IL 111

I-55/I-70

Monks Mound

Collinsville   Road

Cahokia Mounds Historical Site

N

Moellenbrocks), a popular summer vacation and fishing resort. On weekends, St. Louisans rode to and from the lake aboard the Horseshoe Lake–St. Louis–Yellowhammer trolley line. Once there, they rented small boats and launches by the hundreds.

In 1964, a local politician proposed linking the island with the nearby Cahokia Mounds State Historic Site to create an 8000-acre historic and recreational area, an expanse six times the size of Forest Park in St. Louis. And Sam Vadalabene, the late Illinois state senator, proposed renaming Horseshoe "Lake Karandjeff," in memory of a prominent Granite City banker. Both ideas fizzled.

"The main thing about Horseshoe Lake is that it has so much wildlife in an area that is so heavily populated," says former park superintendent Lynn White. "We are surrounded by Granite City, Madison, Fairmount City, Venice, and East St. Louis. When I give talks, I ask the question: 'When was the last time you visited Horseshoe Lake State Park?' Eighty to 95 percent of our neighbors say they've never been here."

Park visitors come in six guises: fishers, hunters, birders, hikers, picnickers, and campers. The best fishing place is right off the causeway, where catfish, carp, bluegill, and bass lurk; the best place to hunt ducks in-season is behind one of the lake's 23 or so blinds, assigned annually to hunters through a state-run lottery; the best place to see the birds is on the trail that rings the island.

A checklist prepared by Ronald E. Goetz of Webster Groves contains 284 bird species that have been seen in and around the park. Goetz explains in *Illinois Birds and Birding* that the lake "is perhaps best known for its herons; virtually all species recorded in the state have been seen here, and species such as snowy egret and little blue heron are found here in large numbers." July and August are top heron-viewing months: The lake south of the causeway (known as the water management or impoundment area) is drained, and millet seed is spread by plane on the mudflat below, where herons and egrets wade in the mud to locate succulent snails and small clams. As the millet grows, water is let back in.

Eurasian tree sparrows, short-legged birds with black ears and throat patches on chestnut-brown bodies, exist in the St. Louis metropolitan area and nowhere else in America. They are seen throughout the year in the hollowed-out cottonwood trees that line Horseshoe Lake's banks along the first section of the trail.

"The very best thing about Horseshoe Lake is that it is only 10 minutes from downtown St. Louis," says Bill Rudden, a St. Louis fireman who goes birding on the island. "I've seen many rare birds at Horseshoe Lake. Sometimes I call the bird hot line to tell others to get over here to see what I've just seen. A few years ago, I used the hot line to report a marbled godwit [a member of the sandpiper family]. We got 33 birders here in half an hour." (To report a rare bird in greater St. Louis, call Dick Anderson at 314-868-2009. To learn of current bird migrations and sightings, call the Washington University Tyson Research Center Nature Line, 314-935-8432, a service of the Friends of Tyson and the Webster Groves Nature Study Society.)

But it is the Eurasian tree sparrow that tempts determined out-of-town birders. "If serious birders fly into the St. Louis area, I tell them to see the Eurasian tree sparrow along the Missouri Bottoms near Lambert Field. If they drive to the area, I tell them to drive straight to Horseshoe Lake," says Paul Bauer, who in 1968, with Anderson, wrote *A Guide to Finding Birds in the St. Louis Area.*

Access

From downtown St. Louis, take I-55/I-70 into Illinois; drive to IL 111 North. Turn left on IL 111; drive 3.2 miles to the park entrance. Inside the park, take the road to your left that spans the causeway onto Walker Island. Park by the picnic shelter. The trailhead is across from the parking area in front of a hiking/bird trail signboard.

Trail

Early along the trail, you'll pass the cottonwood trees where, with luck, a fast-flying Eurasian tree sparrow might pop into view. Along this stretch the lake is deepest along the banks. In fall and winter, diving ducks might demonstrate how they forage for fingernail clams and other food. Just past the northern tip of the island—as your walk takes its first leftward turn—are more tall cottonwoods, coveted by a large population of woodpeckers, nuthatches, and red-winged blackbirds.

In the spring, anglers line the causeway to Walker Island at Horseshoe Lake State Park.

As you walk the shoreline, always on your right, the front grille of a mostly submerged and well-oxidized 1964 Chevrolet Nova smiles up through the mire. Before the state took over the park in 1974, people used the island for a dumping ground.

The northern part of the trail traverses hardwood ponds—swampy ponds surrounded by hardwood trees—and open fields. Six hundred of the island's 3200 acres are leased to farmers. Contracts with the farmers stipulate that part of their yield is to be used to feed island wildlife, especially over the winter.

Off to your right, across the water, are smokestacks of Granite City Steel Company. The company has been a thoughtful neighbor; its water purification plant keeps the lake relatively pollution-free and more enticing to aquatic life.

Once you pass the park benches, you reach the island's southern tip, another place where herons, bitterns, and ducks convene. This section is dominated by rangy trees; subtrails lead into swampy areas filled with cattail, arrowroot, and smartweed, all providing food and cover for permanent and migrating waterfowl. Past the island's south-ernmost point, on your left, is a grassy campground. The shallow banks on your right offer year-round protection and shelter for thousands of ducks.

A dirt path that parallels the lake on your right begins the final lap of the hike. Ahead are three footbridges; the most tree varieties in the park (from mockernut hickory to sour gum); the main wildlife management area; and more of the resident ducks.

In its final stages, the trail heads inland to another majestic cottonwood stand that canopies the parking area. It's not unusual to see birdwatchers pointing tripod-mounted telescopes into the tops of the cottonwoods for signs of the tree sparrows.

"We often call parts of this island a 'three-story forest,'" says Rudden. "That's when you have solid undergrowth, medium high trees, and very tall trees or highballs, where the birds like to stick around to catch insects." In a sense, the Horseshoe Lake walk ends with highballs. Here's to you!

John M. Olin
Nature Preserve

Location: Godfrey, Illinois
Hiking distance: 3 miles
Hiking time: 1½ hours
Bicycles: not permitted

I f you weren't invited to stroll the rear grounds of industrialist John M. Olin's estate during his lifetime, you're cordially invited to do so now. In 1990, the 300 acres that form the back sections of Olin's former estate were designated an official Illinois nature preserve, an act that means the wildflowers, trees, and prairie remnants on a property such as this will never be disturbed except by nature itself.

Olin, once chairman of the Olin Corporation and its predecessor, the Winchester Western Division, makers of arms and ammunition, died in 1981. Years before his death, he gave his land to the Illinois Department of Conservation, which in turn transferred it to Southern Illinois University–Edwardsville (SIUE). The Nature Institute in Alton now leases part of the property from SIUE and manages the rest.

For wildlife protection purposes, the Olin Preserve is usually closed to visitors from November 1 to mid-March in accordance with Illinois Nature Preserves Commission policies.

Access

From its intersection with I-270 East in north St. Louis County, take US 67/MO 367 North over two river bridges into Alton, Illinois. At the Alton bridge, take a left onto US 67, following it about 3 miles north through Alton to its junction with IL 3. Turn left onto IL 3; drive 2.5 miles to Levis Lane and turn left again. In about 0.5 mile, turn left at South Levis Lane, then drive nearly another 0.5 mile to

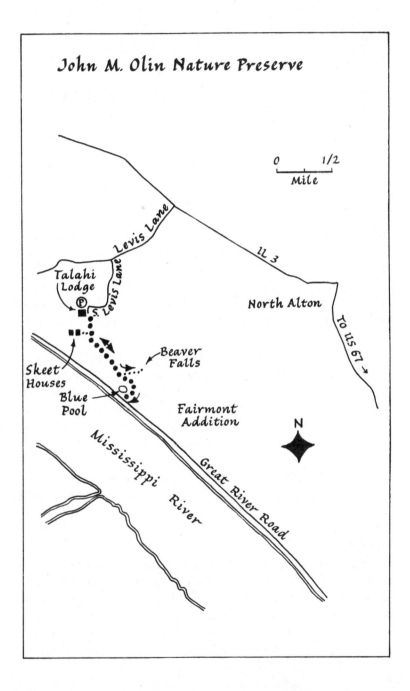

John M. Olin Nature Preserve

0   1/2
Mile

Levis Lane

S. Levis Lane

Talahi
Lodge

Ⓟ

North Alton

IL 3

To US 67 →

Beaver
Falls

Skeet
Houses

Blue
Pool

Fairmont
Addition

N

Mississippi River

Great River Road

the Olin Nature Preserve. Turn left and park near the brown structure on your right, the old Camp Talahi lodge.

Trail

Begin exploring the Olin preserve at the lodge, the former Alton YWCA Camp Talahi, dedicated in 1926. "When I was a girl, it was a big event to go to Camp Talahi for 3 or 4 days," recalls Marjorie Dintelmann of Godfrey. "We ate in one of the four screened-in porches; we swam in the pool (now covered with vines and populated by snapping turtles); and we hiked down to the Mississippi River."

Once past the lodge and the Nature Institute field office on your left, follow the path (an old service road) south to a fork. Stay to the left on the service road, which shortly gives way to ancient blacktop, a forest road that Olin himself plotted in the 1930s. As the road begins a descent, turn right onto another old blacktop lane that heads directly to Olin's prized high and low limestone skeet houses, built in the 1930s.

Olin loved to shoot skeet, recalled the late Alton naturalist and author John Madson, who worked for 21 years as assistant director of Olin's pioneering conservation department at the Winchester Western plant in East Alton. Olin invited the world's best skeet shooters to join him at the skeet houses and the magnificent limestone patio and barbecue pit on a terrace above the Mississippi. No guest list has survived, but it is probable that some of the world's leading diplomats, militarists, and industrialists visited the estate and perhaps did some skeet shooting.

"Mr. Olin was a true conservationist," said Madson, who knew him reasonably well. "He was one of the finest hunters I've ever known. He used to go duck hunting at Calhoun Point just up the river from here. He would hunt quail in Georgia in the classic fashion. He was a member of a marlin fishing club in Peru and a salmon fishing club in Quebec." And he was able to develop an estate rich in wildlife (nearly 200 species of birds are here, according to Nature Insitute counters) and flora (at least 425 species of wildflowers, some of them on a rare blufftop hill prairie, the gem of the preserve—but so rare it's off-limits to hikers). After looping (in occasionally high grass) around the skeet houses, and viewing the remains of the barbecue pit with its river overlook, retrace your steps to the main paved trail. Walk straight ahead, mostly downhill.

Back on the main trail, the path begins a descent to the bottom-land forest near the river. Separating you from a deep hollow on your left is what Madson called "an Olin-type fence [with heavy posts and steel rope]. You can see the engineering in it. Olin had much concern for his guests, many of them from the social set or from other walks of life who came here to tour by car or walk as we do." When the downward trail levels off momentarily, "a splendid hillside view," in Madson's words, appears on your right. "The trees on this hillside need high, clean stems to reach the sun. You can see a long way through the forest under the tops of the slender oaks, ironwoods, and the old box elders in there, and their shading canopies retard under-growth."

After this majestic view, the roadway drops again and finally reaches—at a creek—the real bottom of the hill. Once there, take the wide dirt path to your left and head to Beaver Falls, a beautiful loop detour of about 1¼ miles. At about ²⁄₁₀ mile, take a narrower dirt path to your right; it carries you along a creek and a series of smaller falls all the way to Beaver Falls. The surrounding bottomland forest, predominantly maple, includes rare Kentucky coffee and ironwood trees as well as hollowed-out trees that offer shelter and food to the pileated woodpeckers you will see and hear along the way. (If the trail is muddy, you may wish to turn around about 75 yards before Beaver Falls, since the remaining distance can be treacherous after rain. At this point, the full view of the spring-fed falls is just as striking as if you were right next to them.)

Madson said he had found on the Beaver Falls limestone shelves pottery shards that may predate the Woodland Indians, and occasionally some projectile points from spears used by ancient warriors. Madson advised caution in the falls area, however. Not only have black widow and brown recluse spiders been seen there, but copperhead and timber rattlesnakes as well. After a breather at the falls, retrace your steps to the main trail. Turn left and follow the main trail to the river.

Walkers pass one of John Olin's skeet houses at Olin Nature Preserve.

At a rather deteriorated fork, a closed road leads to your left, over a dislodged stone bridge and toward the former Olin mansion on a blufftop in Alton's Fairmount Addition. Continue walking straight ahead toward the river. Thirty-five feet ahead a one-time wagon or livestock trail, narrow and steep, heads straight up the hill to your right. "Nobody knows that road's history any more," said Madson. In the river forest, thousands of black ash tree seedlings are massed on the left side of the road, entwined in vines and kudzu. Shortly, Blue Pool appears on your right below a giant bluff.

"Nearly every kid who grew up in Alton in the '40s, '50s, and '60s came to Blue Pool," says attorney and historian L. James Struif, a founder of the Nature Institute. "It had a reputation of having a bottomless pit where railroad cars and old trucks and automobiles could be dropped with free abandon and never seen again. But Southern Illinois University disabused that idea when it drained the 25-foot-deep pool a few years ago and found nothing on the bottom." The pool, now covered with duckweed, a free-floating plant that looks like scum or algae, was originally a limestone quarry. In a move to discourage trespassers, SIUE erected a chain-link fence around the pool, but it was "vandalized, stolen, and completely gone within 2 weeks," said Madson. In the winter, eagles roost in treetops above the pool. Peregrine falcons are said to nest nearby.

After you've seen Blue Pool, retrace your steps up the hill to your parking spot by the lodge.

Julius J. Knobeloch Woods Nature Preserve

Location: St. Clair County, Illinois (near Belleville)
Hiking distance: less than 1 mile
Hiking time: 30 minutes
Bicycles: not permitted

This oak-hickory forest, with its old-growth appearance, opened as an Illinois nature preserve in 1983 after having been owned by the family of Balthezar K. Knobeloch since 1874. Even at a comparatively small 44 acres, there is no existing presettlement stand of timber comparable to this woodlot in the Metro East area, says Vic Hamer, site superintendent with the Illinois Department of Conservation. Knobeloch, an immigrant farmer, paid $160 an acre for the rolling woodland, which reminded him vividly of woods in his native Germany.

In 1908, farmer Julius J. Knobeloch bought the land from the estate of Balthezar, his older brother. The property, which the family called Hazel Creek Woods, was nurtured by Julius's 20 heirs until 1980, when The Nature Conservancy bought it at auction for $226,000.

At the auction, the Conservancy bid against furniture makers from Belgium, Germany, and Japan who wanted to log the rich white oaks in the woods to make veneer. Later, the Conservancy sold the property at a loss to the state of Illinois so that Knobeloch's original landscape "will be protected to provide habitat for native plants and animals and opportunities for future generations to study and appreciate our natural heritage," said Preston Schellbach, former chairman of the Illinois Nature Preserve System. "Those bids from foreign countries ought to prove to the public just how scarce timber is in the world," says Hamer.

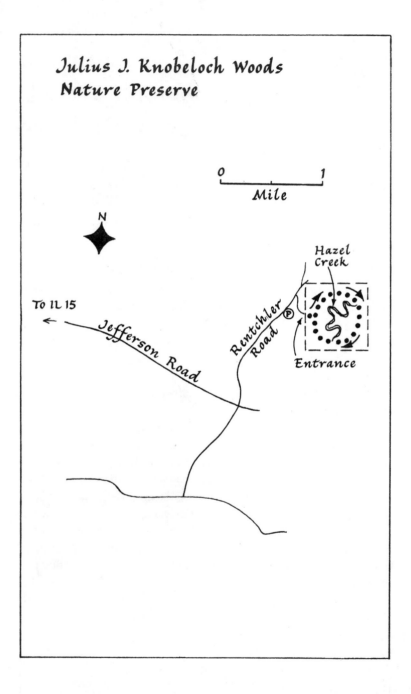

"I personally call this land 'The Timber,' " says Roy Knobeloch of Belleville, a retired farmer and a nephew of Julius. "My dad used to tell me that when he was a young boy, he would go up to 'The Timber' for hazelnuts. Maybe that's where Hazel Creek, which runs through the woods, got its name."

As a footnote, Knobeloch Woods has been a neighbor of Scott Air Force Base since the base's establishment in 1917. Woods walkers back then might have seen or heard army biplanes training for the American Expeditionary Forces in Europe. In the 1920s, they might have been startled to see lighter-than-air ships, or dirigibles, floating overhead. They, too, were based at Scott, which boasted the world's second largest dirigible hangar—after the one in Lakehurst, New Jersey, where the *Hindenburg* exploded and burned.

Access

From its intersection with I-255 in Illinois, take IL 15 East for 13 miles to Jefferson Road. Turn left; drive 1.6 miles to Rentchler Road. Turn left onto Rentchler. In about 1 mile, the Knobeloch Woods sign appears on your right, partially hidden. Park on the Rentchler Road shoulder near the entrance. Enter the woods via a narrow dirt path.

Trail

A 150-year-old split-rail fence marks the starting point of the walk, which makes a near-perfect clockwise loop. Almost immediately, you see what enthralled the foreign furniture makers: a huge spread of white oaks standing serenely in the upland forest. Near the oaks are lesser stands of elms and hickories, which form such a dense canopy that autumn leaves take a full year to begin their decomposition process. (In a forest this dense it takes about five years for a leaf to decompose fully.)

White oak leaves in spring seemed to transport Mrs. J.K. Hudson, who wrote in her 1905 book, *In the Missouri Woods:* "The [new] white oak leaves are pure green without any shading, and they develop to their full size so thin and delicate that a tree hung with new leaves looks as if it were dressed with tissue paper."

Hamer's crew clears the trail twice a year. "Nothing is ever removed from the woods," explains Ed Anderson, Illinois Conservation Department natural heritage biologist. "All we really do is clear off the trail, but only to the edge of the path." Anderson once brought foreign visitors here to inspect this microcosmic parcel of rich timber. "Though you may hear sounds of planes on a glide path to Scott Air Force Base, you can't see any houses or other buildings. This is pretty much what Illinois looked like before it was settled 200 years ago or so. From nature's viewpoint, there's been very little disturbance in these woods."

In a slow descent, the trail heads for Hazel Creek, which alternates between wet and dry, and thus meets the definition of an intermittent stream. The stream lies in a moist bottomland that supports cottonwoods and sycamores, which are often loaded with woodpeckers and bluejays, the most prevalent birds in the woods. Anderson adds that migrating warblers "put on a show in the treetops here during their southward migration in early fall." Ferns are more evident at Knobeloch Woods than in many other nearby park sites. Christmas, rattlesnake, and maidenhair are the three fern species seen most often.

A climb from the Hazel Creek area back to the upland forest is only moderately difficult if done slowly. Atop the hill, the trail rolls a bit, and takes a few curves to complete its loop. White-tailed deer and both red and gray foxes live nearby and probably walk the trail after the human usurpers leave. "I have reason to believe that we have a family of flying squirrels in here," says Anderson, who hasn't personally seen one.

In the last span of the trail are thick groves of dogwoods that, in part, form the understory, which plays second fiddle to the giant white oaks. "If you hike in here at a certain time in the spring," says Hamer of the dogwoods, "it will look like fresh snow has fallen. The showiest wildflowers in the woods flourish along this span." Included among them are the somewhat hard to find red trilliums.

Back at the split-rail fence, the trail ends. Serious walkers who seek more exercise or mileage often hike the trail three or four times in a row, clockwise or counterclockwise.

Leclaire Village Historic District

Location: Edwardsville, Illinois
Hiking distance: 2½ miles
Hiking time: 1½ hours
Bicycles: permitted

In 1875, Nelson Oliver Nelson took a job as bookkeeper for a wholesale hardware and plumbing goods company in St. Louis. Within a year, Nelson became a partner in the firm. Lifted by a vision of a company all his own, he later formed N.O. Nelson Manufacturing Company, eventually the largest plumbing supplier in the Midwest.

A man with a mission far beyond the wooden toilet seats, brass fixtures, architectural marble, woodwork, and metal fittings that his firm produced, Nelson was intrigued by the cooperative movement that had taken root in Europe. He sympathized with new concepts such as worker profit sharing, pension plans, employees as partners, and industrial villages, where employers and employees worked, learned, and played together. When his St. Louis firm's quick growth required expansion, Nelson chose "a country location" near Edwardsville, Illinois, for his own version of a profit-sharing community.

Named for Edmond Leclaire, father of profit sharing in France, the village was dedicated in 1890 and thrived through the early 1900s. "The cornerstone of Leclaire's social and economic design was housing for the worker, education for all ages, recreation, beautification of the environment, and profit sharing," writes Carl S. Lossau, a geology professor at Southern Illinois University–Edwardsville (SIUE). "Nelson believed that nothing contributed so greatly to the American workingman's welfare and contentment as the possession of a comfortable home," Lossau adds. "Leclaire is unique in American history," says John Abbott, former director of libraries for SIUE and a Leclaire

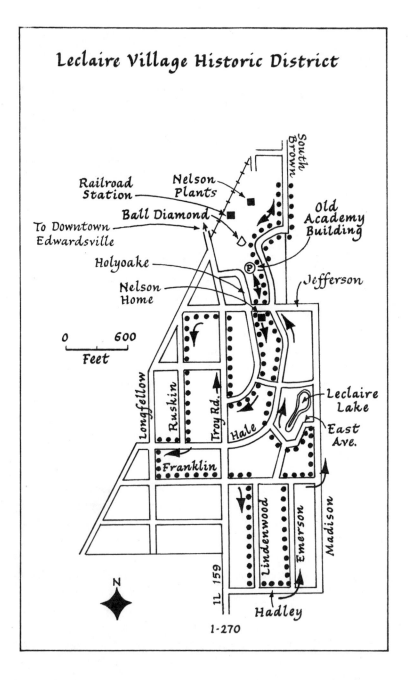

Leclaire Village Historic District

historian. "It's the only community experiment [in America] based on capitalistic cooperative principles."

Access

From downtown St. Louis, take I-55/I-70 over the Poplar Street Bridge to I-255 North, about 10 miles. Take I-255 North for 7 miles to I-270 East. Turn right on I-270 and drive 5.5 miles east to IL 159, exit 12. Drive north for 3.5 miles. IL 159 becomes Troy Road in Edwardsville. Turn right on Hale Avenue. Take Hale to the Little League ballpark that's just past the beige Academy Building. Park on Hale Avenue's gravel shoulder.

Trail

Leave your car and walk north on Hale to the old Nelson factory complex. If the gate is open you can walk in and explore the area. If the gate is closed, continue on Hale, following the chain-link fence around the property and turning left onto South Brown Avenue. Soon another gate will appear; if this one is open, enter the grounds there.

Originally, there were five ivy-covered brick buildings, all well ventilated and windowed. In their prime, "the great factories," as Nelson called them, made for popular public tours. Much of the woodwork and plumbing for the village cottages was made in the factories, which employed 700 people. For many years, the SIUE art and design department occupied the surviving buildings, which hold in storage much of the university's nationally known Louis H. Sullivan ornament collection. "We have several thousand ornaments, many of them from demolished buildings in Chicago, designed by the architect who gave the modern skyscraper its form," says Eric Barnett, assistant director of the University Museum. Local leaders have committed themselves to preserving the historic buildings and finding productive uses for them.

Next to the factories is the former Nickel Plate railroad station, which functioned from the 1890s to 1967. In its early days, the simple combination freight and passenger station served the Toledo, St. Louis & Western railway. Its "Cloverleaf Route" brought into Edwardsville trains headed to St. Louis from Toledo and points in

It's May Day, in about 1910, at the Leclaire Village academy building.
(Southern Illinois University at Edwardsville archives)

Illinois and Indiana. Later, the New York, Chicago & St. Louis—the Nickel Plate Road—took over. For at least 30 years, passenger trains from St. Louis to Buffalo stopped at the station. In its last years, the line handled freight only. After exploring the factory area, retrace your steps to the academy area where you parked your car.

Once outside the factory complex and back on Hale Avenue, you'll see on your right a hedgerow of nine osage orange trees, planted in Nelson's time to screen the factories from adjacent residential areas. In 1922, the St. Louis Cardinals were scheduled to play an exhibition baseball game on the still-existing diamond near the academy building, but Nelson's death at a tuberculosis sanatorium in California canceled the event. Now used mostly for storage, the dilapidated academy was once where Nelson trained his workers and stimulated their minds. Nelson taught a course in bookkeeping; Mrs. Nelson taught sewing and cooking. Journalist Nellie Bly, orator Edward Everett Hale, and pioneer social reformer Jane Addams were guest lecturers at the academy.

There were once 375 or so white frame, one-floor, two-bedroom cottages, which workers bought for $4 down and payments of $10 to $15 a month. Most remain, though many have been altered, says local architect Ed Kane, who lives in Leclaire. Architecturally, these "castles of upright people and beautiful children" (Nelson's language) can be classified as "modified, simplified Victorian," says Kane. All homes, averaging 900 square feet, were set back 30 feet from the street to produce, in the opinion of street and landscape designer Julius Pitzman, "an artistic effect." Earlier, Pitzman had helped to lay out Forest Park as well as Portland and Westmoreland Places in St. Louis.

Following a Victorian tradition, many Leclaire cottage owners planted dual trees in their front yards, one for the husband, the other for the wife. Such a planting might assure good times ahead for the household, says Kane, who has two such original maples on his own front lawn. Look for dual trees throughout your walk through Leclaire; there are many of them.

Walk south on Hale past the academy, then turn right at Jefferson. Nelson lived in the home at 402 Jefferson from 1890 to 1911. Pillars are a late addition to the 12-room home, largest in the village. Nelson's son-in-law, Henry Lawnin, who succeeded Nelson as company president, lived across Jefferson at 311.

In a short block, turn left on Holyoake Road, named for George Jacob Holyoake (1817–1906), an English social reformer whom Nelson considered the father of the cooperative village movement. Most of the village streets, such as Ruskin, Franklin, and Jefferson, are named for people Nelson idolized. Many original Nelson homes are found on Holyoake. Among them are 821, 836, 840, 848, 850, 918, and 926. Follow the curving Holyoake until it meets Troy Road, once famous as "Highway 66."

Turn right onto Troy. The home at 837 Troy was depicted in advertising circulars for Leclaire around 1910. Those ads, and others, pitched $1400 homes in the village (you didn't have to be a Nelson employee to live there) and claimed that Leclaire had "proportionately more paved streets than any other city in the world, every street being paved by cinders and oiled to make it a perfect thoroughfare." The ads also said Leclaire is "the most modern city of its size ever founded." This is pretty heady talk since Leclaire, annexed to Edwardsville in 1934 when the Nelson Company began to fade, was never a city. In fact, Nelson boasted that Leclaire had no government, no police, no churches, "no paupers or idlers, no jails, no vacant houses for rent, and no signboards, unsightly buildings or objects."

Turn left on Jefferson near the village water tower. Leclaire had its own electricity and water plants and a greenhouse to supply flowers and plants to villagers. Turn left at Longfellow. Across the tracks on the right is Nelson's original 27-acre stake in Leclaire; reportedly the tract contained a coal mine and lake, now dry. Bear left onto Ruskin. At 918 Ruskin is an original Nelson-made fire hydrant (which may already have been replaced by the time of your walk, since the local fire department is upgrading its equipment). Take a right at Hale; walk one block west to Longfellow. Turn left onto Longfellow, then left onto Franklin.

Cross Troy Road, then continue straight ahead to Lindenwood, turning right. One block south of the Troy/Franklin intersection, at First and Troy, is a building that housed the Edwardsville depot of the Illinois Terminal Railroad. Until 1956, electric and interurban trains dropped off passengers at Leclaire; the trains went on to Peoria, Springfield, Decatur, Champaign, and Danville. "In the old days, you could buy a weekly pass from Leclaire to the 12th and Delmar station in St. Louis and the average trip would cost 24 cents," recalls George Kottwitz, who joined Illinois Terminal in 1946.

Walk a short block on Lindenwood, where there are more Nelson worker cottages and plenty of aging shade trees. Just south of the home at 1239 Lindenwood is the former trackbed of the Illinois Terminal road, visible as a grass berm that extends diagonally through this section of the old village. Turn left at Hadley. On the south side of Hadley are "new" homes, built in the 1950s. At Emerson, take a left. In front of 1243 Emerson is another original N.O. Nelson fire hydrant.

Turn right onto Franklin and walk to Madison, where you turn left. Make another left at East Avenue, which will take you around Leclaire Lake and eventually to Hale Avenue on your return lap to the parking area.

*Students pose with their teachers and two dogs
at the academy building in Leclaire Village, about 1910.
(Southern Illinois University–Edwardsville archives)*

Fresh-air-minded Nelson brought boys and girls from poor St. Louis families to campouts around the lake and concerts by the Nelson Company's 23-member band. The WPA built the brick walk to the beach in the 1930s. During the Depression, stones were laid along the banks to keep them from eroding.

Hale continues to be the showcase street in Leclaire Village. It has the most trees, some of them century-old elms and oaks; the best-engineered Pitzman street curve; and the most classic cottages and restorations. The home at 913 Hale won a local restoration award; the home at 919 is a Leclaire bungalow in pristine condition. A maverick, however, is the brick residence at 813 Hale; it was moved to Leclaire from Edwardsville about 1968.

Why did the village ultimately fail? "It was a victim of forces it couldn't control including the Depression, but particularly the lack of a tax base and a governmental structure," says SIUE sociology professor Robert Blain, who lives on Hale and—with his wife, Mary—wrote the village's 1990 centennial booklet, *The Historic Cooperative Village of Leclaire.* "It was a noble experiment, though," says Blain.

National Shrine of Our Lady of the Snows

Location: Belleville, Illinois
Hiking distance: 3 miles
Hiking time: 1½ hours
Bicycles: not permitted

Metro east residents know the Shrine of Our Lady of the Snows as the place to drive through the Way of Lights, a spectacular display of more than 300,000 tiny white Christmas lights on hundreds of trees, bushes, and statues. Nearly 350,000 people annually follow the 1.5-mile Way of Lights. It takes Shrine workers 2 months to string the lights, 2 more months to remove them.

This 200-acre development contains one of America's largest outdoor shrines. Its owner is the Missionary Oblates of Mary Immaculate, a 180-year-old, 6000-member religious society that is the eighth largest such group in the world. Help for "the wounded society, the unchurched, the poor in spirit" is the order's mission. The founder of the Missionary Oblates, Blessed Eugene De Mazenod, was expected to be canonized in 1995.

The late Father Edwin J. Guild founded the Shrine. In the late 1950s, he and his associates searched for a site for the shrine they envisioned. For $1150 an acre, the order bought the first parcel of land in 1958, assisted financially by a large and enthusiastic lay organization.

To its altars, amphitheater, gardens, exhibits, gift shop, prayer walls, and restaurant come nearly a million visitors annually from around the world. Many organized "pilgrimages" of church or community groups arrive at the Shrine in a quest for peace, comfort, and

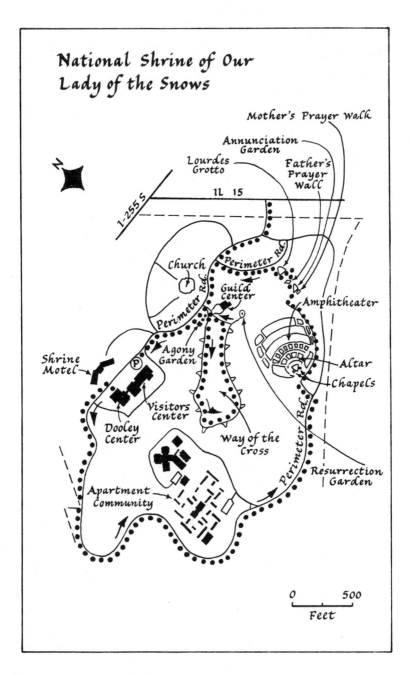

National Shrine of Our
Lady of the Snows

Mother's Prayer Walk

Annunciation
Garden

Father's
Prayer
Wall

Lourdes
Grotto

1L 15

I-255 S

Church

Perimeter Rd.

Perimeter Rd.

Guild
Center

Amphitheater

Shrine
Motel

Agony
Garden

Altar
Chapels

Visitors
Center

Dooley
Center

Way of the
Cross

Perimeter Rd.

Resurrection
Garden

Apartment
Community

0   500
Feet

solitude. The Shrine, in fact, has a full-time pilgrimage director, a clergyman who leads a large pastoral team. Most Shrine programs are ecumenical: Its operations are financed by donations from people of all faiths. Among those who have appeared in the amphitheater are the Dave Brubeck Quartet, the St. Louis Symphony Orchestra, the US Air Force Band, and Ray Doiron, a truck driver from Renault, Illinois.

Doiron claims to have seen visions of the Virgin Mary while at the Shrine and says he speaks with Mary there on the 13th of most months. After Doiron's initial announcement of Mary's appearance, in 1993, he visited the Shrine at least 16 times. Each visit drew more and more observers, capped by an audience in the amphitheater of 6700 in August 1994. Some people arrived as early as 4 AM for good seats at the 1 PM service, says Jo Kathman, Shrine public relations director. Catholic church authorities have not authenticated the apparition, which they describe as "a private revelation."

Access

From downtown St. Louis, follow I-55/I-70 East across the Poplar Street Bridge into Illinois to I-64. Drive east on I-64 to the I-255 South exit. Take I-255 South to IL 15 (exit 17A), then take IL 15 two miles east to the Shrine entrance. Follow signs to the visitors center. Park, then enter the visitors center. Walk through the corridor to the Tom Dooley Center, then exit by the front entrance, turning left onto "the perimeter road." (Across from the visitors center is the Shrine Motel, formerly Pilgrim's Inn.)

Trail

From the Tom Dooley Center, the walk along the sweet-gum-lined perimeter road is a good introduction to the Shrine landscape: beautiful trees, correctly clipped lawns, stunning gardens, rolling hills. "I took a personal interest in seeing every tree and shrub as each was planted," recalled Father Guild, the Shrine founder, in his 1988 memoir, *Dreams Realized.*

The 174-unit Apartment Community (the real name of this retirement center, not a generic term) appears on your left. Father Guild got the idea for the complex from an article about a Methodist retirement home in *Reader's Digest.* Slightly beyond it is an unusual collection of fitzer bushes that is spread over the hillside near the stop sign. Past the sign is a clump of Austrian pine.

Turn left into the outdoor altar and amphitheater area. Father Guild wrote that the Blatz Brewery Band Shell in Milwaukee partially influenced the design for the 2400-seat amphitheater. Extending upward some 50 feet above the shell that covers the altar is a concrete "M" representing Mary. In the summer, the altar is framed by beds of orange roses, whose propagation and patenting were personally requested by Guild. "The rose is the flower of Our Lady, and we make special efforts to mulch and fertilize our roses to keep them free of insects and diseases so that they might continue to reflect and enhance our devotion to Mary," Father Guild wrote.

Christ the King and Blessed Sacrament Chapels adjoin the altar. "The gem of the Shrine" is what Father Guild called the Blessed Sacrament Chapel. Two bronze doors at either end are "the largest single cast bronze portals ever made in the United States," Guild wrote. "Each (door) consists of two panels which weigh 275 pounds each. It took an 11-man crew, led by the designer, St. Louis artist Rodney Winfield, to cast the doors."

Walk up to the upper level of the amphitheater and heed signs that point to the Annunciation Garden. At the garden is a triangular reflecting pool shaped like the Arch in downtown St. Louis. Four turreted bells at the pool ring hourly; they once occupied the belfry of old St. Bruno's Church in Chicago. Coins pitched into the pool end up in the Shrine's general treasury. A mother's prayer walk that features a wall embedded with plaques dedicated to individual mothers is a fixture at the south end of the garden.

Next, find signs pointing to the father's memorial garden. After the mother's prayer walk had been open for several years, people asked where the father's wall was, says Kathman. "So we put in the father's prayer wall and memorial garden." Once past the father's wall, take the path that meanders down to a replica of the Lourdes Grotto, this one about two-thirds the size of the original in France. Neighborhood joggers and walkers and "visiting pilgrims" often stop at the grotto to meditate.

In 1961, a small crowd gathers at the replica of the Lourdes Grotto along the walk at Our Lady of the Snows Shrine. (National Shrine of Our Lady of the Snows collection)

From the grotto, walk west to the perimeter road, then make a left. On your right is the Church of Our Lady of the Snows, designed by the St. Louis architectural firm Hellmuth, Obata, and Kassabaum, Inc. At a V in the road, take a left and walk straight ahead to the short loop path into the Agony Garden, described as "a prelude to the Way of the Cross." After you've looped the garden, return to the perimeter road, turning right. Check out the garden benefactors' plaque on your way out; one contributor is old-time crooner Perry Como.

Soon you will arrive at the ½-mile-long Way of the Cross, which graphically depicts the story of Christ's passion and death at 15 stations rimmed by pines and other evergreens. Before their installation at the Shrine, the stations belonged to the Old Cathedral in Alton, Illinois. After the 14th station, cut across the street and walk to your right to the Resurrection Garden, the final station, whose centerpiece is the Resurrection Cave, where a flame burns continu-

In 1961, visitors filled the amphitheater at Our Lady of the Snows Shrine. (National Shrine of Our Lady of the Snows collection)

ously "as a symbol of the everlasting life that Christ promised."

Upon leaving the Resurrection Garden, walk to your right back to the perimeter road. The Edwin J. Guild Center, containing the 20-minute, multisensory presentation "The Journey," is on the corner. Walk through the three rooms of the presentation, which, according to the Shrine, "leads people on a pilgrimage through creation, the fall, and humanity's search for meaning and redemption." Originally, the display area was purchased from officials of the 1982 World's Fair in Knoxville, Tennessee. At the fair, the display was known as "The Power" and was described by fair officials as its "most technologically sophisticated and mind-boggling exhibit." "Father Guild personally went to Knoxville and said, 'This is what I want for our Shrine,' " says Kathman. "We had to build a building to put 'The Power' in."

Leave the Guild Center; resume your walk on the entrance road, which takes you back to the visitors center and trail's end.

Pere Marquette
State Park

Goat Cliff Trail

Location: Grafton, Illinois
Hiking distance: 2⅔ miles
Hiking time: 1½ hours
Bicycles: not permitted

Pere Marquette Park, at 8035 acres, is the largest Illinois state park. Native Americans lived here as far back as 9500 B.C., say archaeologists, who have found projectile points dating from that period. More than 100 individual Native American burial mounds and countless "habitation sites" are located within the park, says Dan Goatley, field director and archaeologist at the Center for American Archaeology in nearby Kampsville, Illinois. Father Jacques Marquette and Louis Joliet, pursuing a water route to the Pacific Ocean, first touched Illinois territory in 1673. An unpretentious white dolomite cross on IL 100, four miles east of the park lodge, marks the spot.

An ancient Native American village once occupied the site of the park lodge, which opened in 1941. On duty from 1933 to 1939, Civilian Conservation Corps workers, paid $30 a month and assigned to a barracks where the visitors center parking lot is today, built the lodge and 12 cabins behind it. Inmates from Illinois prisons crafted the wrought-iron lighting fixtures and much of the original lodge furniture. Six hundred tons of limestone, quarried near Grafton, are packed into the lodge chimney. It is said that the chessboard in the lodge's sprawling guest lounge is the largest in the world; its pawns are nearly 2 feet tall. A long flagstone terrace faces the Illinois River valley.

In the park's formative stages, nearly 300,000 trees and shrubs were planted. More than 120 different kinds of fossils have been identified on park bluffs, many near the 10 popular hiking trails,

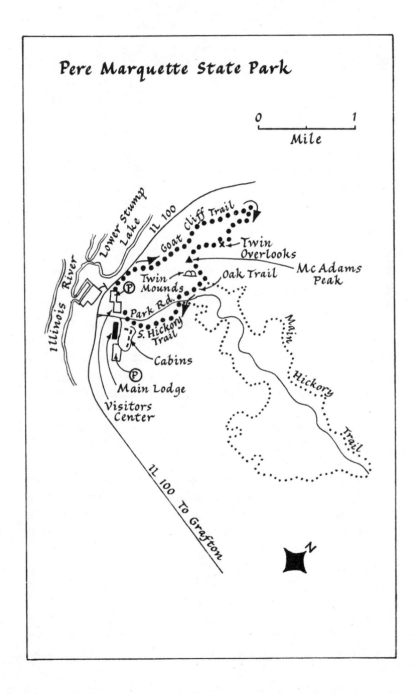

which total about 12 miles. Richard Keating, a botany professor at Southern Illinois University–Edwardsville, enjoys hiking in the park's backcountry, away from the popular trails. In his walks, he has found a valley with 12 species of ferns, and near the park's east end, "giant, detached dolomitic limestone blocks with narrow, straight passages wide enough for one person to pass at a time." On the St. Andrew Ridge Trail, which starts in Rosedale at the northwest corner of the park, he found a very mature oak-hickory forest in a section that reminds him of the Blue Ridge area of Virginia.

Birds love the park. Celebrated birder Helen Wuestenfeld of Jerseyville, Illinois, has helped park managers compile an official list of 230 species, including the American bald eagle, dozens of which are seen here each winter. She has personally seen at least 315 bird species, mostly around Pere Marquette as well as nearby Gilbert and Swan Lakes. "Recently, I saw a goshawk flying over the park," she said. "It wasn't a fly-by, either. It was circling as if looking for food. Then, it flew over the bluffs to hunt in the woods. You see one of these only every three or four years."

Goat Cliff Trail is the oldest park path. It was laid out in 1934 by members of the National Youth Administration, one of President Franklin D. Roosevelt's Depression-era manpower programs. Alton resident Jack Buese watched the trail develop. "They used army trucks and elbow grease to carve it out," he remembers. Buese and the late Alton attorney Bruce Quackenbush hiked Goat Cliff and other trails most Saturdays, usually capping their walks with a picnic lunch while seated on "lunch logs" deep in the forest. The pair were *the* experts on the trail system, often asked by park and conservation officials to upgrade maps or identify little-known spots in the park.

Access

From St. Louis, take I-270 to MO 367 North in north St. Louis County. Drive on MO 367 into Alton, Illinois. Turn left off the bridge. Follow IL 100 through downtown Alton to access the Great River Road for the ride to Grafton. Continue west through Grafton on IL 100 to the park lodge entrance, about 5 miles away. Turn into the visitors center lot, just west of the lodge.

Trail

The yellow-marked Goat Cliff Trail—recommended by Scott Isringhausen, longtime park naturalist/interpreter, as the best way to sample the park's natural treasures—starts west of the visitors center, which was once a corn crib. Early on, the trail parallels IL 100; then it begins its climb to Goat Cliff itself. The first trail landmark (on your left, near the two benches) is Twin Springs, which flow from rocks deposited 300 million years ago, archaeologists estimate. On your right, where large boulders appear to be split, tilted, and dislodged, is visual evidence of the Cap au Gres fault, a 60-mile fracture line extending from Lincoln County, Missouri, east-southeastward into northwest Madison County, Illinois, where it ends. "It flows under the alluvial Mississippi valley," explains David Reinertsen, former senior staff geologist with the Illinois State Geological Survey, Champaign. "When water in the Mississippi and Illinois Rivers struck the hard and shifted rocks produced by the fracture, water was deflected to the east in the area of the fault." This is one reason the two rivers flow east-to-west in the immediate vicinity. Some 200 feet to your right are paw paw and Kentucky coffee trees, which seem to flourish at the feet of the trail's abundant limestone bluffs.

On your way up, the trail widens and big rocks rest along its flanks, a setting reminiscent of trails in the Great Smoky Mountains National Park. In the spring you might see, to your right, much of the hill's north slope spread lavishly with Dutchman's breeches, the white wildflowers whose petals look like baggy trousers hanging on a clothesline. Five rocky landmarks lie ahead before you reach Goat Cliff: a rockpile that offers first-class lake and river views; formidable limestone bluffs, smothered each May with orange wild columbines; Table Rock, a picnic and resting place; Ship's Rock, mimicking a ship's prow; and Fat Man's Misery, which must be walked around or squeezed through to continue uphill. Buese and Quackenbush named these landmarks, but not Goat Cliff itself. "Maybe some ancient goats grazed around here and that's how it got its name," speculated Quackenbush.

Once on Goat Cliff, there is much to see. Straight ahead is AT&T Access Road to Lower and Upper Stump Lakes. Lower Stump

This section of the Goat Cliff Trail in Pere Marquette State Park is just below Ship's Rock.

Lake is the predominant sight in the left foreground. It is a former bottomland forest cut by Civilian Conservation Corps people in 1938 and 1939 before construction of Alton Lock and Dam #26, about 15 miles south on the Mississippi River in Alton. The land had been purchased by the Army Corps of Engineers as floodland. The trees had to be chopped down, or they would die once the forest was flooded, then float down the river and possibly choke the new dam, recounts wildlife biologist David Harper. Frequent flooding has erased most of the stumps from public view. Immediately beyond Lower Stump Lake is the Illinois River, flowing to its junction with the Mississippi. In the background is Swan Lake, a federal waterfowl area and home to occasional swans and passing white pelicans. On clear days, you can spot the grain elevators of Hardin, Illinois, on the right horizon, notes Scott Isringhausen, park interpreter.

From the Goat Cliff overlook, continue upward on the meandering trail. Some large northern red oaks rule this part of the trail. Walk right at the next fork onto a spur to Twin Overlooks, the highest point on your walk. Take the stairs that connect the two overlooks. From the upper overlook you may see (between November and March) American bald eagles riding thermal currents between Williams Hollow on your right, where some of the birds roost, and the Illinois River below, where they seek food. From this observation point you can also view Lower Stump Lake in your immediate foreground. Behind it, in succession, are: the Illinois River, Thirteen Mile Island, and Swan Lake. In the far distance is the town of Brussels, Illinois. Just below the overlooks are rather uncommon blue ash trees, whose young twigs often sprout square stems; ironwood bushes; and chinquapin oaks, which love rocky, arid ledges. Aromatic sumac bushes flank the path between the overlooks.

An old hilltop prairie, one of several in the park, also rests below Twin Overlooks. These gladelike tracts, often called "grassland oases," contain native plants and grasses that have grown relatively undisturbed for more than 8300 years, botanists say. About 30 prairie plant species are found here, including sky blue aster, yellow puccoon, purple prairie clover, little bluestem, and showy goldenrod. Follow the trail back to its junction with the main Goat Cliff Trail and turn right.

Take the trail to McAdams Peak, named for an early Illinois state geologist, Professor William McAdams, grandfather of prominent Washington attorney Clark McAdams Clifford, once President Lyndon B. Johnson's Secretary of Defense. McAdams dug up some

100 Native American skeletons around this site in 1892, then gave them to the Smithsonian Institution in Washington. The McAdams observation platform is perfect for watching south-migrating broad-winged hawks fly by in the fall, advises Helen Wuestenfeld. "You'd better be there between September 17 and October 1 to see them." Just below McAdams Peak is the largest (2.4-acre) hill prairie at Pere Marquette. Sky blue aster, sideoats grama, purple prairie clover, little bluestem, and showy goldenrod are well represented there.

After McAdams Peak, take the Main Hickory Trail (red markers) east to Twin Mounds, accessible via a flight of limestone stairs constructed by CCC volunteers in the 1930s. "This may be the best place in the park to see trees flowering in the spring and the turning leaves in the fall," says Isringhausen. You may also see the Arch in downtown St. Louis, about 45 miles away, on a cloudless day. "Thousands of years ago," says archaeologist Goatley, "Native Americans passing the area in canoes could look up, see the mounds, and know that they were a marker of someone else's territory." From Twin Mounds return to the main Hickory Trail and walk east to the Oak Trail (red-and-white blazed). Turn right for a leisurely forest descent that crosses the main park road. Not far after the crossing, you will meet the South Hickory Trail, where you must veer right for a short walk through a gulleylike area that ends by the lodge and visitors center parking lot.

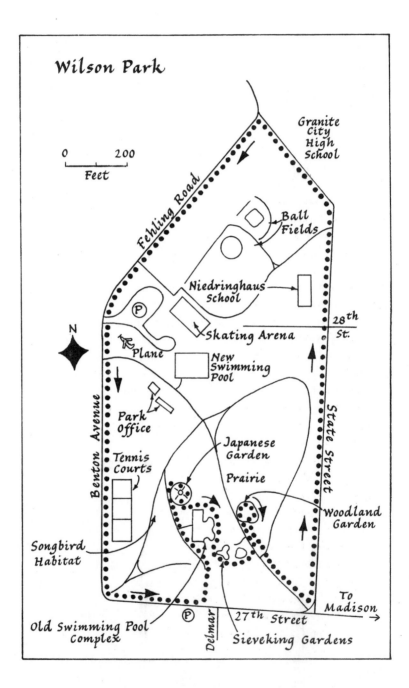

Wilson Park

Wilson Park

Location: Granite City, Illinois
Hiking distance: 1¼ miles
Hiking time: 20 minutes
Bicycles: permitted

Walkers have trod the four corners of Wilson Park since its opening in 1923. Named for President Woodrow Wilson, who campaigned for the presidency here in 1912, the 73-acre facility is to Granite City what Francis Park is to south St. Louis: a walker's paradise.

Focal point of Wilson Park is Sieveking Gardens, a stunning array of rock and flower gardens interlaced with unusual stone sculptures by Ernst Sieveking, park superintendent and advisor from 1923 until his death at 96 in 1962. Within the gardens are a miniature castle and moat, inspired by a Sieveking trip to Europe; cement urns and toadstools; miniature waterfalls and fountains; and evergreens that in Sieveking's day were pruned to the shapes of swans, flower baskets, chickens, eagles, and the Statue of Liberty.

"In the old days, everyone in town drove past to see the evergreens," says Sue Champion, former park district office manager. "At the end of the summer, Mr. Sieveking would give away most of his gardens to the public—annual slips, seeds, even goldfish," recalls Conrad Eads of Granite City, a friend of Sieveking. "We called this 'Flower Giveaway Day' and it was something to behold." Though Sieveking has long departed, Flower Giveaway Day continues, the gardens still looking empty in its wake. In the last three years, 80 new species of trees have been introduced to Wilson Park, as has a woodland garden, east of Sieveking Gardens.

As for wildlife, the park has its own red-tailed hawk. "He lives here, but we don't know where," says birder David Polivick, Granite City director of parks and recreation, who has an office in the park. "His favorite meals are pigeons from our ice rink next door, and squirrels."

Access

On I-70 in downtown St. Louis, drive north to exit 248 A/Salisbury Street. From the exit, turn left and drive to the entrance to McKinley Bridge. Take the bridge (50 cents per auto) to Illinois. From the bridge, it's 4.2 miles to Wilson Park. Follow IL 3 south, then quickly bear left on Broadway Avenue. Stay on Broadway, which, in a mile, becomes Madison. Continue north on Madison to 27th Street in Granite City. Turn left on 27th; drive 2 blocks to the park. Park on either side of 27th Street near the center of the park and near Delmar Avenue.

Bicyclists and in-line skaters may use the asphalt trail from sunrise to 9 AM and from 11:30 AM to 5 PM only, says Polivick, who estimates that at least 1000 people hike the park on a normal weekend.

Trail

The walk begins opposite 27th and Delmar at the midpoint of the park. Walk north into the park on the paved path that bends left and passes (on your right) the old art deco–style swimming pool complex and pavilion. Just beyond the songbird habitat, turn into the new sunken Japanese Garden, on the site of the park's original swimming pool in the 1920s. The vertical central tower/sculpture is what remains of the lime green diving tower, minus the diving board. It is topped with stones put there by Sieveking, and purple fountain grass installed by Bill Monical, grounds supervisor.

"Every tree in the Japanese garden has its roots with the Japanese," says Monical, who has supervised the planting of a weeping pink pussywillow; two purple weeping willows; an upright English oak "whose form was developed by the Japanese"; Japanese black pines; and two dwarf-variety Scotch pines, "improved on and made dwarf by the Japanese culture." Once you've looped the Japanese Garden, walk back in the direction of 27th Street through Sieveking Gardens, taking note of the gazebo at their east end. At least 50 local couples are married annually in the gazebo. Each April on Prom Day, couples from next-door Granite City Senior High School have their photographs taken there. Walk across the path to the Woodland Garden, slightly to your left.

In this new garden, ringed by a mulched path, are a grove of oaks, a white redbud, a Japanese snow drop, and a forest pansy redbud, the latter three quite rare. Along the woodland loop are sections of fallen, decomposing trees, partially sunken and surrounded by spring perennials. "As a tree deteriorates, it sets up its own biological community, and it's worthy of display," says Monical, who designed the garden. After looping this garden, walk back on the diagonal path, which ends at the intersection of 27th and State Streets.

What may be "the finest collection of gingko trees in the area" lies along 27th Street just before State. According to park gardener John McDaniel, Sieveking himself planted the gingkos and some sycamores in this section of the park. A few years ago, the sycamores were removed to give the gingkos more room to breathe.

Turn left onto State Street. Stroll past the picnic area, cross 28th Street, and pass Niedringhaus Elementary School. Opened in 1929, it was named for the "founder" of modern Granite City, George W. Niedringhaus of Granite City Steel Company. (Early in the 20th century, steel and related industries were so formidable in the area that Granite City was called "Pittsburgh of the West.") The blacktop path soon swings to your left past a grove of tall and shady pin oaks on your left. Pin oaks are the park's dominant tree; there are more than 500 of them. Over on your right is the Granite City Senior High School complex, in the same location since at least 1915.

Soon after the path rounds a corner to your left and begins to parallel Fehling Road, you will pass the ball diamond where Granite City High graduate Del Maxvill supposedly started his baseball career. Maxvill signed his first contract with the St. Louis Cardinals in the park, recalls Harold E. Brown, former Granite City director of parks and recreation. Eventually Maxvill became a respectable infielder for the Cards and later their general manager.

A "new"—vintage 1967—indoor skating arena, which cost $450,000, is situated farther along on the walk. Next to the recreation center is the city's new state-of-the-art swimming pool, opened in 1994. "We actually call it a water park," says Polivick, speaking mainly of the 16-foot, figure-eight slide that more than 71,000 youngsters slid down in the first few months it was operative. And plans are being developed for the Earl H. Iberg Park and Playground, a contemporary, handicapped-friendly playground partially funded by a $300,000 gift from Iberg's estate. It will be located behind the new pool.

An elevated F84F Thunderflash fighter bomber, used in the Korean-War period, pops up next. The plane was accepted by the park district in 1970 when Amvet Post 51 found it didn't have enough room to display it on its own lawn. Steve Conkovich is the plane's guardian. Every year, he mails up-to-date snapshots of the plane to the US Air Force. "They want to know what condition the plane is in," says Conkovich. "The Air Force doesn't want a piece of junk out there," adds Conkovich, who says he has personally put more than 100 new parts into the plane since it went on exhibit. "The citizens of Alton also wanted this plane," he says, "but I spent five years writing letters to get the Air Force to give it to the people of Granite City."

Straight ahead on the asphalt trail are the tennis courts where superstar Jimmy Connors practiced in the early 1960s. "His mother and grandmother would bring him here from Belleville so he could play tennis with some of the good college players who lived in Granite City," recalls his friend John Van Buskirk, now the Granite City Senior High basketball coach. Turn left onto 27th Street by the redwood benches and a cluster of memorial trees (the park plants 100 such memorials each year). Finish your walk near the trio of flagpoles and your parked car.

"The Wilson Park trail is used by people pushing baby carriages as well as the very, very old," observes Rosemary Brown, a strong local advocate of the park trail. "The park has always been like this. It is right in the heart of our community."

Bibliography

Denison, Edgar. *Missouri Wildflowers.* 4th edition. Missouri Department of Conservation, 1993.

Gass, Ramon. *Missouri Hiking Trails.* Missouri Department of Conservation, 1990.

Haller, Karen S. *Walking with Wildflowers.* University of Missouri Press, 1994.

Hernon, Peter and Terry Ganey. *Under the Influence: The Unauthorized Story of the Anheuser-Busch Dynasty.* Simon & Schuster, 1991.

Jackson, Kenneth T. and Camilo J. Vergara. *Silent Cities.* Princeton Architectural Press, 1989.

Knittel, Robert E. *Walking in Tower Grove Park.* Grass-Hopper Press, 1978.

Loughlin, Carolyn and Catherine Anderson. *Forest Park.* University of Missouri Press, 1986.

Madson, John. *Tallgrass Prairie.* Falcon Press, 1993.

Madson, John. *Up on the River.* Penguin Books, 1986.

Miller, Howard S. (text) and Quinta Scott (photos). *The Eads Bridge.* University of Missouri Press, 1979.

Mormino, Gary Ross. *Immigrants on the Hill.* University of Illinois Press, 1986.

McCue, George and Frank Peters. *A Guide to the Architecture of St. Louis.* University of Missouri Press, 1989.

Pryor, R. Roger, John A. Karel, Charles Collison, and Susan Flader. *Exploring Missouri's Legacy.* University of Missouri Press, 1992.

Stadler, Frances Hurd. *St. Louis Day by Day.* The Patrice Press, 1989.

van Ravenswaay, Charles. *Saint Louis. An Informal History of the City and its People, 1764–1865.* Edited by Candace O'Connor. Missouri Historical Society Press, 1991.

Winter, William C. *The Civil War in St. Louis.* Missouri Historical Society Press, 1994.

Books from The Countryman Press and Backcountry Publications

The Countryman Press and Backcountry Publications, long known for fine books on travel and outdoor recreation, offer a range of practical and readable manuals.

Walks & Rambles Series:

Walks & Rambles in Southwestern Ohio
Walks & Rambles on Cape Cod and the Islands
Walks & Rambles in Dutchess and Putnam Counties
Walks & Rambles in Westchester & Fairfield Counties, 2nd Ed.
Walks & Rambles in Rhode Island, 2nd Ed.
More Walks & Rambles in Rhode Island
Walks & Rambles on the Delmarva Peninsula
Walks & Rambles in the Upper Connecticut River Valley

Hiking Series:

Fifty Hikes in the Adirondacks
Fifty Hikes in Central New York
Fifty Hikes in Central Pennsylvania
Fifty Hikes in Connecticut
Fifty Hikes in Eastern Pennsylvania
Fifty Hikes in the Hudson Valley
Fifty Hikes in Lower Michigan
Fifty Hikes in Massachusetts
Fifty Hikes in the Mountains of North Carolina
Fifty Hikes in New Jersey
Fifty Hikes in Northern Maine
Fifty Hikes in Northern Virginia
Fifty Hikes in Ohio
Fifty Hikes in Southern Maine
Fifty Hikes in Vermont
Fifty Hikes in Western New York
Fifty Hikes in Western Pennsylvania
Fifty Hikes in the White Mountains
Fifty More Hikes in New Hampshire

We offer many more books on biking, fishing, and canoeing plus books on travel, nature, and many other subjects. Our books are available through bookstores, or they may be ordered directly from the publisher. VISA/Mastercard accepted. To order, or for a complete catalogue, please contact: The Countryman Press, Inc. P.O. Box 175AP Woodstock, VT 05091 or call our toll-free number, (800) 245-4151.